SOCIOLOGICAL PERSPECTIVES ON GLOBALISATION

SOCIOLOGICAL PERSPECTIVES ON GLOBALISATION

Edited by
AJAYA KUMAR SAHOO

PUBLICATIONS
KALPAZ PUBLICATIONS
DELHI-110052

Sociological Perspectives on Globalisation

Rs. 750

ISBN: 81-7835-580-9

Published in 2006 in India by
Kalpaz Publications
C-30, Satyawati Nagar,
Delhi-110052
E-mail: kalpaz@hotmail.com

Lassertype Setting by: Rudra Computer Graphics, Delhi
Printed at: Salasar Imaging System, Delhi

Contents

Preface

Prevailing literature on globalisation and its impacts remains a highly contested terrain. Supporters of globalisation celebrate its progressive character: its promise of abundance, socio-economic empowerment, cultural diversity and general improvement in the human condition. Critics of globalisation, on the other hand, lament its potential to generate spatial, social, economic and digital inequalities. Globalisation processes, it is argued, strengthen those who have and marginalise those who do not. India is a relative latecomer to globalisation, having only embarked on its globalisation journey around fifteen years ago. The impacts of this globalisation embrace are still being played out although certain trends are now beginning to become apparent. The subjects covered in this new edited book by a promising young scholar, Ajaya Kumar Sahoo, engage with some of these emerging trends and provides important and pertinent sociological perspectives on differential impacts of globalisation in India.

The first set of papers in the book, from chapter one to chapter eight, include interesting perspectives on the interplay between tradition and modernity, ethnic and gender relations and tension between empowerment and marginality. Given that most of the geographical focus of the book is on eastern and north-eastern regions - generally thought to be lagging behind in the globalisation stakes – the authors provide many interesting insights on emergent trends. What becomes clear on reading these chapters is that the traditional exclusionary practices in India – through caste, gender, tribe, religion, property and education – are all still alive and kicking, albeit in a modified form, despite the impact of over 60 years of democratic politics and pro-active grassroots level political and social movements among subaltern groups in the marginalised localities. It is especially interesting to note the inclusion of a paper on Business Process Outsourcing, as this amply illustrates the tensions between modernity and globalisation. Although outsourcing activity seems, superficially at least, a modernising activity since it leads to the construction of transnational identities, it nevertheless positions a segment of the young urban Indian labour force into the category of an exploited global proletariat.

An important early form of globalisation of India was through the export of labour to the expanding areas of the British Empire which created the 'old' Indian diaspora. In the post-independent period, despite India's development trajectory which emphasised 'global isolation' and self-sufficiency, a large number of Indians, both unskilled and skilled migrated to north America and Europe in cyclical waves associated with trends in demand and skill shortages in these metropolitan areas to create the core of the 'new' wealthy Indian diaspora. Growing awareness about the developmental roles played by diaspora communities in their homeland in countries such as China, Africa and Latin America and the realization that diasporas are a strategic asset which needs to be harnessed finally awakened the Indian state to embark on a constructive dialogue with its 20 million strong diaspora communities located in over 70 countries around the world. India's strategic shift from indifference to a pro-active dialogue with its diaspora has now begun to have a profound impact on the Indian economy at rural, regional and national levels. Thus whether it is through socio-economic development in the central districts of Punjab, in Kerala or Gujarat or in sectors such as IT and Software or medical services diasporan influence has become clearly visible. A focus only on the low NRI inflows of Foreign Direct Investment (say relative to China) to India grossly underestimates the diaspora's contributing to Indian foreign exchange reserves, stock market investment and bank deposits. Given this growing interest in diaspora's potential contribution to India development, two chapters of this book speculate on the potential and strategic role that diaspora communities can play.

It needs to be remembered that diaspora-homeland relations are not necessarily all economic. A further two chapters discuss the issues of ethnicity and identity of Indians in the diaspora and cultural exchanges between diaspora communities and India. These demonstrate both the emergence and significance of global networks and transnational practices over the past two decades or so. We are also reminded that despite the well-deserved hype associated with the economic successes of the Indian diaspora and their 'model minority' status in the USA, diaspora communities have got there through long protracted struggles as illustrated by the paper on Indians in Trinidad some still suffering racial tensions.

It has been a pleasure to peruse this rich and varied collection of papers included in this volume. Ably edited by Ajaya Kumar Sahoo this edited collection of readings by both established and young scholars embarking on their professional careers, provides a significant contribution to the growing literature on uneven and differentiated sociological impacts of globalisation. This book will be of great interest not only to sociologists but scholars working in the field of social anthropology, political science, cultural and ethnic studies and of course the rapidly growing fields of diaspora studies and transnationalism.

A.K. Sahoo

Acknowledgements

It gives me immense pleasure to express my sense of gratitude and sincere thanks to all those who directly or indirectly helped me in completing this book.

First of all I thank all the authors in the book for their timely cooperation and encouragement, without which this book would not have been possible.

I am thankful to all my well-wishers, friends and family members who have rendered their love, patience, tolerance, and thus helped in the process of making this book a reality.

Ajaya Kumar Sahoo

Contributors

Ajaya Kumar Sahoo, Senior Research Fellow, Department of Sociology, and, Research Fellow, Centre for the Study of Indian Diaspora, University of Hyderabad, Hyderabad.

Biswajita Padhi, Lecturer, Department of Economics, Aeronautics College, Orissa.

Eswarappa Kasi, ICSSR Doctoral Candidate, Department of Anthropology, University of Hyderabad, Hyderabad.

Jayanta Choudhury, Assistant Professor, State Institute of Public Administration and Rural Development (SIPARD), Agartala, West Tripura.

Jeetendra D. Soni, Ph.D. Research Scholar, Centre for the Study of Regional Development, Jawaharlal Nehru University, New Delhi.

Mukesh Kumar, Lecturer, Post-Graduate Department of History, Gaya College, Magadha University, Bihar.

Neena Rosy Khalon, Senior Lecturer of Sociology, Centre for Immigration Studies, Guru Nanak Dev University, Punjab.

Nihar Ranjan Mishra, Ph.D. Research Scholar, Department of Anthropology, University of Hyderabad, Hyderabad.

R. A. Mangathai, Faculty, State Institute of Public Administration and Rural Development (SIPARD), Agartala, West Tripura.

R. Siva Prasad, Associate Professor, Department of Anthropology, University of Hyderabad, Hyderabad.

Samir Dasgupta, Professor and Head, Department of Sociology, University of Kalyani, West Bengal.

Sarbeswar Sahoo, Doctoral Candidate, Department of Sociology, Faculty of Arts and Social Sciences, National University of Singapore, Singapore.

Soubhagya Ranjan Padhi, Lecturer, Department of Sociology, Aeronautics College, Orissa.

Surendra D. Soni, Lecturer in History, Government Lohiya (P.G.) College, Rajasthan.

Taruna Upadhyaya, Shree Institute of Science and Technology, Bhopal, Madhya Pradesh.

V. Basil Hans, Teacher Fellow, Department of Studies and Research in Economics, Mangalore University, Karnataka.

Introduction - Globalisation: A Sociological Dimension

Ajaya Kumar Sahoo

The phenomenon of globalization in recent time has attracted more significant global attention than perhaps any other issues. Ronald Robertson (1996: 8) points out that, "in academic circles 'globalization' was not recognized as a significant concept, in spite of diffuse and intermittent usage prior to that, until the early, or even middle, 1980s. During the second half of the 1980s, its use increased enormously, so much so that it is virtually impossible to trace the patterns of its contemporary diffusion across a large number of areas of contemporary life in different parts of the world."

Globalization is a multifaceted process that manifests itself in the various aspects of life: economic, political, social and cultural. The advantages and disadvantages of globalization have been debated heavily in academic and policy circles in recent years. While the supporters of globalization theory refer to the emergence of the "middle-class" especially in developing countries, economic growth within peripheral economies, democratization and the emergence of a "global culture," the critics point to the rising gaps of inequality between nations, increased environmental degradation, the loss of sovereignty, cultural imperialism and the rise in extreme nationalism (Ramsaran and Price 2003). Joseph Stiglitz (2002: 4) argues that "globalization has reduced the sense of isolation felt in much of the developing world and has given many people in the developing countries access to knowledge well beyond the reach of even the wealthiest in any country a century age."

Robertson has formulated the question of globality as a duality of objective and subjective processes. According to him, "globalization refers both to the compression of the world and the intensification of consciousness of the world as a whole. The processes and actions to which the concept of globalization now refers have been proceeding, with some interruptions, for many centuries, but the main focus of the discussion of globalization is on relatively recent times" (Robertson 1996: 8). At the core of most discussions on globalization is the role of information and communication technology, in ways that have considerably reduced the distance between "time and space" (Harvey 1990). Globalization has made it possible for the "closer integration of the countries and peoples of the world," facilitated through the "enormous reduction of costs of transportation and communication, and the breaking down of artificial barriers to the flows of goods, services, capital, knowledge, and (to a lesser extent) people across borders" (Stiglitz 2002: 9). Globalization has brought sweeping changes on the life of the individual. Today an individual's life is structured less by the past than by his/her anticipated future. Habit, custom and tradition play less of a role than they did for the previous generations. Similarly the beliefs and practices of individuals have also been changed significantly.

Different scholars have analysed and interpreted the concept "globalization" from different perspectives. Sharma (2004: 102) for instance, considers globalization "as Neo-capitalism propelled by modern technologies of mass production of weapons of mass destruction and of goods for mindless conspicuous consumption as well as their free international trade under the 'benign' regime of W.T.O." According to Friedman (1996: 199) "globalization refers to processes that are usually designated as cultural, that is, concerned with the attribution of meaning in the global arena."

Another form of globalization can come from below (such as the environmental, women's and anti-nuclear movements, or in the case most relevant to this discussion, human rights struggles). The human rights movement has long laid claim to a universalizing mission. This is evident in the assertion that the regime of rights and freedoms established through the Universal Declaration of Human Rights extend beyond the arena of purely national concern. The globalization-from-below activists have the potential to add a democratic dimension to the debates about globalization from above (United Nations 2000: 5). The Universal Declaration and other human rights instruments are unequivocal in their declaration that all persons are equal, and that the right to non-discrimination is a basic and fundamental human right. The grounds upon which non-discrimination is prohibited are also clear, and have been expanded over time to accommodate new forms and expressions of an insidious practice that unfortunately is as old as humanity. Especially important are the prohibitions of discrimination based on race, colour, gender, religion and ethnicity (ibid.: 13).

The subject of globalization and its impact on women – both locally and globally – became of considerable interest among scholars in most countries. Few observers will deny the fact that the general issue of gender relations globally, and the question of women's human rights specifically, has undergone significant transformation. Needless to say, while much has been achieved, there remains a considerable amount yet to be accomplished (ibid.: 15).

The process of globalisation and its impact on social relations is the feature of most of the diasporic communities. While discussing globalization from Indian perspective, Sharma (ibid.: 99) points out that "India offers a good example of movement of peoples and ideas. It has both received and dispatched men, materials and messages. These processes did not add elements of other cultures to Indian culture in India – thereby 'globalizing it' – but also spread Indian culture world-wide." The process of globalisation and the inevitable expansion of "markets, transportation, communication, capital and skills have challenged the geographic hegemony of national governments" and their borders (Centre for Development Enterprise, 1997: 17). Globalisation transcends territory, location, distance, and borders, and has been accompanied by rapid migration of people across borders, and has raised questions about identity, citizenship and nationality.

Scholars of diaspora studies have argued that, globalisation and other forces have resulted in the formation of large numbers of transnational communities. Today, diaspora has made a dynamic comeback in the debates around ethnicity, nationality and nationhood, boundaries and identity. A concept that has transformed in time, diaspora has returned to address and assist the understanding of migration, post-migration and reterritorialization, people's multiple senses of belonging and loyalties beyond national boundaries. It has been argued that the links between globalization and the rise of diasporas are not necessarily direct. However,

> [g]lobalisation has enhanced the practical, economic and affective roles of diasporas, showing them to be particularly adaptive forms of social organization. As diasporas become more integrated into the cosmopoli, their power and importance are enhanced. Their relative solidarity and integration are particularly evident in relation to the local populations among whom they work (Cohen, 1997: 176).

According to Vertovec (1997: 277) the term "diaspora" is often applied to "describe practically any population that is considered 'deterritorialized' or 'transnational' that is, which has originated in land other than that in which it currently resides, and whose social, economic, and political networks cross the borders of nation states or, indeed, span the globe."

Relationship of any diaspora with the homeland/ motherland falls under the broader domain of international relations as it involves at least two countries to formally accept to permit their subjects to interact with each other. Even in the absence of such formal understanding and other constraints, relations of imaginary kind could exist through building structures and institutions that recreate the places of origin by diaspora communities (Bhat and Sahoo 2005: 64). Toady the diasporic communities go beyond the host nation-state and motherland to network with their communities dispersed around the globe. The emergence of such networking, cutting across several countries is most appropriately described by the term "transnationalism." Transnationalism has been defined as a "social process whereby migrants operate in social fields that transgress geographic, political and cultural boundaries" (Glick-Schiller, et al., 1992: 9). Levitt (2001: 14) has argued that the "impact of transnational migration differs from, but must be understood within the context of, the heightened globalisation in which it is embedded. Changes prompted by migration and globalisation mutually reinforce one another."

The present book *Sociological Perspectives on Globalisation* provides an interesting collection of essays by specialist scholars on the above themes. I hope the collection of essays in this book will interest to the students, scholars and researchers in social sciences and open up further debates on the above issues both at micro and macro level.

The Essays

The book is consists of thirteen chapters. Chapter one gives a general understating of the subject "Sociology" and its applied status in the present context. The second chapter deals with the civil society and role of subaltern groups. The third and fourth chapter examines the issue of gender in two different societies from a socio-anthropological perspective. The fifth chapter deals with the role of self-help groups in poverty alleviation. The sixth chapter deals with the changing patterns in religious beliefs and practices of village communities, and the seventh chapter focuses on the social realities of health systems in the rural setting of Punjab. The eight chapter deals with the socio-economic developments processes of Sugalis. The ninth chapter focuses on the Business Process Outsourcing. The tenth chapter deals with the globalisation and its impact on Indian diaspora. The eleventh chapter focuses on the Indo-Black relationships in the Caribbean from a historical point of view. The twelfth chapter examines the role of Indian diaspora for the development of homeland. The last chapter focuses on the migration, community formation and transnational networks of Oriya diaspora.

Samir Dasgupta's paper examines critically and methodologically the history of the growth of the discipline "sociology" and its present status. The paper discusses several critical issues that the discipline has undergone over the years to achieve its present applied status in the academic arena. The early history of the growth of the discipline has hardly noticed the disciplines' applied status which is realized recently as a result of the research carried out by intellectual sociologists. After tracing the works of several pioneer scholars such as Max Weber, Herbert Spencer, Emile Durkheim, Lester Ward, Jay Weinstein, the paper compares the growth and development of applied sociology in the America, Europe and India. According to the author, the status of applied sociology in India is still suffering from the crisis of professional stability, lack of scientific and methodological knowledge and the crisis of theoro-empirical blending. The paper concludes that, there is a need to rethink the purpose and definition of applied sociology as it differs from "time and space." This is an interesting paper especially for those who are interested to learn more about the discipline's past, present and future.

The notion of civil society today is commonly identified with a non-statist, somewhat romanticised, set of institutions that stand for liberalism in the form of free market in economic sphere and democracy in political sphere. Sarbeswar Sahoo's paper examines the changes that have taken place in the nature of civil society in India especially over the last one and half decades as a result of growing socio-political mobilisations and large scale transformations. He talks about the Habermas's concept of "public sphere" where democratic participation plays an important role. He argues that although Indian constitution has established the foundation for a universal public sphere by recognising the rights of individuals, the civil society has divided on power relations and public sphere remain confine to a small section of bourgeois middle class interest groups. Similar points of departure has also been made by scholars like Sudipta Kaviraj, Javeed Alam, Partha Chatterjee and slightly different forms by scholars like Dipankar Gupta, Andre Beteille and Ashis Nandy. According to the author, caste, gender, tribe, religion, property, and education are the basis of exclusion, inequality and exercise of power in India. Thus he suggests that, there is a need for alternative public spheres what Nancy Fraser calls *subaltern counterpublics* which represent "parallel discursive arenas where members of subordinated social groups invent and circulate their counter discourses based on oppositional identities, interests, and needs." With the arrival of globalisation, the subaltern struggle around identity and exclusion took a new turn. The 1990s, for instance, witnessed electoral upsurge of the disadvantaged groups and radical transformation in the nature of politics in India with increasing participation of the marginalized people and rising grassroots political movements.

India is home to one third of the poorest people on earth, and has the largest concentration of tribal populations in the world. Under the Indian Constitution, such groups are referred to as "scheduled tribes," and in regional context they are known as *adivasis*. Soubhagya Padhi and Biswajita Padhi in their paper discuss the issues of health and human rights of tribal women in the Koraput district of Orissa. They argue that, in comparison to the earlier period where tribal women used to enjoy privilege positions in the society, today in this age of globalization they are identified to be the most exploited classes. The paper is based on the qualitative data collected from 23 remote tribal villages in the Koraput district of Orissa. The survey found that tribal women in the Koraput district are deprived of basic health facilities. Their accessibility to professional standards of health is severely limited. The authors have taken into consideration several indicators to analyse the health, human rights conditions of women that prevails among the tribal communities such as lack of communication facility, fertility and infant mortality rate, maternal mortality rate, nutrition rate, early marriage and maternal malnutrition, registration of pregnancy, distribution of work, economic situation, education, language and other infrastructure problems. One of the many strategies pointed out by the authors to overcome the gender disparities in the tribal societies is the involvement of different communities in decision making and mutual interaction between the service providers and the beneficiaries. The paper also urged the international community to reconsider the situation of Orissa and take into action to secure a representative government, which can be committed to international human rights standards including the equal rights for women.

Tribes have their own peculiar culture, civilisation, language or dialect in comparison to the general population. The North Eastern States of India have other than geographical uniformity, remained predominately tribal population with many languages, dialects, religions, and histories. R.A. Mangathai's paper focuses on the dimensions of gender inequality among the tribes of Tripura *especially* in the realm of personal law, inheritance of property and political participation. Although the literatures suggest that, there is a shift towards sanskritisation among the tribal women, as the practice of the rigidity of matriarchy is gradually breaking down as a result of the impact of modernisation, the author argues that women in Tripura still suffer from various discriminations. For instance, access to education among tribal women is limited due to lack of enabling environment and inaccessibility of schools, employment at government sector jobs are very less for women, they are denied of equal property rights, domestic violence is common among tribal women, and last but not the least the status of tribal women has worsened due to the change in their terms and levels of interaction with non-tribals. The author argues that, although globalization has changed the socio-economic conditions of tribals, it led to the gradual marginalisation of tribal women in socio-economic, political and traditional forums.

A significant development in recent years has been the mushrooming of community-based organizations and initiatives at the grassroots level. In India, in the recent past, self-help groups have been formed as part of the developmental strategy with primary focus on poverty alleviation and empowerment of women. Self-help groups are voluntary, small group structures for mutual aid and the accomplishment of a special purpose. They are usually formed by peers who have come together for mutual assistance in satisfying a common need, overcoming a common handicap or life-disrupting problem, and bringing about desired social and/or personal change. The initiators and members of such groups perceive that their needs are not, or cannot be, met by or through existing social institutions. Self-help groups emphasize face-to-face social interactions and the assumption of personal responsibility by members. They often provide material assistance, as well as emotional support; they are frequently cause-oriented, and promulgate an ideology or values through which members may attain an enhanced sense of personal identity.

Jayanta Choudhury in his paper argues that, strengthening of self-help groups (SHGs) is one of the important strategies for poverty alleviation in rural areas. The author has analysed the processes and stages of formation of SHGs in Tripura into three stages such as Government initiatives, NABARD initiatives, and NGOs initiatives. He has highlighted the factors that hinder the process of sustaining the SHGs in each of these three initiatives. The main reason for slow growth of self-help groups in Tripura, according to the author, is the autocratic leadership style of founders and a bureaucratization that preclude membership participation. The paper offers few suggestions and policies of how to sustain the SHGs. According to the author, the strength of SHG approach lies in mobilizing small savings of the poor, utilization of fund optimally through collective action (such as creation of rural infrastructure), participation of NGOs, regular meetings with banks and governments, transparent and democratic participation.

Niharranjan Mishra's paper focuses on the dimension of religious rituals and festivals associated with agriculture that are celebrated in Orissa and their changing patterns in the present context of globalisation. Beliefs in gods and goddesses and worshiping idols have become an inseparable part of the socio-cultural life of the people in Orissa. The author argues two important points in his paper, firstly, most of the rituals and festivals observed in Orissa are basically agro-centric, as the life in Orissa largely revolves around agriculture, and secondly, rituals are primarily observed to reduce or evade the evil influences on agriculture caused by the cyclic changes of nature. The paper has substantiated with primary sources of data such as personal observations of author as well as opinions of respondents regarding the importance of rituals, beliefs in gods and goddesses and their linkage with the agricultural practices in the rural areas of Orissa. The author argues that, although globalisation has made significant impact on the life of villagers today, the rituals and festivals associated with agriculture have still play an important role and celebrated among villagers today with much fanfare. The paper is an interesting attempt, as it covers some of the important aspects of village life through micro studies.

Neena Rosy Kahlon's paper focuses attention on the understanding of the social realities of health systems in the rural setting of Gurdaspur district of Punjab. The approach towards disease and its curative aspects have been inextricable linked to religious and cultural norms and practices in India. The paper argues that the perception of the villagers regarding health and illness is traditional and is governed by extra medication norms. The study, based on the data collected through primary sources reveals that, the modern health care delivery system has not made much impact in the rural areas and that the traditional faith healing practices still play an important role in the treatment of diseases. The paper in a way highlights certain important aspects of etiology, diagnosis and therapy.

The role of governmental and non-governmental organizations for the socio-economic development of tribal population in India has taken considerable attention by academicians and policy makers in the recent time. Eswarappa Kasi and R. Siva Prasad in their paper try to examine the socio-economic changes that have brought about as a result of the intervention of governmental and non-governmental organizations in the lives of marginalized tribal communities in Andhra Pradesh, especially focusing on a particular tribal group called *Sugalis* of Anantapur District. After examining the role of factionalism and faction politics in the implementation of development interventions, the authors focus on the types of change that the tribals have experienced as a result of the implementation of different schemes by both government and other agencies.

Taruna Upadhyaya's paper discusses about the Business Process Outsourcing (BPO) which has today become a global phenomenon. Today, companies that are leader in strategic thinking are using BPO to achieve important objectives that go beyond reducing the cost and attention given to non-strategic business processes. According to the author, Business Process Outsourcing is the delegation of one or more IT-intensive business processes to an external provider who, in turn, administers and manages the selected processes based upon defined and measurable performance metrics. It allows an enterprise to just focus on its core competency and by outsourcing all the other support based facets that generally consumes a substantial amount of a firm's time and energy.

V. Basil Hans's paper examines the socio-economic and political changes that has brought about as a result of liberalisation in the early 1990s in India, its impact on Indian diaspora, and the role of Indian diaspora for the development of homeland. According to the author, despite the impact of globalisation, Indians in the diaspora has retained their emotional, cultural and spiritual links with the motherland, which is symbolised through their socio-economic and political participations. The best example could be remittances of NRIs to their family members back home as well as involvement of diaspora in the developmental activities such as establishment of educational institutions, hospitals, and creation of "model villages." The paper addresses the central issue of formulation of policies of government of India towards Indian diaspora over the years. The author argues that, post-liberalisation consensual economic reforms especially after 1990s has led India to become a truly globalise economy and has resulted in the active participation of the Indian Diaspora. Efforts thus are being devoted to the mobilisation of the global NRI/PIO communities and resources for political, social and economic goals including developmental, philanthropic and educational activities of the NRI/PIO communities. The paper examines further the success story of Indians in the field of education, business, politics, and media in the diaspora as well as the ethnic conflicts of Indians with their counterparts on the issues of maintenance of culture. The paper concludes with few suggestions of how to bridge the cultural gap between India and the Indian diaspora.

Mukesh Kumar's paper focuses on the history of migration and construction of cultural identity of Indians in the Caribbean. It examines how the Indians in the plantations became the easy targets of discrimination, hostility, and violence in the hands of indigenous groups, and the lukewarm response of Indian government towards Indians in the Caribbean. The author argues that, despite the antagonistic and discriminatory policies of the Caribbean society, and despite the impact of globalization, Indians have still retained their ethnic and cultural identity which is expressed through their observation of cultural festivals and religious rituals. The paper concludes with the assertion that, a multicultural structure would be created which foster better social tolerance towards minorities, make them more visible and thereby ease ethnic and religious tensions and conflicts in the Caribbean.

Globalization has increased the mobility of human capital and high skills individuals as knowledge is becoming an integral part of the global economy. The mobility of human capital has both positive and negative impact on both host as well as sending countries. In host countries for instance, the contribution of skilled immigrant workers to economic growth, and in particular, to research, innovation and entrepreneurship is increasingly recognized, while to the sending country, migration of highly skilled workers often resulted in brain-drain, causing significant economic loss.

Jeetendra D. Soni and Surendra D. Soni in their paper developed a multilevel modular scheme to draw a strategic framework to address the issues of harnessing the potentials of diasporic community. According to the authors, in the recent years the Indian attitudes toward overseas Indians have undergone significant changes as a result of two important reasons. They are such as: 1) despite the socio-economic and political problems in the host society and despite the lack of concern of Indian government towards her people abroad, Indians have retained their cultural identity, and 2) it is because of the sizeable contribution of Indian diaspora in the form of remittances for the socio-economic development of the homeland. The authors argue that Indian diaspora is an invaluable asset for India and India should formulate strategies for the responsive and productive engagements of this diasporic community in the multifaceted fields. The paper calls for a new policy formulation that could trace the potentials, capabilities, aptitudes and attitudes of the Indian diaspora and to draw a strategy for their more productive engagements.

Ajaya Kumar Sahoo's paper examines the emergence of transnational networks of Indian diasporic communities. Taking the case study of one of the regional diasporic communities of India i.e., Oriyas in the global context, the paper traces the history of Oriya migration, perpetuation of Oriya culture in the host society and the present day transnational networks. The paper does not focus much on the abstract issues of "Oriya identity" in the host society, rather it emphasizes on the emerging transnational networks of Oriyas.

References

Bhat, C.S. and A. K. Sahoo. 2005. 'Transnational Networks of Indian Diasporic Communities: The Case of Telugu Diaspora'. *Man in India,* Vol. 85 (1 & 2): 61-80.

Centre for Development Enterprise. 1997. People on the Move: Lessons from International Migration Policies. Johannesburg.

Cohen, Robin. 1997. Global Diaspora: An Introduction. London: UCL Press.

Firedman, Jonathan. 1996. *Cultural Identity and Global Process.* London: Sage Publication.

Glick-Schiller, N. Basch, L and Blanc-Szanton, C. 1992. *Towards a Transnational Perspective on Migration: Race, Class, Ethnicity and Nationalism Reconsidered.* New York: New York Academy of Sciences.

Harvey, David 1990. *The Conditions of Postmodernity.* Oxford: Blackwell

Levitt, P. 2001. *The Transnational Villagers.* Berkeley: University of California Press.

Ramsaran, Dave and Derek V. Price. 2003. 'Globalization: A Critical Framework for Understanding Contemporary Social Processes'. *Globalization,* Vol. 3, Issue, 2.

Robertson, Ronald. 1996. *Globalization: Social Theory and Global Culture.* London: Sage Publication.

Sharma, K.N. 2004. 'Globalization: How Novel? How Noble?'. In: Surendra K. Gupta (ed.) *Emerging Social Science Concerns: Festschrift in Honour of Professor Yogesh Atal.* New Delhi: Concept Publishing Company.

Stiglitz, Joseph H. 2002. *Globalization and its Discontents.* New Delhi: Penguin Books

United Nations. 2000. *The Realization of Economic, Social and Cultural Rights: Globalization and its impact on the Full Employment of Human Rights.* Preliminary report submitted by J. Oloka-Onyango and Deepika Udagama in accordance with Sub-Commission resolution 1999/8.

Vertovec, S. 1997. 'Three Meanings of "Diaspora" Exemplified among South Asian Religions'. *Diaspora,* Vol. 6, No. 3: 277-99.

1
Academic-Sociology and Use-Sociology: A Dilemma

Samir Dasgupta

Sociologists should not trouble themselves more to open new avenues for intellectual stimulation and intellectual barbarism. If such process continues then we will be on the borderline of post risk society and simulacra-fashioned 'sociological imagination'. The reality of unreal has already been dominated over the field of sociological theoretical puzzle. And we are ignoring the fact that "*the character of any sociological inquiry depends upon by and for whom it is conceived and applied*".

Intellectuals no longer legislate they just interpret. It is undeniable that sociology today is suffering mostly from the disease of language. But if we back to our original roots, we could notice that sociology was very much concerned with the idea of progress, humanity, freedom and peace. Here lies the importance of practicing applied sociology.

Status of Contemporary Sociology

The philosophers discussed much of the subject matter of sociology without thinking of it as a distinct subject. In the early 19th century all the subject matter of the social sciences was discussed under the heading of moral philosophy.

Even after Auguste Comte's coinage of the word sociologie in 1838, the matter was mingled with other social sciences for some sixty years. In 1890 Albion Small, taught a course called sociology, as did Franklin H. Giddings in the same year. But 1892 was the year of the first real commitment to the creation of a field of sociology that took place in the University of Chicago.

In the following year or two, departments in the subject were flowered at various universities. By the late 1890s nearly all of the educational institutions in the United States either had departments of sociology or offered courses in the subject. The history tells us that the similar developments of the growth of Sociology have occurred in various other parts of the world. After 1945 a strong revival of interest in sociology took place in various academic and professional institutes in Europe and USA. German sociology had a strong base in the late 19th century and afterward, and the writings of Ferdinand Tönnies, Max Weber, Georg Simmel, and others were influential in all parts of the world. By the early 1930s, however, official Nazi hostility had impeded its development and by the time of World War II had destroyed it as an academic subject in Germany.

Immediately after the war a new generation of scholars, aided by visiting sociologists, imported the new empirical research methods and began the development of a style of applied German sociology much different from the classical theoretical traditions. At the University of Frankfurt, Max Horkheimer's Institute was revived. By 1970 most West German universities began to cultivate applied sociology like administrative research of use to planning, studies of unemployment, youth problems, and delinquency. In Great Britain, Sociology was mainly concentrated on studies of the poor, and much of it was undertaken by social workers in the United States. In the postwar period, a considerable revival of sociology took place in the London School of Economics, Oxford and Cambridge. A parallel growth took place in Canada, Australia, and New Zealand. Canada, Japan. Israel, India, Africa, Philippines, Indonesia, Pakistan, the Scandinavian countries with some apparent reluctance, allowed itself to be much influenced by American sociology.

The dispute about the main purpose of sociology, whether it works to understand rhetoric discourse, or to cause human progress. In contemporary society there has emerged a radical movement among sociologists in various countries involving advocacy of complete commitment to action and practice on current social problems. Applications of sociology now appear to be spreading in a variety of directions, and here the possibilities of applied activities continue to spread.

C. H. Cooley (1924) states that "I will not attempt at this time to estimate the contribution of Herbert Spencer—he certainly had a vast and on the whole salutary influence—but I will call attention to one aspect of his work which is pertinent to what I have to say. His sociological theories, it seems to me, were not well suited to be the starting point for detailed scientific investigation, on account of the somewhat remote and analogical character of their relation to actual life. They did not spring primarily from social observation; they sprang rather from the wish to extend over the social field conceptions drawn from physics and biology. As they were not tools forged to deal with social facts they could not readily be used for the purpose by other students.

I take it, then, that the younger generation of students at that time felt, vaguely perhaps, that the right start had not been made, that there was no practical basis for applying the evolutionary ideas of the time to human life, and that it still remained to build a satisfactory frame-work upon which the growth of a modern social science could proceed. His point is that, thoroughness of detailed investigation was not at that time a practicable ideal, because if at-tempted, it would have proved unsound for lack of sound general premises to base it on. "We all feel, I think, that a good deal of detailed work has actually been done, by biologists or others not in touch with the progress of sociology, which is nearly or quite worthless because not soundly based."

Cooley (1924) continues, "The rising generation is the best judge as to what its task is. It would seem, however, if what I have said is sound, that not much of its best energies is likely to get into general works on the principles of sociology. Text-books we shall no doubt have—a constant flow of them—and that is well because a teacher can be most effective when he uses his own book. But I conceive that original work is likely to take the direction of more limited but thorough studies. This work will be theoretical—I for one am not interested in any work that is not—but the theory will spring from a more circumscribed and penetrating study of fact. There is room for many such books, and, if they are really well done, a technical public ready to appreciate them. Let me ask, finally, whether the time has not come for a more stringent criticism of our product? We elders have "got by" and now we would like to raise the standard. When everybody was trying to do everything we were all so superficial that no one ventured to cast stones at any one else. But the new generation will not tolerate "arm-chair sociology." There is altogether too much foundation for the impression prevailing in other fields that work in sociology is hasty and pretentious. Let us have no journalism, but insist that whatever a man's subject, or whatever his conception of scientific method, he give us no work that is not, in one way or another, a thoroughly good job" (Cooley, 1924).

Applied Sociology-What does it Sense?

It is often said that ideas rule the world, but this is true only of world ideas. The highest and brightest ideas, the most profound and important thoughts of any age or people, have scarcely any influence upon the world. This is because such ideas are always confined to a very few of the most developed minds and are not shared by the mass of mankind. They do not belong to the world. There is supposed to be no way by which they can be conveyed to mankind at large. No thought has any appreciable social effect except it be actually possessed by society. The whole of society, i.e., all sane persons of mature minds, must themselves think it, otherwise it is socially ineffective. But any idea that permeates the whole mass and becomes the thought of society itself sways the mass and shapes the action of society in its entirety (Lester Ward, 1906: 40). This is the philosophy behind the dialect of applied sociology.

The history of the metamorphosis of sociology is unique. The transformation of the discipline from the philosophical tradition to the empirical and applied fields has given the discipline the highly valued status in modern society. Sociology, from the academic orbit has now stepped into the applied world where intellectual stimulators have merged with practitioners. Though applied sociology is the product of American temper it is undeniable that each and every word of sociology has an applied bearing. Practically, sociology builds on a triadic paradigm i.e. truth, reality and reconstruction. The growth of sociology from the earliest roots in enlightenment, through the philosophers, positivists, social surveyors, and theorists is now again getting back to its applied roots. From the technical dialect for which sociologists have earned dubious notoriety (Peter Berger, 1963), sociology, at present, is gaining its applied status and moving into the realms of the first step of freedom.

It is sometimes viewed by a section of so called *intellectual sociologists,* who claim themselves as the initiators and modifiers of sophisticated abstract theories, that the applied use of sociology be neglected. But the classic thinkers of sociology use their intellectual temper with a view to remove social anarchy and chaos. They had in mind to use sociology for a better world with the notion of applying its common sense. Their 'common sense sociology' might be historical or theory-based but it represents applied consequences and usage. The social sciences are important to a democracy because they encourage the open discussion and the sociologist can make the contribution only if his situation affords him reasonable freedom and security (Gunner Myrdal, 1953).

To move within the orbit of theoretical and academic demarcations is intellectual barbarism. Sociology becomes an applied discourse if sociologists step out of line. Weinstein (2005) argues, "Many of us were educated in this "pure science" tradition. We were strongly encouraged to seek academic careers in which the number of articles published in referred journals was used as primary measure of our worth. And we were vigorously discouraged from entertaining the "adolescent fantasy" that sociology was to be used to improve the world (p.7). Philosophers have only interpreted the world, in various ways; the point is to change it. (Karl Marx, 1978 [1888]) Recently sociologists have become concerned not just about the lack of a guiding paradigm but about their very futures as members of a *subsidized* academic discipline. As universities are swiftly entering into vocational paradigms and slowly dismantling sociology departments around the country especially in the Third world countries, and so we have all been pressing the question what is sociology, why should it exists, and how can we protect ourselves from the fear of loosing identity.

The loudest voices speaking to this question have, so far, been those who helped get us into this fix those who are searching for a paradigm rather than a purpose, for a model rather than a method, for science rather than usefulness, for the middle ground rather than the marginalized voices (Stoecker, 1992). As a result we are either absent or seen as useless. Sociologists now claim and raise their voice of protest: "*Why does our discipline abrogate its responsibility for creating a better world, or why does it do so by adopting hierarchical, exclusionary modes of gathering and distributing.*" But alas! Sociology is still remains as a sophisticated academic discipline, living in the shelter of university, confined in the academic prison. They are serving as free scholars, teaching the borrowed concepts, doing their self styled research, producing mostly unproductive, nasty, repetitive and journalistic Ph.D. theses, which have no link with national development and social conditions. They are; therefore, free to neglect their obligation to human beings. The mastermind sociologists began sociology with its theoretical frame of references, putting stress on applied underpinnings of the theoretical context. So the beginning of sociology had practical implications for human lives, which Mills (1959) emphasizes when developing his idea of the sociological imagination. The sense of conviction and commitment are the prime movers in use-sociology. The metamorphosis of the approach from creative imagination to practical usage is important to be considered for reaching the root. It is claimed, 'Sociology, of course, purports to be an intellectual discipline that seeks to understand our experience of society' (Peter Berger & Brigitte Berger, 1972: 3). But side-by-side, society is our experience with other people around us. So facing, interacting and encountering other people are our daily experiénces. And, as sociologists, we should not hide ourselves under the box of intellectual puzzle rather we should apply our theoretical intellect for the betterment of the human species.

Finally, increasing numbers of the next generation of sociologists are asking for something different from their sociological training. They want a greater diversity of voices, from the ground up; involved in their academic socialization

The Objectives and Missions

Developing understanding and appreciation for the diverse actions, challenges, and accomplishments of community-based service providers, organizers, and activists in grappling with social issues; and familiarizing with the methods of applied sociology such as: problem exploration, policy analysis, problem mapping, and program and action evaluations; and lastly engaging in active learning experiences and exercises to develop the one-on-one skills (e.g. negotiation) and group skills (e.g. envisioning processes) necessary to effectively interact with others in public life If sociology gets its professional status the question of knowledge application will come into fore and then the subject will be made either through method oriented-research or its application through the process of interaction with the "client".

Alvin Gouldner and S.M. Miller (1965) state, "*It is the historic mission of the social sciences to enable mankind to take possession of society*" (p.VII). Of course applied sociology does not necessarily mean the science of social problems. It is very much open like the sky. And theory building without evaluation does not cover the meaning of sociological study. There should be a balance between theory and fact and the result will produce the practical utility of sociological know-how. It is undeniable that the applied sociology is always beyond the intellectual classical stimulation. The classical thinkers had in mind the practical reasoning of knowledge-sociology, which was hidden, owing to the intellectual pressure of theory building.

Jay Weinstein (2002), rightly states, "Applied (or practicing) sociologists tend to embrace an essentially pragmatic philosophy of science in which the ultimate test of theory is the extent to which it can produce knowledge that works" (p.1). He does not admit that making a commitment to applied approaches is tantamount to proportional suicide rather this is the only key to professional success and commitment to social being. The root of applied sociology lies embedded in the theories and approaches of the classical thinkers. This 'Third World' knowledge locates the senses of applied sociology. In the 1920s logical positivism, which had developed from radical positivism, starting from the investigation of the 'Vienna circle' continued its struggle against 'metaphysics' from the positions of empiricism. Evidence of the senses and this criterion of the fact and its verifiability haunted the mind of the philosophers. Comte observes that all scientific knowledge can only be obtained through observation, experiment, descriptions and generalizations with the help of mathematical means. So "inherent in the (actual) doctrine of positivism is the understanding that until and unless our theories are applied, we will never know if they are valid" (Weinstein, 2002). Spencer's idea on Progress marks the significance of practical sociology.

Emile Durkheim also uses a clinical paradigm of sociology. Durkheim was also an activist – a practicing sociologist. He was very concerned with the issue of educational reform, study of suicide and theory-empirical findings that put him on the map of applied sociology. Max Weber presses on the application of interpretative sociology to empirical analysis. He develops a paradigm where the particular action concerned is "*placed in an understandable sequence of motivation, the understanding of which can be treated as an explanation of the actual course of behaviour*". Lester Ward (1906) who happens to be the ideal progenitor of applied sociology establishes its philosophical truth.

Practically, the university academic draws a line of demarcation between sociological theory and practice or otherwise between abstractions and applications. A metamorphosis has just happened. From macro thinking to micro thinking - from broad based philosophical generalization to pin point and specific empiricism – from university academic stimulations to social practicing – from theorist to professionals. This transformation is necessary to keep safe the autonomy of the discipline-it is necessary to make the discipline an applied one like engineering, medical and law. People trained in sociology are to be found as industrial consultants, urban planners, social workers and personnel managers as well as in many other practical jobs.

So with the changing situation of time and space, the nature and context of applied sociology have also changed. Applied sociology should be assessed in terms of the social, cultural, valuational, economic and spatial settings of the people. Here lies the real linkage between social being and professionals – between sociology and social policy and between social order and human behaviour. It is an undeniable reality that sociology is not just an abstract intellectual phenomenon but has major practical implications for people's lives. So the applied sociologists say that Sociology refers to different theoretical trends, but also based on a diversity of research and practice models, related to different theoretical presuppositions and methodological issues. For example, a participatory survey, an autobiographic approach (life story), action research, group interviews are techniques to be put in a broader context to become a applied process of producing knowledge. It has to be much more than techniques. "Learning to become a sociologist should not be a dull academic endeavour. The best way to make sure it does not become so is to approach the subject in an imaginative way and to relate sociological ideas and findings to situations in your own life" (Anthony Giddens, 1992). It appears that public interest in the development of sociological knowledge increases as a consequence of rising awareness of its promise for human safety and welfare.

With the emergence of globalization domestic problems within nations, regions, cities, and towns appear to become increasing sources of human crisis. A tendency of increasing severity of ethnic hostilities and conflict, rise of fundamentalism and religious bigotry, and of internal conflicts between generations, political factions, and other divisions of the populations are also coming into the fore. There are also threats to human peace and better living from various forms of general social disorganization, reflected in the spread of pockets of poverty, delinquency, crime, vice, political corruption, community disorganization, homelessness, sex assault, age old problem, and family disorganization. The threats of overpopulation, degradation of the ecological environment and loss of bio diversity have added a further reason for public alarm.

Academic or journalistic sociologists do not yet provide the solutions. Here lies the need and growing demand of applicable knowledge of sociology. Applications of sociology also appear to be spreading in multifaceted directions, and here the scopes seem unlimited. Sociologists aid industries, hospitals, banks, NGOs, rural administrations, help unions, organize protest movements of students and youth, reform disadvantaged villages, counsel persons, addicts and families, and gives or sells services to a wide variety of consumers. To what extent these applied activities will continue to spread will doubtless depend on their effectiveness relative to other means of gaining the same effects. Freeman and Rossi (1984) invoked, "it is not possible to train students in applied sociology without on-going faculty involvement in the work we are training them for". To encourage such training, they lay out a list of specific illustrative changes needed in sociology departments to accommodate applied sociology, such as a openness to publications in non-sociology journals as well as technical and proprietary reports; flexibility to allow a colleague to take an applied, public service assignment; and adequate support staff to help to ensure the quick and quality turnaround applied clients require. Their and other ideas for shifts in graduate education will be taken up by an exceptional panel of sociologists at the ASA's Directors of Graduate Study conference in August on "Preparing for Applied Careers." A 1998 ASA report on "Applied Programmes" profiles a number of MA-only programmes that have been particularly creative in addressing actual or simulated client-driven research agendas. Many of these programs include a sociological research centre at the hub, where faculty and students engage in collaborative research. Freeman and Rossi made the point, and I concur, that not all sociologists or sociology departments should turn to applied activity, but, as in economics, the strength of our discipline can derive from high quality "training" for and "doing" of both academic and non-academic work (Felice J. Levin, 2005).

The classical sociologists thought they would explore the causes of social problems and policy makers would gobble up the knowledge, embrace new solutions and create a better world. *These early social scientists had no idea that the powers that be would actively seek to suppress and distort their knowledge.* Reflecting on society eventually leads to conclusions about the causes of social problems and effective remedies. But in a world where the turf has already been divided up, any solutions are likely to step on toes of powers that be who are profiting off the way things are. Even if it would benefit everyone in the long run, the ultimate conservative agenda is to leave things alone.

Sociology, argues Bauman (1990) offers us a commentary-a refinement on the knowledge we possess and use in everyday life. It extends the social map beyond our personal experience so that we have a scope to perceive and internalize areas of human activity. The sociology of use is reentered as a substantive body of knowledge relevant to the work of all sociologists and essential for ameliorating social problems. Weinstein (2000) develops a twin paradigm of use-sociology and academic sociology. He argues, "*Applied (or practicing) sociologists tend to embrace an essentially pragmatic philosophy of science in which the ultimate test of theory is the extent to which it can produce knowledge that 'works'. Academic Sociologists employ the nomological model that focuses on the development of theory for its own sake*".

The practical knowledge is valued. "*This account of practical knowledge has its immediate roots in the pragmatist epistemology of the late nineteenth and early twentieth centuries*" (Weinstein, p.11). If we view knowledge as the source of human existence then it can be assumed that man's cognitive activity and its results are the organic part of practice. It is the result of man's cognitive activity, a collection of objective reality.

Applied Sociology is the use of sociological principles and research methods to analyze and suggest solutions to various social problems and difficulties. This term tends to imply a more active use of research. Many a sociological writing opens with a definition of a new concept (or relationship) and a discussion of methods to be employed to measure it. This is then frequently followed by presentation of some data relevant to the new concept. For the resurgence of applied sociology to occur, it needs to be mindful of the socio-historical documents and chronology of social change. One should not be the servant of power. Sociology without freedom of thinking is meaningless. Unless the negotiation between theory and empirical research, between study of macro problem and micro problems, between freedom and bonded choice take place, the arena of applied sociology will be confined within its boundary.

Applied Sociology in the Shrinking World

We never go to remedy social problems by just insisting individuals try harder (Durkheim). Individual problems are not the result of moral failings. It is the system that has to change. The vision of a society in crisis, which is the result of postmodern irony, can easily be perceptible and can be tackled by using the methods of applied sociology. Here, method does not imply the jargonic or confined written methods rather it means the application of the scientific method with openness of mind and vision. To put it simply we should start with the question: Sociology for whom? When trained sociologists consider the question it can either trouble them on open up new avenues for intellectual exploration, self-awareness and historical perspective. Lee (1976) calls upon professional sociologists, as individuals and members of schools, to struggle to obtain a hold upon the discipline.

"They (the Professional Sociologists) are caught up in the practical experiences of careerism and therefore, inclined to act robot-like in terms of the mandates of the marketplace" (Lee, 1976: 926). In Europe, sociologists use the theoretical pretensions under the mask of intellectual stimulation. It is only in America where the cultivation of applied sociology

took its own room. The rest of the continents were very much identical with the theoretical study of social reality. Pitirim Sorokin (1941) in his excellent work explores the vast expanse of human affairs and points out the surfacing crisis of modernity. With the mission of crisis eradication, the concept of globalization dominated over the intellectual arena. It is about reacting out and encompassing the whole globe and drawing everybody in. But in reality it is more like deciding who to pick to be part of the central economy and who to exclude. In the era of globalization, we witness the tragic division of humanity and hostile groups. Terrorism, bigotry, fundamentalism, ethnic violence, fanaticism, severe famine, economic genocide, moral and ethical corruption, debt burden - all are the gifts of globalization, which compounds the crisis in society. The nature and extent of social problems have changed its character and dimension. Our society has now become a postmodern forest of social problems in which lives the majority who are suffering from the pain of crisis of existence and identity. Two global wars and a series of major revolutions and civil wars had already taken place and the world is embroiled in what would become the Third world war. As a result the moral fibre of society is weakening. People are loosing faith in the objectivity and value of their systems of truth, justice and law. Codes of right and wrong are no longer valued as appropriate standards for conduct; instead, they have become devices by which the rich and powerful could consolidate their privileges and manipulate disadvantaged under class (Barry V. Johnston, 1998). The post war society thus faces unobtrusive and deadening conditions. The crisis of our age therefore needs a moral and applied social reconstruction. Here lies the necessity of having applied sociological knowledge. It should be the right choice and responsibility of the applied sociologists to educate people and stimulate commitment to development. This is the empirical philosophy of the interaction between the professional (sociologist) and the client (social being). "Applied sociology, involves the implementation of discoveries of theoretical sociology to ameliorate problems created by social change" (Sorokin, 1937: 22). The activity is very much concerned with problem making and problem solving, linking theory with action.

An applied sociologist leaving behind his interpretive inequity should be concerned with the need-oriented problems of the clients. In that case he must be an altruist, a humanist sociologist and a solidary interactionist. Secondly, applied sociology should have a close link with the cultural pattern, cultural diversity and cultural particularism of a society. The professional-client relationship as the prime expression of applied sociology mostly depends on each cultural type, which ultimately shapes its institutional complexes and social variability with proper truth and reality.

William Kolb (1951), notes, "Atomization fragmentation, alienation, bureaucratization, terror, and the loss of human choice are all realistic of our time" (P.268). These modernization phenomena make our society more complicated. So the applied sociological field should not be confined in the cage of *problem–specific behaviour* but rather, it should cover the macro aspects with its macro vision and insights.

Theory and Practice: A Synthesis or Dichotomy?

Hundreds of years have passed but we have not yet been able to explore the practical uses and usages of the discipline. "We have not yet learned enough about how to permit the growth of necessary institutionalization of our discipline without diminishing opportunities for creative dissent" (Alfred McChung Lee, 1976: 925). Two steps have only outlined by the sociologists i.e. conceiving sociological inquiry and applying the conceived academic temper. The strange 'interlude of such dual orientations makes purely knowledge-based theoretical stimulation and practice based applied stimulation. The intellectual knowledge based sociology got its room in European sociological arena and America gives birth to applied sociology. And the debate between university intellectuals and professionals still continues. In America, sociologists are mostly professional "they are disposed to obligate themselves to the demands of academical administrators, to political and business establishments that operate educational and research organizations, to book publishers and to those who provide subsidies for special projects of research, writing and consultation" (Lee, 1976: P.926). Fletcher (1970) observes that the most serious and searching discussions of sociological theory have taken place in America and "we need to deplore the misplaced intellectual snobbery with which American scholarship has seemed, sometimes, to have been greeted by British Scholars – though this, for a long time now, has very definitely been declining". The *theoretical-applied continuum paradigm* of American sociology is at present undeniably positive, critical and cosmopolitan in its character. It is certainly generous in its appraisal of the contributions of scholars of other countries (Fletcher, 1970).

British sociology on the other hand, is very historical by its approach and content. It has a tendency to carry the sociological bag empty applied content. Only Geddes, Becker, Charles Booth, Peter Townsend and Rowntree had opened the petals of applied sociology in Britain. The period from 1880 to 1920 was one of the deep involvements of middle class people in U.K. and America in human efforts to perceive and to reform the living conditions of the distressed people living in urban areas. Charles Booth in his "*Life and Labour of the People of London*" explores the factual conditions of life style of the poor in London. The study documents the reform, a fact-based paradigm of social policy, and develops the practice of empirical social study. Jane Addams, in the U.S.A, pioneered practicing urban social work specifically for the establishment of housing settlements among the industrial poor. W.E. DuBois' in his study "*The Philadelphia Negro in 1899*" contributes much to the field of practical research in social science. The social survey tradition that developed by classical British sociologists entered into the arena of American Sociology with the work of Ogburn in 1930. The old style survey has developed into empirical social research. It regards itself as a systematic method of examining hypotheses. The technique of practical social research aims at reducing the variety of subjective opinions, attitudes, and behaviour form which it claims to establish the nature of objective social institutions and processes (Heinz Maus, 1962).

The practical roots of applied Sociology are embedded in the hydra-headed expansion of the discipline. It touches biology, geography, medical science, ethnology, social psychology, anthropology, etc. It also extends its antenna to touch criminology, social work and epistemology. The symbiosis and the synthesis ultimately lead to the study and perceive social reality. Secondly, most of the universities in developed countries begins to teach the practical social research. "It is now regarded as the only suitable scientific form for modern sociology and incidentally one which has earned sociology the approval of those who control large-scale industry and government (Heinz Maus, 1962). The shifting visions of Sociology make a dichotomy between content and purpose for the discipline. Lee (1976) states, "*how can sociology continue to survive and thrive unless sociologists see themselves as part of the social and intellectual struggles to make more dignified human life and living possible for our grandchildren*" (pp.933-934). Herein lies the importance of practicing applied sociology. Sociology is certainly a broad ranging, daring, adapting, searching, problem-locating and problem-solving instrument. The question 'sociology for whom' needs rethinking and the easy answer i.e. "sociology for the service of humanity" should be re-evaluated in the context of modernization crisis. This refers to the need to develop the knowledge of direct service to people as citizens, as consumers and as neighbours. It is not our vision to see the world in terms of facts and things but rather to connect these with social and individual needs and desires. The changed vision of applied sociology is the product of the unfolding debate about its subjectivity and objectivity. "*Practice follows the truth, not vice versa*" (Marcuse, 1960: 322).

Applied Sociology: What does it sense?

Depending on our commonsense knowledge we can view the historically changing society and perceive our own views and outlook. The synthesis of our own views about us and the views of the social being of changing society, which occurs by the process of mutual transformation and transmission, denotes applied sociological know-how. The necessity of applied study of society and social beings, which crosses the borderline of our common-sense knowledge through careful and humane investigation, covers practical need and moral and value oriented feelings for purposive action. Fletcher (1970) observes, *"As soon as we become involved in particular conflicts with other groups in society; as soon as we are brought face to face with particular social problems; we are at once made aware how little we really know about social reality, and at once realize that a more painstaking study of the facts is necessary............. We would like to eliminate from society war, poverty, crime and delinquency. ... We would like to improve matters; to remove these obstacles to social justice; and would therefore like to know the underlying causes of these social facts"* (pp.35-36). The knowledge of sociology serves the purpose of perceiving the problems and helps sociologists to formulate effective social policies. This is the prime rationale of practicing applied sociology. Very recently the term "*Sociologic Practice'* has been defined as the content of both applied and clinical sociology. Practicing sociologists "use sociology as the solution to practical problems, as appeared to doing research and/or teaching sociology in a relatively abstract academic setting, such as a university or research institute". Applied sociologists, in particular, use the broad canvas of theoretical principles in sociology and sociological research techniques in their attempts to resolve these problems. This clarification is a little bit unclear. The definition is partially correct in terms of its concept bearing. It is a new academic stimulation – a revised paradigm of the application of orthodox sociological theory and scienticism. The applied sociologist mostly analyzes the notion of sociological application in the context of problem-solving study. They observe that applied Sociology is the use of sociological principles and research methods to analyze and suggest solutions to various social problems and difficulties. This term tends to imply a more active use of research. The professional-client interaction is the prime agenda of applied sociology. For example, when a patient feels sick he calls a physician. The physician (a professional) detects the disease adopting different methods of research like pathological test,

X-ray, Scan etc. The findings of this test help the physician to prescribe appropriate medicine to his patient for his recovery. Here a patient (client) seeks the assistance of a doctor (professional) in resolving his organic problem. Likely, a family or a group of families (client) may seek assistance of a sociologist (professional) in resolving family problems. Industrial organizations, corporate houses, banks, community organization, rural management organization etc. may also seek help of a sociologist to explore and resolve their problems.

Here applied sociologists have to depend on research and secondly, on the basis of findings they can supply policy guidelines and policy recommendations to the concerned clients. So it is observed that applied sociologists who normally employ social research methods may often be called upon to take recommended changes to their clients in the course of their works. It is also to be noted that most of the individuals who certainly belong to any type of organizations have some problems, which are more than individual i.e. social. It is also the responsibility of an applied sociologist to trace immediately the origin of social problems. It is called applied research method, which is very much scientific and problem-specific, by nature. The deductions that might be theoretical or empirical will satisfy the demand of the social clients. Of course, the professional-client interaction, as the base of applied sociology, undeniably should have a strong theoretical knowledge and insight to use theory in the applied paradigms. In a word, applied sociology should bear a theory-action linkage and theory-empirical orientations. Contemporary Sociologists therefore begin with the assumptions that an use-sociology is nothing but the applications of generalizations, developed by pure sociology to concrete and practical cases.

Status of Applied Sociology in India

Sociology in India is mostly the product of the west. So in the beginning there was a trend of studying western societies. The influence of British tradition had implications for the unit of analysis and even the choice of problems (Y.B, Damle, 1982). The practice, teaching and research in sociology in India because of certain degree of western, Euro centric and American bias have not developed with its own character and lost its own approach. But logically speaking, the societies studied by sociologists have mainly been their own; they have given most of the attention to their own contemporary societies. This is the prime point of departure of the nature of Indian sociology from others. Secondly, because of the intellectual vertigo and elitist mind-set (who have taken training or doctoral degree or advanced courses either in U.K. or in U.S.A), the growth of Indian sociology has followed a slow and tortuous path. But it had a background of indigenous applied sociology. Sociology and social anthropologies in the seventies made its value felt by the planners, administrators and policy makers.

The discipline has found a legitimate place in the major research institutes, institutes of technology, NGO sectors, management, planning commission, some ministries and institutes of tribal development and also in industries (M.S.A. Rao, 1982). In the 1970's, India's sociology had made a useful contribution to the applied fields like health, nutrition, education, welfare, industry, rural and urban development. "The professional status of sociology is yet to be firmly established" (Unnithan, 1982: 75). So it can be argued that sociology in India is still suffering from the crisis of professional stability, lack of scientific methodological knowledge and the crisis of theoro-empirical blending. Thirdly, sociology in India suffers from identity crisis and the sense of intellectual elitism of the theory-cultivators. The country, which is the victim of globalization gloom and where we see the cloud of poverty, illiteracy, health hazard, industrial risks, unemployment, dowry death, malnutrition. Family disorganization, urban poverty, child abuse, sex assault etc., there we can perceive the immense scope of applied sociological research and do-good motivation. With this motivation we have formed the organization to explore the vast potentials of applied or practicing sociology in India.

The time has come for the sociologists to be engaged in the practice of our profession and its application to address issues of societal importance should be committed to the following principles of professional ethics and standards: the right of all individuals to be treated with culturally sensitive respect and dignity, regardless of their relationship to the professional activities being conducted, the right of members to engage in free inquiry and publicly clarify their research and findings if either is misrepresented , the responsibility of members to be sensitive to their personal beliefs and advocacy regarding an issue as it relates to their ability to objectively perform professional activities related to that same issue, the responsibility of members to evaluate the potential positive outcomes of their professional activities and act in a manner consistent with the principles of this code.

The practice of sociology, it is the responsibility of members, above all else, to knowingly do no harm to those they serve or their research subjects. This responsibility includes all individuals and social groups regardless of the member's assessment of the legitimacy or role in society of that person or group.

It can be argued that sociology in India is suffering from the crisis of professional stability, lack of scientific methodological knowledge and the crisis of theoro-empirical blending. It also suffers from identity crisis and the sense of intellectual elitism of the classical theory-cultivators. A group of Indian sociologist deals with the western theoretical puzzle and another section expresses interest to cultivate indigenous sociological theory based on the concept of historicity of Indian reality, tales of nationalist consciousness, and movement, ideological puzzles, ethnographic and village studies, Panchayat, caste and clan mapping, cultural continuity and change etc.

So, sociology in India, as in many parts of the world, is in need of renewal (Andre Beteille, 2002). Regional sociology in India, for example sociology in West Bengal, excepting the classic and applied works of a few, is mostly social policy support oriented. The practitioners always show a trend of writing research papers, monographs or books on either village Panchayat or on the issue of rural development, Dalit Sociology, village organization, caste mapping or on the issue of political movements. But most of them have practically contributed a very little to the current and complicated field of Indian applied Sociology. The works of rural reconstruction or elimination of rural vices or reform (Structural and functional) of village Panchayat is the agenda of the Government. Neither the Government's policy of rural reconstruction or land reform or village Panchayat, so far the reality is concerned, has made successfully possible on the basis of any sociological theory or empirical data or sociologists' participation as a practitioner to supply theoro-empirical inputs to the Government for rural development programmes and other national development policies.

In India Sociologists, are not involved in the work of policymaking – if involved, their opinion is mostly being ignored. Secondly, social reconstruction policy suffers mostly from the lack of having sociological knowledge of the practitioners. On the contrary most of the sociological research in India is 'non-relevant' to policy issues and the findings are generally unproductive in the matter of policy formulation and policymaking. But sociologists sometimes show intellectual gesture (which I call elitist snobbery) to be associated invisibly with such two or three or four specific fields, which are the concern of the Government. Regional sociology in India, as such, suffers from academic puzzle, professional identity crisis, and classroom confinement. The country, which is the victim of globalization gloom and where we see the cloud of poverty, illiteracy, health hazard, industrial risks, unemployment, dowry death, malnutrition, family disorganization, urban poverty, child abuse, sex assault etc., there we can perceive the immense scope of applied sociological research and do-good motivation.

The sociologists of the period of emergence were less concerned with the professionalisation of sociology in respect of concepts, theories, methodologies and practice. Their only interest was with the issue, of social relevance (Y. Singh, 1986). S.C. Dube (1977) notes, "Even after three decades of independence both teaching and research in sociology continues to be cast in the colonial mould. It is incredible but true that sociologists in India did not react to the advent of freedom in any significant manner. In fact they began initiating the western pattern under the guise of cultivating international science without any sense of guilt or even qualms of conscience" (p.10) Andre Beteille (2002) distinguishes sociology from social engineering and social activism. He comments that sociology is not blended with social engineering or social activism rather it serves a larger social purpose by advancing main critical understanding of his social circumstances. He notes, *"I can not think of many sociologists who have contributed substantially to the solutions of practical problems or used their specialized knowledge to spearhead an effective social movement. But the best among them, such as Max Weber, Raymond Aron and in our own country M.N. Srinivas, have enriched our critical understanding of our own social circumstances. .... I have never been attracted by the idea of sociology as a policy science. It can contribute something to policy analysis but very little to policy prescription. Sociologists who place their services at the disposal of the government often come to grief; their advice is either ignored or put to use contrary to the ones intended"* (p.8). The thinking of Andre Beteille is certainly real but still the question comes into mind: Sociology for whom? Will it move around the orbit of theoretical abstraction only? It is the reality that we have neither developed any theoretical paradigm, which is truly global or local, nor any specific world-view school of thought, which have been accepted and became popular. It is mainly because of the fact that we have re-cultivated the western sociological doctrine and ours sociology did not emerge from any critical stage like cultural or economic or political crisis. Only Nationalist consciousness and the spirit of Nationalist movement shaped and influenced our sociological body of knowledge.

So, sociology in India has become the analytical history of Indian social reality and social structure. For the reason perhaps, it has become very much academic and university-centric. It is evident from a project report that around 100,000 undergraduate, 6000 postgraduate and 200 doctoral students come out of Indian Universities every year. But most of them do not get opportunities to be associated with practicing sociology. Problems of unemployment, lack of scope of professional sociology and identity crisis of the discipline make the students frustrating. The University Grants Commission has recently framed the undergraduate and postgraduate curricula with the notion of job orientation, knowledge orientation and social orientation. Keeping these orientations in mind, the National curricula committee emphasizes the following as objectives of sociology education: *"to equip the students to critically understand and interpret social reality, to generate in students a distinctly sociological perspective on socioeconomic and cultural reality and to enhance the social sensitivity and sensibility of the students and to help students acquire skills that will be useful to them in their personal and professional life"* (UGC model curriculum, Sociology, 2001).

But still the question arises as to what new challenges does India society encounter as it seeks to explore the emerging new conditions of society and social being? To what extent have its theoretical and methodological factors responded to deal with new social realities? This can only be possible by employing professional sociologists through the process of interaction between social activists and non-sociologists on the one hand and attuning the curriculum with the emerging social conditions of India on the other. Organic intellectuals are certainly needed for developing their free sociological thinking but intellectual labours are also needed to justify and demand their need in intellectual market. So using Sociology for good purposes reflects the renewed status in the practice of sociology at the present changed moment, for making a better world. It is doubtless to comment that mirroring other faces and using our mindset for a better world is the only key to knowledge sociology which links with the truth and then merges with the reality which ultimately paves the path of social reconstruction and lights the spirit of altruism and humanity. Sociology in India has *"a floor and a ceiling ....and its ceiling remaining open to the sky"*.

So sociology from above and from below is a befitting paradigm of use and practicing sociology in India, which should be explored by the users of good sociology with the open sky above, and wide mud below.

References

Adams, Bert, N. and R.A. Sydie. 2002. *Contemporary Sociological Theory*. London: Sage Publications.

Albrow, Martin. 2001. "Globalization after Modernization: a New Paradigm for Development", in Frans Schuurman (ed.) *Globalization and Development Studies*. New Delhi: Vistaar Publications.

Allen Tim and Thomas Alan (eds.). 2000. *Poverty and Development into the 21st century*. London: The Open University.

Anderson, Perry. 1998. *The Origins of Postmodernity*. London: Verso.

ASA Newsletter, 2005.

Atal, Yogesh. 2003. *Indian Sociology from where to wherein*. New Delhi: Rawat Publications.

Barnerd, Cohn and M. Singer (eds). 1968. *Structure and Change in Indian Society*. Chicago: Aldine Publishing Company.

Bauman, Zygmunt. 1987. *Legislators and Interpreters*. Cambridge: Polity Press.

Bauman, Zygmunt. 1992. *Intimations of Postmodernity*. Cambridge: MIT Press.

Beck, Ulrich. 1992. *Risk Society*. London: Sage.

Berger, Peter L. 1963. *Invitation to Sociology*. England: Penguin Books.

Berger, Peter L. and Brigitte Berger. 1972. *Sociology – A Biographical Approach*. New York: Basic Books.

Best, Steven and Douglas Kellner. 1991. *Postmodern Theory*. London: The Macmillan Press Limited.

Beteille, Andre. 2002. *Sociology Essays on Approach & Method*. New Delhi: Oxford University Press.

Blerstedt, Robert. 1965. "Social Science and Public Service" in Alvin W. Gouldner and S.M. Miller (eds.), *Applied Sociology: Opportunities and Problems.* New York: The Free Press.

Brownstein, Henry and Merton, Robert K. 1986. Footnotes. ASA, December, p.11

Callinicos, Alex. 1990. *Against Postmodernism.* New York: St. Martin's.

Callinicos, Alex.1999. *Social Theory: A Historical Introduction.* Cambridge: Polity Press.

Collins, Randall. 1994. *Three Sociological Traditions.* London: Oxford University Press.

Comte, Auguste. 1855. (H. Martinue trans). *The Positive Philosophy.* New York: Blanchard.

Cooley, Charles Horton. "Now and Then" in *Sociological Theory and Social Research: Being Selected Papers of Charles Horton Cooley.* It was also published in *Journal of Applied Sociology* Vol. 8: 259-262 (1924).

Dadayan, V. 1988. *The orbits of the Global Economy.* Moscow: Progress Publication.

Damle, Y.B. 1982. "Theoretical Orientations and Methodological Perspectives for Sociology in India in the 1980's" in P.K.B. Nayar (ed), *Sociology in India.* Delhi: B.R. Publishing Corporation.

Desai, A.R. 1980. Presidential Address, XVth All India Sociological Conference, Meerut, India.

Desai, I.P. 1981. *Craft of Sociology and other Essays.* New Delhi: Ajanta Publisher.

Durkheim, Emile 1933. *The Division of Labour in society.* New York: Glencoe III. The Free Press.

Durkheim, Emile.1950. *The Rules of Sociological Method.* NY: The Free Press.

Fletcher, Ronald. 1970. *The Making of Sociology: A Study of Sociological Theory*. New Delhi: Rawat Publications (2000).

Giddens, Anthony. 1990. *The Consequences of Modernity*. Cambridge: Polity Press.

Giddens, Anthony. 1992. *Sociology*. Cambridge: Polity Press.

Gouldner, Alvin, W. 1965. "Explorations in Applied Social Science", in Alvin W. Gouldner and S.M. Miller (eds), *Applied Sociology: Opportunities and Problems*. New York: The Free Press.

Gouldner, Alvin, W. and S. M. Miller (eds). 1965. *Applied Sociology: Opportunities and Problems*. New York: the Free Press.

Hunter, J.D. and J. Yates. 2002. "In the Vanguard of Globalization: The World of American Globalizors" in Peter L. Berger and Samuel P. Huntington (eds), *Many Globalizations: Cultural Diversity in the Contemporary World*. New York: Oxford University Press.

Inkeles, Alex. 1982. *What is Sociology?* New Delhi: Prentice Hall of India Pvt. Ltd.

Johnston, Barry, V. (eds). 1998. *Pitirim Sorokin – on the Practice of Sociology*. Chicago: The University of Chicago Press.

Kolb, Williams L. 1951. "Review of Social Philosophies of an Age of Crisis", in American Sociological Review. Vol. No.16.

Lee, Alfred McLhung. 1976. 'Sociology for whom?' *American Sociological Review*, Vol. 41. Number 6 December, USA.

Mckee, James B.1969. *Introduction to Sociology*. New York: Holt, Rinehart and Winston.

Maus, Heinz. 1956. *A Short History of Sociology*. London: Routledge and Kegan Paul.

Miller, S.M. 1965. "Prospects: The Applied Sociology of the Center-city" in Alvin W. Gouldner and S.M. Miller (eds), *Applied Sociology: Opportunities and Problems*. New York: The Free Press.

Mills, C. Wright. 1959. *The Sociological Imagination.* London: Oxford University Press.

Mukherjee, Ramkrishna. 1973. 'Indian Sociology; Historical Development and Present Problems'. *Sociological Bulletin,* Vol. 21, No.1.

Myrdal, Gunnar. 1953. 'The Relation Between Social Theory and Social Policy'. *British Journal of Sociology,* XXVII.

Parsons Talcott. 1949. *The Structure of Social Action.* New York: Glencoe.

Pieterse, Jan Nederveen. 2001. *Development Theory.* New Delhi: Vistaar Publications.

Popper, K.R. 1972. *Objective Knowledge: An Evolutionary Approach.* Oxford: Clarendon Press.

Powell, Jim. 1998. *Postmodernism for Beginners.* Hyderabad, India: Orient Longman.

Rao, M.S.A. 1982. 'Sociology in the 1980s: Retrospect and Prospect' in P.K.B. Nayar (ed.), *Sociology in India.* Delhi: B.R. Publishing Corporation.

Rock, Vincent, P. 1965. "The Policy Makers and the Social Sciences" in Alvin W. Gouldner and S.M. Miller (eds), *Applied Sociology: Opportunities and Problems.* New York: the Free Press.

Singh, Y. 1986. *Indian Sociology Social Conditioning and Emerging concerns.* New Delhi: Vistaar Publications.

Sorokin, Pitirim, 1941. *The crisis of our Age.* New York: E.P. Sutton.

Sorokin, Pitirim. 1929. *Some Contrasts between European and American Sociology* in Barry V. Johnshon (ed.), Pitirim Sorokin on *The Practice of Sociology* (1998). Chicago: The University of Chicago Press.

Sorokin, Pitirim. 1937. *Social and Cultural Dynamics* (3 vols.). New York: American Book Company.

Spencer, Herbert. 1857. "Progress" in Westminister Review. Vol. LVII (N.S. Vol.XI) April.

Stoecker, Randy. "Sociology and Social Action" cited in http// comm.-org.utoledo.edu

Toynbee, Arnold. 1954. *Study of History*. London: Oxford University Press.

UGC Model Curriculum. 2001. Sociology: New Delhi.

Unnithan, T.K.N. 1982. "A New Sociology in the 1970's and Perspective for the 1980's" in P.K.B. Nayar (ed), *Sociology in India*. Delhi: B.R. Publishing Corporation.

Ward, Lester. 1906. *Applied Sociology*. Boston M.A.: Ginn.

Weber, Max. 1947. *Theory of Economic and Social Organization*. New York: Oxford University Press.

Weber, Max. 1973[1917]. "The Meaning of Ethical Neutrality in Sociology and Economics" in Max Weber on Universities (ed.), and Trans. by Edward Shils. Chicago: University of Chicago Press.

Weinstein, Jay. 2002. 'The Place of Theory in Applied Sociology: A Reflection'. *Theory & Science*, U.S.A.

Weinstein, Jay. 2001. file://A:\01 weinstein_revised.html

2

Civil Society, Citizenship and Subaltern Counterpublics in Post-colonial India

Sarbeswar Sahoo

Taking into account the growing socio-political mobilizations and large-scale transformations in the society and polity in last few decades, this paper[1] examines the changes in the nature of democracy in India. The central argument of the paper is that when passive citizens who were merely the consumers of state welfare programmes turn into active citizens, being aware of their oppressive social conditions and rights, an active civil society movement emerges at the grassroots level which transforms the nature of democracy. Defining civil society in Habermasian perspective, the paper argues that the idea of public sphere is grounded on the principles of active citizenship, and it is difficult to create a universal bourgeois public sphere (as argued by Habermas) in a plural and unequal society like India where exclusion and welfare has created a mass of passive citizenry, and thereby calls for the mobilization for multiple interest groups. It is evident that in the past few years, as a response to the rolling back of the state and onslaught of globalization, various marginalized groups have been active in the political arena. The rise of these 'subaltern counterpublics'[2] or 'proletarian public spheres'[3] have been the major catalysts in democratizing and decentralizing Indian democracy. Simultaneously, Indian society has also witnessed the upsurge of various communal and sectarian movements which undermine the edifice of democracy. As the Indian case suggests, despite the existence of such uncivil social elements within the civil society, the marginalized interest groups have been successful in carving out a space for themselves which changed the nature of governance from a nationalist elite serving model to a more radical form of social democracy[4] through political mobilization and grassroots political movements and there by transforming towards what Giddens (2000) calls the *democratization of* (Indian) *democracy*.

This paper is organized in eight sections. The second section deals with the Habermasian understanding of public sphere and civil society as a bourgeois rationality. The third section explains the politics of exclusion and exploitation which ceased the possibility of a universal public sphere in India. The fourth section looks at citizenship rights and the mobilization of subaltern counterpublics. Increasing proletarian participation in electoral politics, and the rise of grassroots movements have been examined in fifth and sixth section respectively. The seventh section examines the rising anti-democratic forces within civil society, and the final section provides some concluding remarks.

Civil Society as Bourgeois Rationality

Jurgen Habermas's public sphere belongs to the same theoretical family of civil society which provides a common platform for the representation of common interest in the public. For Habermas, the coffee houses in England, salons in France, and table societies in Germany embodied the public sphere, and provided significant ground for democratic participation in the eighteenth century Europe. In his book *Structural Transformation of the Public Sphere,*[5] he focuses on the bourgeois public sphere which was conceived as a sphere where private people transcending their private preoccupations come together as public and form an interactive body of citizens engaged in rational-critical discourse addressing common purposes. Communicating with each other, social actors learn to share ideas and create a unified public. Their communication was marked by certain features, by rationality, by disinterestedness, by irrelevance of inherited identities to their deliberation, and by rigorous separation of private and public spheres (Rudolph and Rudolph 2003: 3).

The classical bourgeois public sphere was constituted around rational-critical argument where the exercise of reason occupied supremacy. For Habermas (2000: 29), the educated middle class learnt the art of rational-critical debate through their contact with the modern 'elegant world'. Public sphere is not based on the common sense of the ordinary people. Tracing back the intellectual history, he argues that the core ideas that shape the constitution of public sphere are the development of the notion of 'public opinion' as opposed to 'mere opinion'. Mere opinions are the arbitrary views of isolated persons taken in the aggregate (Calhoun 1990: 313). It consists of '"things taken for granted, normative convictions", and "collective prejudices"' (quoted in Rudolph and Rudolph 2003: 4). Where as the public opinion is the outcome of 'the deliberated, reflective consideration of the bourgeois educated persons' (quoted in Rudolph and Rudolph 2003: 4), or/and communicative rationality which is 'the unconstrained, unifying, consensus-bringing force of argumentative speech' (quoted in Flyvbjerg 1998: 212).

Habermasian public sphere presents a catalogue of fundamental rights in defense of public sphere (freedom of speech, opinion, press, assembly, association, etc.) and the intimate sphere (inviolability of person and residence, etc). Emphasizing the autonomy and citizenship rights of the Individual, he recognizes the constitutional rights of individuals to engage in political activity in the public sphere (right of petition and suffrage, etc) and economic activity in the private sphere (equality before law, right of property, etc.).[6] In public sphere, the idea of 'publicity' in principle is opposed to all domination (Cohen and Arato 1995:227). Habermas's account of bourgeois conception of public sphere requires bracketing inequalities of status and to deliberate 'as if' they were social equals (Fraser 1990:62). The only 'force' which is active in the ideal speech situation and in communicative rationality is 'the force of the better argument' (Flyvbjerg 1999: 213). For Habermas, the proliferation of multiplicity of competing publics is necessarily a step away from, rather than toward, greater democracy, and that a single, comprehensive public sphere is always preferable to a nexus of multiple publics (Fraser 1990: 62). He also assumes that the discourse in public sphere should be restricted to the deliberation about common good, and that the appearance of 'private interests' and 'private issues' is always undesirable (ibid).

To summarize, Habermasian understanding of public sphere is an arena where citizens agreegate voluntarily in the public sphere to discuss common issues as opposed to private interests. This is a comprehensive and universal sphere of literate people who belonged to the bourgeois middle class engaged in deliberative exchange in which rational-critical arguments rather than inherited ideas and personal statuses could determine agreements and actions. Thus, the notion of public sphere in civil society implies: (a) it is universal in nature; (b) it is accessible to all; (c) people come together in an arena of common concerns; (d) it is an independent sphere outside the state; (e) it belonged to the bourgeois middle class; (f) it is a space for the literate people who have the monopoly over producing 'public opinion'; (g) people in the public sphere exercise certain rights.

Civil Society, Citizenship and Public Sphere in India

Indian Constitution, by recognizing the rights of Individuals and ensuring equality, established the foundations for a universal public sphere. Despite of these provisions, civil society was divided on power relations and public sphere remained confine to a small section of bourgeois middle class interest groups who, unlike Habermasian public sphere, happened to be a part of the state. The public sphere was in true sense a kind of *burgerliche gesellschaft* which was inaccessible to the ordinary masses. There could be two interrelated reasons which closed the 'space' for public participation and created an exclusionary public sphere. The first is the development of a strong welfare state and the legacy of colonialism which kept the politicized Indians apolitically busy and produced a *depoliticized* citizenry, and the second is the exclusion of the common people from the public sphere on the basis of standards set by the virtues of modernity.

Sudipta Kaviraj (2001) argues that the confinement of civil society to a certain section was due to the belief of the masses in the nature of the post-colonial state and the illusion provided by the state and ruling elites. It was the modern elites who mobilized the masses and spoke for them against the tyranny of the colonial state, and thus enjoyed unquestioned legitimacy to power in the post-colonial period. Thus, as Alam (2004: 3) points out, post-colonial democracy in India began as a tryst between the elites and the masses where the masses were promised of welfare and in return delegated the elites the power to rule. The emergence of a strong welfarist post-colonial state ensured the provision of services such as social, economic, education, health, and cultural aspects of governance. Since the state and the elites assumed the role of provider, protector and regulator of social welfare, the citizenry became passive and *depoliticized* which created an illusion of consensus that an active civil society distinct from the state was unnecessary. Civil society as a sphere of rights legitimized the domination of the upper castes, and upper classes. And it is through the same civil society, as Gramsci argues, capitalist state established its hegemony over society in India.

The second reason was more contradictory to the very nature of citizenship rights ensured by the Constitution and democratic state. As Partha Chatterjee (1998, 2004) argues, Indian civil society was confined to a small section of English educated middle class elites who dominated the social, literary and political life and played an important part in the anti-colonial struggle. For him civil society refers to 'those institutions of associational life originating in Western societies that are based on equality, autonomy, freedom of entry and exit, contract, deliberative procedures of decision making, recognised rights and duties of members and such other principles' (Chatterjee 1998: 42). Although the Indian Constitution[7] and the laws guarantee everyone as a citizen with fundamental rights, but, most of the inhabitants are deprived of exercising such rights due to the pervasiveness of various traditional exploitative practices related to caste, tribe, class, community, religion, ethnicity, education, gender, etc, which ceased the possibility of developing a common and comprehensive public sphere, as proposed by Habermas. Gupta (2000: 243) argues that these bonds are not, in themselves, conducive for creating ties of citizenship that the public sphere promotes. And 'the greatest threat to civil society in India today comes from the intrusion of collective identities based on caste and community into domains that ought to be governed by the rights and obligations of individuals' (Beteille 1999).[8]

Under Indian Constitution, every individual is guaranteed with citizenship rights (Article 5 –11) and fundamental rights (Article 12 –35) such as right to equality, liberty, right against exploitation, right to freedom of religion, and cultural and economic rights. Any kind of discrimination against citizens on grounds of religion, race, caste, sex, place of birth is prohibited under law. The question arises that to what extent have the liberal spirit of constitutional provisions, institutional guarantees and the language of rights, strengthened and shaped the public sphere in India? As Ashis Nandy (2002: 4) observes, the mainstream social theories give everyone the right to vote, but not the right to bring their odd cultural ideas and morality into the public sphere. It is observed that despite of all these legal and constitutional provisions, social relations are inherently hierarchical, and certain groups are denied of basic liberties to education, freedom of speech, freedom of opinions, and the equality of opportunity in the civil society on the grounds of ascribed identity. Thus, the mere acceptance of rights does not mean that the problem of inequality and exclusion has been resolved.

Caste is one such factor which discriminates the people of lower castes[9] and strictly denies their participation in the public sphere. As R.M Pal observes[10] that the caste system has created impregnable walls between groups of human beings where birth solely determines the social position in society. Caste system denies basic education to lower castes and women. The literacy rate for Scheduled Castes (SCs) in 1991 was 37.4 per cent as compared to 57.7 per cent for others.[11] They were excluded from the mainstream life of the village and forced to live as untouchables. They are often denied the right to vote and forced to work without remuneration as bonded labourers. For example, on the Independence Day during 1998, a woman *sarpanch* (elected village council leader) was striped naked while unfurling the national flag in a district of Rajasthan.[12] Dalit officers and elected leaders are publicly humiliated, for which they believe that public sphere is full of caste discrimination that denies them equal social standing. It is this apprehension of humiliation that prevents them from participating in the political realm, and makes them 'exiled citizens' or 'stigmatized citizens' (Guru 2005: 267). Thus, the public sphere in India is imbued with the ideology of purity-pollution which destroys the possibility of any intimacy (ibid).

Not only the caste, but also gender, tribe,[13] religion,[14] property and education were other basis of exclusion, inequality and exercise of power in India. Women are considered as the symbols of the private. Education for girls is not accorded a high importance by many families. The disparity between male and female is very high (21.70 percent) in terms of the literacy status.[15] In the patriarchal ordering of society, the relegation of women to the private sphere of family based on compassion, affection, emotion and unreflective loyalties are in sharp contrast to the rational-critical principles of public sphere. They are denied of equality and agency in the public sphere of civil society. The *purdah* (veil) system denies women of Muslim community from the public space. The practice of *sati*[16] was very much a part of the tradition. Violence[17] acts as a weapon through which society exercises its power and keeps a section of the population excluded from the public sphere. Discrimination and hatred also continues on the basis of religion. The wave of sectarianism and communal riots became frequent feature of the society. According to the Planning Commission Report more than a quarter of the Indian population do not own any property and are living below poverty line, which makes them over-dependent on economic activity and deprives them entering into non-economic relations with other human beings. Poverty and lack of property does not allow people to participate in the public sphere in Habermasian sense.

The idea of a universal public sphere as the site for dialogue and communication seemed impossible due to the existing incompatibility and conflict among multiple languages[18] in India. Although Hindi is considered as the national language, is the mother tongue of only 18 percent people. The regional languages of self-determination are either subordinated by the legal and bureaucratic languages or not recognized in the public domain. Many people lack verbal skills to carry on a critical public discussion. Speaking of different languages indicate not only the presence of incommensurable tongues but also incommensurable beliefs which sadly disprivileged certain groups reasons beyond their control and rational-critical communication in the public sphere proved to be the ultimate chimera (Chandhoke 2005: 332). Thus, many subalterns simply 'lack voice' inasmuch as they are unfamiliar with the terms of the dominant language.[19] Speakers of subaltern languages simply loose out in the power of linguistic politics because the spaces of communicative ethics have already been colonized and the procedures of exclusion have already been institutionalized.[20]

Over-dependent on the state for welfare and lack of politicization on the one hand, and discrimination of people on the basis of social statuses excluded a vast majority of population from the public sphere. Individuals placed in unequal conditions are unable to participate in political life on the basis of equality and freedom (Chandhoke 1995: 164), and the non-participation of people implies the restrictive nature of public arena. The long-term dependency on welfare produced a mass of 'passive citizenry'[21] incompatible to the idea of public sphere. Difference in interest and identity did not bring people together into a public domain to engage in rational-critical communication on 'common issues' which potentially concern everybody. The normative ethos of public sphere was fashioned purely out of the inter-personal communication between a certain classes of people, which are not antagonistic to the oppressive state as it was in 18th century Europe, but were in conjunction with it for the fulfilment of sectarian collective interest. As Gramsci conceptualizes, the state in India exercised its hegemony through the bourgeois public sphere. It provided moral and ideological legitimacy to state and bureaucracy to exercise power and the common masses in society were protected neither by the state, nor by the civil society. The bourgeois middle class attain the political legitimacy of the common people either through consent by providing economic opportunities or through coercion by using oppression and violence.

Thus, the very essence of universal public sphere of Habermas was not realized in the empirical context of India as (a) it is not accessible to all, (b) ascribed identities are not bracketed but play significant role in inter-personal exchange, (c) majority of the population are illiterate and property less (poor),[22] (d) conflicting of interest and identity does not recognize common issues, (e) groups are excluded on ascriptive statuses to participate in rational-critical debate, (f) there is no 'common language' for communication, (g) the public dimension to constitutional rights on the autonomy of the individuals are not accomplished, (h) the logic of power is never absent from public domain of deliberation, and (i) the 'public' and 'political' was confined among the modern, educated elites and dominant classes in India.

Active Citizenship and Subaltern Counterpublics in India

As a response to the institutional confinement of public life to a single, comprehensive public sphere based on rationality, class status and education, Nancy Fraser (1990: 66-67) develops the idea of multiple public spheres. For her, plurality of competing publics are the result of mechanisms of inequality and domination that are deeply ingrained in modern liberal societies (Rabinovitch 2001: 345) which better promote the idea of participatory parity than does a comprehensive, overarching public in both stratified as well as multicultural societies. The members of subordinated groups would have no arenas for deliberation among themselves about their needs, objectives, and strategies as the public sphere tend to operate to the advantage of dominant groups. Thus, there is a need for alternative public spheres, or what Fraser calls *subaltern counterpublics* which represents 'parallel discursive arenas where members of subordinated social groups invent and circulate their counter discourses based on oppositional identities, interests, and needs' (Fraser 1990).

In a stratified and multicultural society like India where diversity and inequality are the basic norms of everyday social and political life, it could be argued that multiple public spheres could provide space of representation for the subalterns against exclusion and marginalization, and help making claims for citizenship and inclusion. Thus, civil society[23] is defined as a sphere where groups organized on class and other social bases - gender, sexuality, race, ethnicity, environment - engage in political and ideological struggles (Chandhoke 1995: 168). Along the lines of Nancy Fraser, it is argued in India that if the different identities are not recognized and measures not adapted to protect their distinct interests, then equality of rights and equality of treatments would effectively reinforce the dominance of majority.[24] Informed by group differences and assigning differential system of rights and obligations of citizenship, Indian constitution provides the legitimacy for the creation of multiple public spheres. Differential treatment to different groups created differential identity, affiliations and mobilizations. This diversity of interest produced specific community publics for representing different interests.

The question here is that what led to the mobilization of multiple publics in India during the 1990s? And how do the issues become public and political? Although rights were recognized by the constitution since the beginning, the overarching dominance and assurance of the welfare state made people passive recipients of the government programmes. An explanation to this could be made through Alam (2004: 76) while he argues that it is not just the granting of citizenship, but actualizing the exercise of rights, becomes the key component in the ongoing journey of democracy. But, one of the most important reasons of the rising of multiple groups demanding citizenship entitlements is what Rajni Kothari (2001) calls the 'decline of the moderate state'.[25] For him, Indian state after 1960s moved away from the pluralistic and inclusive model of politics followed by the Congress Party which marked the trend towards deinstitutionalization process. The state suffered from both a 'crisis of governability' as well as a 'crisis of legitimacy' (Chandhoke 2003) and failed to keep its promises with persistent poverty (260 million people), malnutrition and hunger (268 million), unemployment (75 million), illiteracy (48%), rising corruption scandals (2.8 CPI), crisis of communalism (80456 affected), caste discrimination, gender inequality, dominant caste democracy, criminalization of politics, rigid bureaucracy, and ineffectiveness in enforcing the rule of laws.[26]

The failure of the centralized state marked two essential developments which had implications for democratic citizenship in India. Firstly, the people in civil society were left to be responsible for their own social reproduction; and secondly, the state had to enter into partnership with organizations in civil society, market, and with transnational organizations. In the first context, the rolling back of the state from many areas of welfare and the decline of political process necessarily involves the decline of interest in the poor (Kothari 1997: 229). This carried serious implication for the disadvantaged groups, who were not in a position to ensure their social reproduction, and who had been enabled to do so by the welfare state, were now thrown upon the not so tender mercies of the market and a rather uncivil society (Chandhoke 2003). This geared up the communities as politically significant rather than being mere ritual status groups, and led to the rise of various social movements concerning citizenship rights at the grassroots to represent the interests of ordinary people and their aspirations for carving out an autonomous space to discuss the essence of freedom, autonomy, and dignity of human existence. It was in this precise context that non-state agencies whether national or international movements, pressure groups, human rights organizations and non-governmental organizations representing the issues on behalf of the disadvantaged in civil society, became a partner of the state in governance. They assumed the role of development work and delivery of services as well as worked with the grassroots movements to advance citizen's rights through legal reform and strategies to empower the poor (ibid).

Although the service delivery by non-governmental organizations provided solutions to the problems of welfarism, it was feared that the society would continue with passive citizenry. But non-governmental associationalism's continuous involvement in empowerment and grassroots mobilization created an active citizenry which provided sites for the development of alternative politics and the circulation of counter-discourses. They also articulated diverse concerns, negotiated alternative views and offered the training ground for participatory democracy which strengthened active citizenship (Brown, Kenny, Turner and Prince 2000: 204-205).

With the rolling back of the state, the marginalized sections became more vulnerable and the legitimacy of the state was questioned. Issues affecting different sections like caste, tribe, gender, ethnic and religious groups, became the part of a generalized discourse of discussion and interrogation which gave them a 'public' character; and the collective demand for rights and the struggle for empowerment made it 'political'. The common good of one group was different from the common good of others. Multiplicity of problems pluralized the public sphere and created multiple sites of collective resistance within the civil society. This did not create a universal public sphere because, as Chandhoke (1995: 199) argues, 'a space can not be public in conditions where the individual is socially unequal and culturally marginalized, edged out ideologically and deprived politically'.[27]

The state which also used to be the single locus of power and authority started sharing power with multiple actors and became pluralized.[28] The people who had been *depoliticized* and remained as passive citizens by the policies of the state rise to demand justice, equality, and freedom. The 'individual' made a transition to the category of 'right bearing citizen'. This transformation came largely from the exploited stratum of society in their struggle for rights and entitlements which provided the institutional channel for (a) the participation of citizens, (b) for the representation of their interests, and (c) for clear lines of accountability (Chandhoke 2003). Citizens represented themselves and their interests, which *politicized* their existence in the public sphere. Rights acquire political edge and political clout when individuals assert and articulate these rights in the form of claims upon the polity; and when the democratic state recognize these rights, when they grant status in the form of law, and when the judiciary defends these rights against violations.[29] The politics of struggle did not remain confined within the political and civil rights but widened to the social and economic rights of the marginalized. The subaltern struggle for rights has expanded the capacity of civil society and widened the scope of democratic participation. The non-party political formations and grassroots mobilizations provided a *political* alternative, opened up a democratic space and transformed the nature of polity from what Rudolph and Rudolph call *command polity* to *demand polity*[30] and Kothari calls *politics of the classes* to *politics of the masses.*

Subaltern Participation and Democracy in India

The 1990s witnessed electoral upsurge of the disadvantaged groups and radical transformation in the nature of politics in India with increasing participation of the marginalized people and rising grassroots political movements. Democracy no longer requires clutches in the shape of powerful leaders – as guardians of democracy and as trustees of people – in order to survive.[31] It has become internal to common people's political consciousness, not because it has solved all the problem of society, but because it has provided them a space to fight for their dignity, rights and entitlements.[32] It has become a mode of organizing power or a space for struggles for the marginalized.

Alam (2004: 27) argues, although the voting percentage has not changed significantly between 1971 and 1996, the internal composition of voting-public has changed in a dramatic manner. In 1971, there were more upper caste, urban and college educated voters, where as in 1996, there are more non-literate people, rural based people, Muslims, tribals, scheduled castes and OBCs. The social foundations of political power today – as distinct from the class character of the state – comprise more of vulnerable sections than in 1971 (ibid). The caste composition of voting pattern reflects that

> ...beginning with the OBCs versus the upper castes, in 1996, there were 59 percent OBC votes against 56 percent upper caste votes. Compared with the average polling of 58 percent, there is 1 percent more in OBC votes and nearly 2 percent less of upper caste votes. The difference becomes more pronounced when we look at the scheduled castes, whose votes are 2 percent above the average, that is about 60 percent of them voted, in comparison to the upper caste votes of 56 percent. In 1971, the difference was not so conspicuous. Both the OBCs and upper castes were 1.5 percent below the average, but the scheduled castes were only half a percent above the average (Alam 2004: 29).

Similarly, there is a more pronounced shift in voting figures between the non-literate and the educated. To quote from Alam (2004: 29)

> In 1996, the non literate vote is half percent more than the voting average, and surprisingly the educated vote is 5 percent lesser than the average. On election day, 60.5 percent of the non-literate, and only 55 percent of the educated choose to vote. In 1971, the educated voted 6 percent above the average of

55 percent, and non-literate voted 3.5 percent below the average.

It is also observed that the Adivasis (tribals) and Muslims are participating increasingly in the election process. To quote

> In 1996, the aggregate vote of the various Adivasi communities was slightly less than one percent (57 percent) below the national average of 58 percent. In 1971, it was below the average by 6.5 percent; on an average polling of 55 percent, the tribal vote was 48.5 percent....In the case of Muslims, it was exactly one percent below the average in 1996; where as in 1971, it was seven percent below the average (Alam 2004: 31).

Although, the urban people have more access to the media networks and seems to be more politically sensitized, it is observed that their voting percentage is lower than the rural people. To see

> The votes of those residing in rural areas is one percent higher than the average in 1996; where as in 1971, it was lower than the average by one percent. This is not significant shift in the case of some of the other pairs we considered. But it acquires significance in relations to the votes in urban areas. In 1996, the vote of the urban residents was lower than the average by about 3.5 percent, but in 1971, it had been higher by 4 percent (Alam 2004: 32).

It is observed that most of the privileged sections of society are getting alienated from democratic process, and the legitimacy of the democratic system, now, derived from the vulnerable sections of society. Thus, today, as Zoya Hasan (2000: 29) claims, the historically disadvantaged groups are among the more active and enthusiastic participants in the political process. As a result of this participation, the locus of power has shifted from the established upper-caste elite to new upwardly mobile groups, and from the centre to regions and localities (ibid).

Globalization and the Politics of Micro Democratic Movements

The collapse of the Soviet Union and India's adoption of the policies of economic liberalization effectively signalled the demise of the hegemony of the language of socialism in Indian politics (Yadav 1999: 23). The subaltern struggle around identity and exclusion took a new form with the arrival of globalization. The entry of the global forces in local spaces without much mediation by way of protection or control from state has brought sharp divide between the classes and the masses[33] and pushed the marginalized into a state of destitution. With the decline legitimacy of political practices and fewer state intervention, the rich getting richer by the logic of accumulation and market, and the poor getting poorer through the logic of exploitation, exclusion, and growing alienation from centres of power and decision-making (Kothari 1997: 229). Globalization was seen as an incarnation of the old idea of development which disrupts communities, cultures, and livelihoods of the poor without offering them any viable and dignified alternative (Sheth 2004). The policies of trade liberalization and corporate globalization led to the rising cost of production and the falling price of farm commodities which resulted in the suicide[34] of many farmers. Large-scale development projects such as construction of big dams and mining industries were devised with international agencies which evicted indigenous people from their land and livelihood.[35] The democratically elected government is now at the service of the corporations, controlling with guns and police the very citizens who 'freely' elected them.[36] Liberal democracy acted as market democracy, and openly protected the interest of the MNCs instead of the citizens. Local democracies were viewed as roadblocks to the expansion of market democracy.

Thus, as a response to the exploitative state and globalization process, multiple grassroots social movements have been active in challenging the prevailing establishment and throwing alternative possibilities. The growing disparity between liberalization's economic agenda for profit and subaltern's empowerment agenda for social justice has translated the submissive language of mass alienation into assertive mass mobilization. According to some guesstimates, there are 50,000 to 100,000 movements groups[37] active in the country today. As Sheth (1995: 32) argues, social transformation for these groups is not an apolitical activity, but a live political agenda for changing the terms of discourse on democracy in India. This, however, does not mean that they define the politics of movements in direct opposition to the institutional framework of democracy. In fact, they view institutional democracy as a necessary, though not sufficient, condition for pursuing their parallel politics of micro-movements, through which they seek to raise the social consciousness of people and democratize the hegemonic structures of power in society (ibid: 32-33). The movements against bauxite mining in the tribal areas of Andhra Pradesh and Orissa, against dams in the Narmada valley, and the peasants and laborers movement against the corrupt political and bureaucratic structure in Rajasthan are some prominent political mobilisation for grassroots democratisation in India today.

The globalization-related policies of the state opened up a space for transnational corporations and help them acquiring the land for their industrial establishment in the resource rich areas. One such project is the bauxite mining project in Andhra Pradesh[38] which planned to displace 50,000 tribals and create massive deforestation. The state, whose prime duty is the welfare and protection of the citizens, is now using sovereign powers to protect the MNCs and TNCs to crush the citizens (Sahoo 2005). In opposing the project, in 1991, a walkathon (padayatra) known as *manya prante chaitanya yatra*, a consciousness raising walk was organized by SAMTA and SAKTI around tribal livelihoods, identity, culture, ecological destruction, and fundamental rights ensured by Indian constitution. Over

50 other social action groups also joined the movement which is still continuing. Largely accepting SAMTA plea, the Supreme Court of India gave a 400 page judgment in 1997, outlining the steps which needed to be taken to make the tribals as partners in the development of scheduled areas. Thus, the court recognized the local people as legal-stake holders in the development of the area they live in (Sheth 2004). A similar struggle against bauxite mining is still continuing in securing the economic, ecological and cultural rights of the Adivasi communities in the tribal areas of Orissa against the Utkal Alumina Industries Limited which plan to displace 60,000 people from their land and livelihood.[39]

In another instance, largely victimized by the political and bureaucratic system, the peasants and labourers, in Rajasthan, have launched a mass-based political movement under the banner of Mazdoor Kishan Shakti Sangathan (MKSS)[40] or organization for the empowerment of the workers and peasants around the issues of corruption, bureaucratic unaccountability, right to information, and minimum wages for the labourers. Besides being underpaid, people in the area did not get enough work through the year, often because sanctioned development programmes often remained on paper, with the allocated money being pocketed by government officials and elected leaders (Sheth 2004). When they demanded to be paid minimum wages, they were refused on the grounds that 'they did not work' as per official records, which led to the demand for having access to public records and right to information. Various sit-ins, rallies, demonstration and public hearings were organized in the state level demanding comprehensive legislation granting citizens the right to information. The struggle of MKSS resulted in the passing of sate legislation on right to information. This culminated in half a dozen other state assemblies passing similar legislation. In the central level, the Right to Information Bill got the assent of the President on June 15, 2005 and has been enforced on October 12, 2005. Thus, being recognized by the state, the creative politics at the grassroots around citizenship rights and entitlements has acquired political edge and changed the nature of democracy in India, making it more participatory and responsive to the demands of the marginalized. The potential of the subaltern classes and their ideologies of discontent and resistance in reshaping the state prevented the bourgeois in instituting its hegemony over civil society.

Saffronization of Civil Society

Not only the subaltern grassroots movements, but also various sectarian and religious fundamentalist movements have become a significant feature of Indian society since the 1990s. The elevation of communal forces (Bharatiya Janata Party and its allies) to power witnessed, what Radhika Desai (2004) calls, a systematic 'saffronization' of state and civil society in India. The civil society was fragmented on religious lines where the minority religious groups were relegated to the status of second class citizens. This period marked the highest point of communalism in Indian history. For example, in a single and intense anti Sikh program (1984) around 3000 Sikhs were butchered in most merciless fashion.[41]

The rise of Hindutva, which stands for the disenfranchisement of those whose loyalty to the nation it holds in suspect, has spread the 'politics of hate' in society and has been responsible for many Hindu-Muslim riots in the country. On 6 December 1992, 30,000 Hindu nationalists demolished the Babri mosque in the Indian city of Ayodhaya which witnessed massive rioting across the country. The Christian communities working in the remote areas were accused of conversion and have also been subject to violence which manifested its brutal form with the burning alive of Pastor Graham Stuart Stains along with his two sons, Philip and Timothy (Ages 11 and 7) in Orissa on 23 January 1999. Recently, in Godhra riot, according to the official acknowledgement 850 persons and as per unofficial estimates 2000 people were killed.[42] As per the National Crime Record Bureau: 2000, the number of riot victims has increased into 80,456. Since 1998 the Viswa Hindu Parishad (VHP) had also been indulging in armed communal mobilization through its trishul (trident) distribution to awaken the Hindus.

From the above discussion, it is clear that the hate politics of the Hindutva project leaves no space for any kind of dialogue, and rational-critical communication within civil society. The public sphere of the civil society has been flanked by communal discourses which have given rise to counter civil society and anti-democratic movements.

Towards Conclusion

It is evident from the preceding discussions that social exclusion and discrimination ceased the possibility for creating a universal public sphere in India. The mobilization of the marginalized grounded on multiple interests, pluralized the public sphere within the civil society. Civil society became the playing field for both democratic forces in the form of subaltern assertion for citizenship rights, and anti-democratic forces in the form of rising communal and sectarian groups. Not only the structure, but also the very nature of the public sphere in India has been transformed. Unlike the homogeneous and universal public sphere of Habermas, the subaltern counterpublics are based on the politics of difference and heterogeneity. The deliberations in these public spheres are neither grounded on the qualifying characteristics of educational achievements nor on property relations reflecting the person's class status. 'Public opinion' is formed out of common sense, which has broadened the scope of public sphere to illiterate mass-public in the rural areas and transformed its nature from being merely a space for opinion formation (weak publics) to influencing the decision-making and public policy (strong publics).

Thus, despite the existence of some anti-democratic communal forces within civil society, the politicization of rights and the social struggles at the periphery made public spheres of civil society arenas of political democracy. The struggle groups who were previously out side the arena of power, in most cases, have been successful in articulating their needs and press their claims in the political terrain not as passive subjects but as self-confident citizens. The publicization and politicization of issues through various grassroots movements have challenged and, in most cases, redressed the arrangements within the civil society and the state. The legitimacy of the modern state and democracy in India is neither any longer dependent on the hegemony of the elites, nor an act of faith granted from above. It is rather now firmly grounded on the idea of popular sovereignty and/ or what Partha Chatterjee (2004) calls 'the politics of the governed'.

Notes

1. The author is grateful to Asso. Prof. Vedi R. Hadiz for dispelling various doubts on the confusing and complex relationship between the idea of civil society and democratization, and to Prof. Bryan S. Turner for comments while writing this paper.

2. As these subaltern and marginalized groups were mobilized under different interests against the dominant classes, and the state, I equate them with Nancy Fraser's (1990) idea of 'subaltern counterpublics', and Negt and Kluge's (1972) idea of 'proletarian public sphere'. Writing a critique of universal and bourgeois public sphere, Fraser develops the idea of 'subaltern counter-publics' as an alternative vision to Habermas. For more see Fraser, N (1990).

3. In opposition to Habermas's bourgeois form of public sphere, Oskar Negt (his student) and Alexander Kluge (1972) advocate for a public sphere which is not bourgeois in form. They saw that a proletarian public sphere has already begun to appear which will assert its claim to leadership in the future. For more see Hohendahl and Russian (1974).

4. For Kothari there has been a shift from Nationalist Democracy to Radical Social Democracy. This is a transition from top-down elites centered model to a more bottom-up, people centered and participatory form of democracy achieved through the struggle of the masses and grassroots political movements for rights.

5. First published in German in 1962 as *Strukturwandel der Offentlichkeit* and translated into English in 1988.

6. Cohen, J and Arato, A (1995), p. 226.

7. To have access to Indian Constitution, see: http://pib.nic.in/feature/feyr2003/fjun2003/f100620031.html

8. To some extent, Beteille is right in his argument. But the evolution of citizenship and citizenship rights in India cannot be understood detached from community-based claims for rights and entitlements. Unlike Western Democracies, in India, rights and entitlements are claimed in the name of communities as well. See Alam (2004). Although Beteille sees ascribed identities as problem for civil society, I would argue, that these identities constitute significant factors for civil society mobilization in India today.

9. As per 2001 census, lower castes or the scheduled caste constitutes 16.2 percent (166,635,700) of Indian population. They are also popularly known as 'dalits' or the oppressed castes.

10. Quoted in Mathew, 2003.

11. http://www.literacyonline.org/products/ili/webdocs/daswani.html.

12. In another case in Melavalavu (Tamil Nadu), the dominant castes of the area murdered the panchayat president and the vice-president who both belonged to a lower caste, merely because they dared to fight the panchayat elections. For a detail analysis on panchayati raj and human right see Mathew, G (2003).

13. According to the 2001 Census the tribals, commonly characterized as the Scheduled Tribes (STs) by the constitution of India constitute 8.2 percent (about 84.3 million) of India's population. See Sahoo, S (2005).

14. As per the 2001 census, there are Hindu 80.5%, Muslim 13.4%, Christian 2.3%, Sikh 1.9%, other 1.8%, and unspecified 0.1%. http://www.cia.gov/cia/publications/factbook/geos/in.html

15. According to the Census of India 2001 only 54.28 percent of the female population is literate while the literacy rate in case of male is 75.96 percent.

16. It means woman committing suicide in the pyre of the husband. Although the practice of *sati* was abolished in 1829 by Lord Bentinck, but it was still prevalent when on September 4, 1987, in Deorala, a nondescript village in Rajasthan, 18 year Roop Kanwar burnt to death on the pyre of her husband Mal Singh. For more details about this case see http://www.countercurrents.org/gen-shukla190304.htm

17. Here I talk about violence against the women and lower caste people. According to the data 4 molestation cases, 1 sexual harassment case, 6 cruelty cases by husband and relatives, 1 dowry case, and 2 rape cases are occurring every hour against Indian women. A total of 143795 crimes against women were reported in the country during 2001 as compared to 141373 during 2000 recording 1.7 percent increase. It is also observed that every hour 2 Dalits are assaulted, every day 3 Dalit women are raped, everyday 2 Dalits are murdered, and everyday 2 Dalit houses are burnt down.

18. There are 18 major languages recognized as "National Languages" by the Constitution of India. There are 22 official languages spoken through out the country. There are 24 languages which spoken by a million or more people. Some of them are Hindi, Bengali, Oriya, Telugu, Tamil, Marathi, Urdu, Gujurati, Malayalam, Kannada, Punjabi, Assamese, etc. See: http://en.wikipedia.org/wiki/Indian_languages. There are 1600 mother-tongues in India (Sheth, 1995).

19. For a brilliant analysis on tribals and the representation of their language in the public sphere see Chandhoke, (2005). Gayatri Spivak also claims that subaltern can't speak in a way that would carry any sort of meaning for us without altering the relations of power that constitutes him/her as a subaltern. Once he or she begins to speak, their constitution as subaltern will no longer hold.

20. When two unequally placed languages meet in the public sphere of civil society, the more powerful of the languages has already set the terms of exchange. The languages that do not meet the standards of the dominant language, or those that express different understandings, are doomed to marginality and loss. For example: languages of women in a male-dominated society, or languages of lower caste in a high caste dominated society. For more details on linguistic exclusion see Chandhoke, (2005).

21. A passive citizen hardly plays any role in the public or the political sphere but receives certain benefits from the state in order to live and act freely (voluntarily) in private spaces protected by the state. The active citizen, on the other hand, takes part in common deliberations on his own good and the good of all, has an interest in who governs him and why, which policies have been adopted and why, and is prepared in the last instance to exercise power himself. For more details on 'active citizenship', see Bhargava, R (2005), and Brown, K, Kenny, S, Turner, B, and Prince, J (2000).

22. For Habermas literacy and property are two of the basic criteria for participating in the public sphere and generating 'public opinion' different from 'mere opinion'.

23. Here civil society is a much broader concept than public sphere. Many public spheres coexist within the arena of civil society. Here public sphere I mean a group

of people mobilized on a particular issue such as gender, caste, religion, environment, which is common to the interest of the community. Multiplicity of issues created multiple public spheres. Public sphere primarily understood as issue based mobilization of people out side the arena of state. Thus, it includes the social movements by the marginalized sections.

24. For a debate on the differential, and universal conception of citizenship rights see Rodrigues, (2005), pp: 209-235.

25. By moderate state he means a state which despite the powerful tendency towards centralization and homogenization, acts as an instrument of social justice and human freedom. The Indian state between 1947 and 1967 (partly up to 1975) was such a state. For him, the deinstitutionalization process inaugurated by Mrs. Gandhi's premiership.

26. For a detail explanation of Indian state and its failure in fulfilling the popular promises see Chapter. 3 on 'State and Development Planning in India: A Critique' in Sahoo, S (2004a). See also Sahoo, S (2004b).

27. Chandhoke (1995) does not talk about multiple public spheres. There existed inequality among different groups which has little possibility of creating a universal public sphere. As the people within a particular groups share more or less equal status, and as the group is affected by common problem, it is possible to mobilize people for a public sphere.

28. For a brilliant analysis of the pluralisation of state apparatus see Chandhoke (2003).

29. Chandhoke (2003). In the section on democratic movements, I will discuss with concrete instances that how different marginalized sections of the society have been able assert their rights before the state through social mobilizations and in turn compelled the state to take positive actions to protect the rights of the

poor and marginalized in India. Some such movements are the tribal movements in Andhra Pradesh, Right to Information in Rajasthan, etc.

30. Command Polity is where state hegemony dominates over society and Demand Polity is in which societal demands expressed as electoral pressure dominate over the state. See Rudolph and Rudolph (1987).

31. Alam, Javeed (2004), p.17.

32. See the series editor Neeladri Bhattacharya's preface to Alam (2004), p. x.

33. See Kothari, R (1986) for an extensive discussion about the relationship between classes and the masses in Indian society. By classes he refers to the upper and middle classes. He argues that the 'classes' are to wallow in the imported mass culture of consumption and the masses are to be left to the playground of the market and that, too, largely in the unorganized sector.

34. It is estimated that more 25,000 peasants in India have taken their lives since 1997 when the practice of seed saving was transformed under globalization pressures and multinational seed corporations started to take control of the seed supply. For details about the impact of globalization on farmers suicide see Shiva, Vandana (2004): http://www.countercurrents.org/glo-shiva050404.htm.

35. According to an estimate in the last 40 years 15.5 million populations have been displaced, and out of which 74.52 percent populations are still awaiting for rehabilitation. For details see Sahoo, S (2005)

36. See Esteva, Gustavo, and Prakash, Madhu Suri (2004). They also discuss how globalization has got legitimacy after four failed Development Decades and constituted a timely substitute for the now frayed flag of development.

37. See Sheth, D.L (1995), p. 31. Some of them are Chipko environmental movements, Save Narmada Movement, anti-mining projects in Orissa and Andhra Pradesh, MKSS's movement for anti-corruption and right to information in Rajasthan, Tarun Bharat Sangh's movement for water conservation in Rajasthan, rights to food by Akal Sangharsh Samiti in Rajasthan, right to health by Jan Swasthya Aviyan, peasants and farmer's movement, women's movement, dalit movements, tribal movements on culture, development and displacement, movements related to identity politics, citizenship and human rights, anti-globalization movements, and several others.

38. The detail description about this movement is reproduced from D.L. Sheth (2004).

39. For displacement and bauxite mining projects in the tribal districts of Orissa, see Sahoo, S (2005).

40. For a case study on MKSS and its struggle for right to information see Sahoo, S (2004b) http://www.commarts.chula.ac.th/revisiting/pdf/32_SARBE.PDF.

41. http://www.countercurrents.org/comm-puniyani150905.htm.

42. On 27 February 2002, 60 passengers most of them are *kar sevaks* (worshipers of lord Ram of Hindureligion) were burnt after the Sabarmati train caught fire near Godhra, Gujarat, while returning from Ayodhaya. Suspecting this an act by the Muslims, a communal carnage was broke out by the Hindus which marked heavy rioting and destruction.
http://66.102.7.104 search? q=cache :ICdD4D8KomQJ: www.hrw.org reports/2002/india gujarat.pdf+Number+ of+ riot+ victims +in+ 2002 + in+India&hl=en

References

Alam, Javeed. 2004. *Who Wants Democracy?*. New Delhi: Orient Longman.

Beteille, Andre. 1999. 'Citizenship, State and Civil Society'. *Economic and Political Weekly,* September 4.

Bhargava, Rajeev. 2005. 'Introduction'. In Rajeev Bhargava and Helmut Reifeld (eds.) *Civil Society, Public Sphere and Citizenship: Dialogues and Perspectives,* pp.13-55. New Delhi: Sage Publications.

Bhattacharya, Neeladri. 2004. 'Editor's Preface'. In Javeed Alam *Who Wants Democracy?,* pp. ix-xii. New Delhi: Orient Longman.

Brown, K, Kenny, S, Turner, B, and Prince, J. 2000. *Rhetorics of Welfare: Uncertainty, Choice and Voluntary Associations.* London: Macmillan Press.

Calhoun, Craig. 1990. 'Civil Society and Political Life'. *Contemporary Sociology,* 19 (2), March.

Calhoun, Craig. 1992. 'Introduction: Habermas and the Public Sphere'. In: Craig Calhoun (ed.) *Habermas and the Public Sphere.* Cambridge: The MIT Press.

Chandhoke, Neera. 1995. *State and Civil Society: Explorations in Political Theory.* New Delhi: Sage Publications.

Chandhoke, Neera. 2003. 'Governance and the Pluralisation of the State: Implications for Democratic Citizenship'. *Economic and Political Weekly,* July 12.

Chandhoke, Neera. 2005. 'Exploring the Mythology of the Public Sphere'. In: Rajeev Bhargava and Helmut Reifeld (eds.) *Civil Society, Public Sphere and Citizenship: Dialogues and Perspectives,* pp. 327-347. New Delhi: Sage Publications.

Chatterjee, Partha. 1998. 'Beyond the Nation? Or within?. *Social Text,* No. 56, Autumn.

Chatterjee, Partha. 2004. *The Politics of the Governed: Reflections on Popular Politics in Most of the World.* New York: Columbia University Press.

Cohen, J and Arato, A. 1995. *Civil Society and Political Theory.* Cambridge: The MIT Press.

Desai, Radhika. 2004. 'Forward March of Hindutva Halted' *New Left Review,* No.30, Nov-Dec.

Esteva, Gustavo, and Prakash, Madhu Suri. 2004. 'Introduction: A Dialogue with Ashis Nandy' in Ashis Nandy, *Bonfire of Creeds: The Essential Ashis Nandy.* New Delhi: Oxford University Press.

Flyvbjerg, Bent. 1998. 'Habermas and Foucault: Thinkers for Civil Society'. *British Journal of Sociology,* 49 (2), June.

Fraser, Nancy. 1990. 'Rethinking the Public Sphere: A Contribution to the Critique of Actually Existing Democracy'. *Social Text,* No. 25/26.

Giddens, Anthony. 2000. *Runaway World: How Globalization is Reshaping our Lives.* New York: Routledge.

Gupta, Dipankar. 2000. *Culture, Space and the Nation-State.* New Delhi: Sage Publications.

Guru, Gopal. 2005. 'Citizenship in Exile: A Dalit Case'. In: Rajeev Bhargava and Helmut Reifeld (eds.) *Civil Society, Public Sphere and Citizenship: Dialogues and Perspectives,* pp.260-276. New Delhi: Sage Publications.

Habermas, J. 2000. 'Social Structure and the Public Sphere'. *The Structural Transformation of the Public Sphere: An Enquiry into a Category of Bourgeois Society,* Translated by Thomas Burger with assistance of Frederick Lawrence, Cambridge: MIT Press.

Hasan, Zoya. 2000. 'Introduction: The Political Career of the State in Independent India'. In: Zoya Hasan (ed.) *Politics and the State in India,* pp. 11-34. New Delhi: Sage Publication.

Hohendahl, Peter and Russian, Patricia. 1974. 'Jurgen Habermas: The Public Sphere (1964)'. *New German Critique,* No. 3, Autumn.

Kaviraj, Sudipta. 2001. 'In Search of Civil Society'. In: Sudipta Kaviraj and Sunil Khilnani (eds.) *Civil Society: History and Possibilities,* pp.287-323. New York: Cambridge University Press.

Kothari, Rajni. 1986. 'Masses, Classes and the State'. *Alternatives,* 11 (2), April.

Kothari, Rajni. 1997. 'Globalization: A World Adrift'. *Alternatives,* 22 (2), April-June.

Kothari, Rajni. 2001. 'The Crisis of the Moderate State and the Decline of Democracy'. In: Niraja Gopal Jayal (ed.), *Democracy in India,* pp. 101-127. New Delhi: Oxford University Press.

Mathew, George. 2003. 'Panchayati Raj Institutions and Human Rights in India'. *Economic and Political Weekly,* January 11.

Nandy, Ashis. 2002. *Time Warps: Silent and Evasive Pasts in Indian Politics and Religion.* London: Hirst and Company.

Pantham, Thomas. 1988. 'Interpreting Indian Politics: Rajni Kothari and his Critics'. *Contribution to Indian Sociology,* 22 (2).

Rabinovitch, Eyal. 2001. 'Gender and Public Sphere: Alternative Forms of Integration in Nineteenth-Century America'. *Sociological Theory,* November.

Rodrigues, Valerian. 2005. 'Citizenship and Indian Constitution'. In: Rajeev Bhargava and Helmut Reifeld (eds.), *Civil Society, Public Sphere and Citizenship: Dialogues and Perspectives,* pp. 209-235. New Delhi: Sage Publications.

Rudolph, S and Rudolph, L.I. 2003. 'The Coffee House and the Ashram: Gandhi, Civil Society and the Public Spheres'. Working Paper No. 15, South Asia Institute, Department of Political Science, University of Heidelberg.

Rudolph, L I and Rudolph S.H. 1987. *In Pursuit of Laxmi: The Political Economy of the Indian State.* Mumbai: Orient Longman.

Sahoo, S. 2005. 'Tribal Displacement and Human Rights Violations in Orissa'. *Social Action: A Quarterly Journal of Social Trends,* 55 (2), April-June.

Sahoo, S. 2004a. *State, NGOs and the Discourse of Development in India: A Sociological Analysis.* An unpublished dissertation submitted to the Centre for the Study of Social Systems, Jawaharlal Nehru University, New Delhi.

Sahoo, S. 2004b. 'Civil Society and Democratization in India: Media Perspective'. Paper presented at the International Conference on *Revisiting Globalization and Communications in the 2000s* at Chulalongkorn University, Bangkok.

Sheth, D.L. 1995. 'Democracy and Globalization in India: The Post-Cold War Discourse'. *Annals of the American Academy of Political and Social Science,* Vol. 540, Local Governance around the World, July.

Sheth, D.L. 2004. 'Globalization and New Politics of Micro-Movements'. *Economic and Political Weekly,* January 3.

Yadav, Yogendra. 1999. 'Politics'. In: Marshall Bouton and Philip Oldenburg (eds.) *India Briefing: A Transformative Fifty Years,* pp.3-38. New York: M.E. Sharpe with Asia Society.

Website Links

- http://pib.nic.in/feature/feyr2003/fjun2003/f100620031.html
- http://www.literacyonline.org/products/ili/webdocs/daswani.html
- http://www.cia.gov/cia/publications/factbook/geos/in.html

- http://www.countercurrents.org/gen-shukla190304.htm
- http://en.wikipedia.org/wiki/Indian_languages
- http://www.countercurrents.org/glo-shiva050404.htm
- http://www.commarts.chula.ac.th/revisiting/pdf/32_SARBE.PDF
- http://www.countercurrents.org/comm-puniyani150905.htm
- http://66.102.7.104/search?q=cache:ICdD4D8KomQJ:www.hrw.org/reports/2002/india/gujarat.pdf+Number+of+riot+victims+in+2002+in+India&hl=en

3

Engendering Health and Human Rights of Tribal Women in the Koraput District of Orissa

Soubhagya Ranjan Padhi
and
Biswajita Padhy

Mankind's experience over the millennia of his life on the earth reveals that women have lived in two parallel worlds ever since the first community habitation. They have occupied positions of eminence and authority and at the same time they have also been object of oppression, hostility and petty tyrannies of the male bread winner. The discrimination against women begins at birth or even from the very womb of the mother.

Gender inequality – an enigma illustrates that mankind has been willing to give women everything but equal status with their male counter parts. Women constitute almost half of the country's population, which has been deprived of self respect and subjugated into existence at whim and mercy of men. Gender inequality prevents women from acquiring benefits that they deserve as one near half of the population of India.

The decade long gender disparities undermines women's health and constrains women's freedom, human rights and decision making power. Truly we are living in a world where gender matters. While human rights itself is about equity, the character of society – its faith and belief system which is for many centuries is dominated by patriarchal and gender bias framework determines the extent of equity that is reflected in reality. The age-old faith based social system, joint family; religious dogma and superstious ideas jeopardize the life of women in our society and put a lot of hardship on women. Gender disparities - which affect many women, have lead to a host of health problems including traumatic injury, unintended pregnancy, low birth weight, sexually transmitted infection (including HIV), depression, exploitation and suicide. The construction of gender roles implies that women have far lesser access to productive resources and decision making compared to men, resulting in unequal balance of power.

The Status of Tribal Women: Myth and Reality

The western concept of development has contributed to an increase in economic and gender inequalities, notwithstanding its promise of providing improved living conditions. However a better health facility and apt human rights for women, especially tribal women, can be viewed as a device in ensuring sustainable development. Despite the rosy picture of greater human rights in recent days, women are facing problems in every sphere of their life. Tribal women are identified to be the most exploited class for obvious reasons of their socio-economic inequalities. Eradication of atrocities against them still remains a distant reality.

Traditionally women have been enjoying a better social status in tribal societies. They are not forced by their husband to give birth a male child. So far as the as sex-ratio is concerned one can find that tribal women are almost equal number as the males.

The women's family receives "bride price" from the groom. Tribal women have a greater freedom to choose the mate for their marriage. Tribal women after the death of their husband can have the choice to remarry one of their husband's brothers. But in spite of all these advantages, tribal women are leading a very miserable life in their society in recent times. Though tribal women constitute half of the total tribal population, still they live in a male dominated society. The women folk work more than the men do. Invariably polygamy is the practice which leads to large number of single women in the society. Frequently they are tortured by their dipsomaniac husbands. All these practices are definitely a mockery at the innocence of tribal women.

Our social context consider gender as a central element of stratification and attempts to understand the position of women and their vulnerability can not examined without a gender analysis in Indian society.

The status of women is intimately linked to the issues of health and human rights. Gender consideration often leads to denial of various human rights – including the access to adequate nutrition and other health services. According to the modern human rights law, which guarantees equality between sexes, many of the health disadvantages of women can be classified as injustice. Maternal death can be regarded as one of the extreme point of a series of injustices that many women face. But in many countries social research has tended to overlook the consequences of these gender biases on health and human right of women and neglected to examine fully the different social, cultural and economic context within which women work and live. To delineate the stress experienced by women one has to probe into the inner world of their experience. This would unearth their sense of identity, role acceptance, compliance, vulnerability and many other personal issues. It is thus crucial that the dominant human rights discourses should address health and gender equality. There is an urgent need to come out with bench marks and indicators to monitor gender concerns in health disparity and human rights violation. The present paper focuses on the emerging human rights and health issues of tribal women in the Koraput district of Orissa. The paper at the end put forward some suggestions and measures to safeguard the status of tribal women.

Objectives

The aim of this paper is to debate and highlight issues of gender inequalities in health and human rights context and to discuss various health practices and strategies to examine the status of tribal women in Koraput district of Orissa. It focuses on the malice of gender inequality and violation of human rights in tribal society due to dominant age-old faith and traditions and to gain an understanding about the dynamics of progressive faith based social change that aim at gender streamlining in recent times.

The Context: Koraput District

As per the Scheduled Area Order 1977, Orissa is one of the Scheduled Areas. The order again specifies that Koraput district is one of the major scheduled areas of the state. Koraput was the largest district of Orissa till 1992 (undivided districts of Koraput), and later it was divided into four districts – Koraput, Nabarangpur, Rayagada and Malkangiri on 2nd October 1992. The district is located between 18°13' degree and 19°10' degree North latitude and 82°23' degree east longitude in extreme south part of Orissa. It is bounded by Rayagada district of Orissa and, Vizianagram and Srikakulam districts of Andhra Pradesh in the east, Malkangiri district of Orissa and Baster district of Madhya Pradesh in west, Nabarangpur and Kalahandi district of Orissa in the north and Vizianagram and Visakhapatnam district of Andhra Pradesh, in the south. According to the 2001 census, the total population of Koraput district is 11, 77,954 (5,89,438 males and 5,85,516 females). The sex ratio of the district is 998 females for 1000 males. The density of population is 134 per sq.km. The district rank 15th among the districts in Orissa in terms of population and contains in it 3.21 per cent of the total population of the state in 2001 census. The district ranks 3rd in the state and 86th among the district of India in terms of geographical area. It has a geographical area of 8807sq.kms, which covers 5.66 per cent of the total geographical area of the state. 83.18 per cent of the total population of Koraput district is live in rural areas (Census 2001).

MAP OF ORISSA

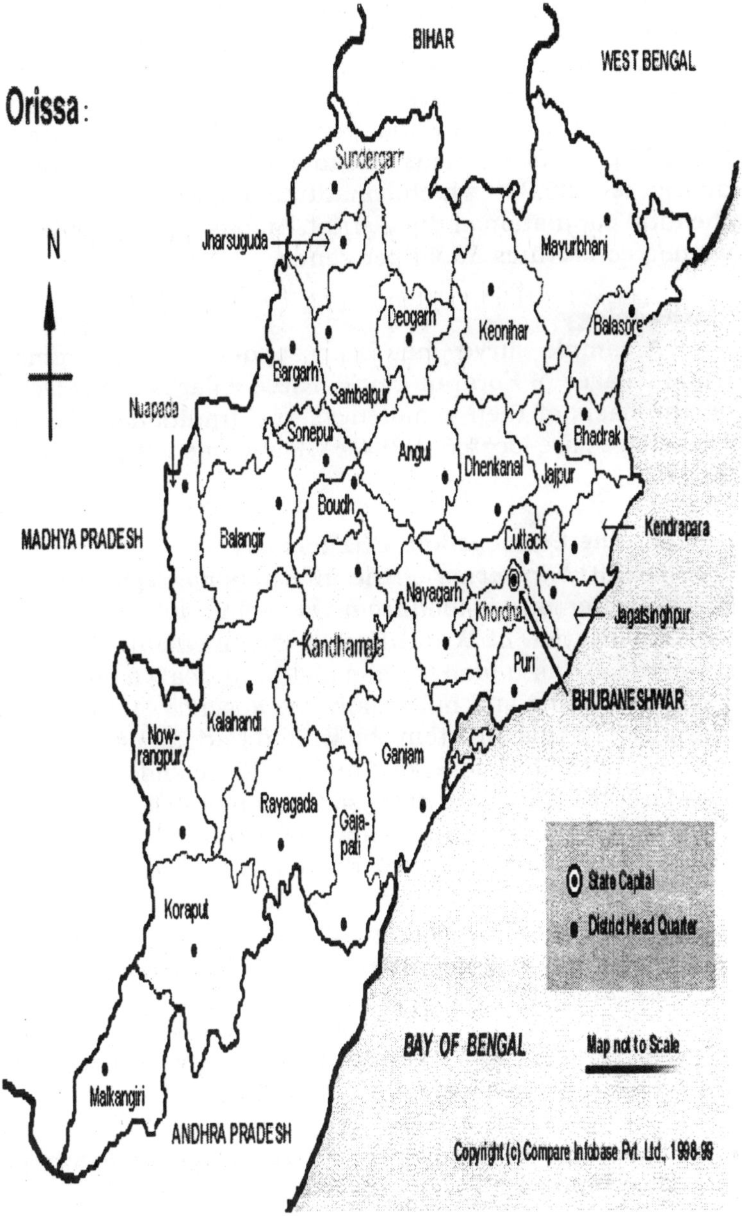

The tribal communities are living throughout the length and breadth of the district. 62 types of tribes inhabit the Koraput district. Majority of the people speak the local language of Kuvi, Gadava, and Paraja. However Oriya language of the state, act as a link language for the people. The major types of the primitive tribes are Paraja, Kondha, Soura, Gadaba, Halva, Bhumia, Koya, Kotia, Pentia, Santala and Bhatada. According to 2001 Census, the total tribal population of the district is 5,85,830 which constitute almost 50 per cent of the total population of the district. Among tribal population women constitutes 50.44 per cent..

Methodology

A sample survey has been conducted in 23 remote tribal villages of Koraput block. These villages are selected on the basis of their remoteness and traditional lifestyle. The villages are located in three GP and one village belongs to NAC.

Health: The Concept and Challenges

"Health" in terms of the international legal practice can be better understood from the definition employed by the Constitution of World Health Organization (WHO). It says: "Health is a state of complete physical, mental and social well-being and not merely the absence of disease or infirmity". In this direction the United Nations pronounces the need of the human rights and health to endorse higher standard of living and better socio-economic conditions of women. The WHO understanding of health of women goes beyond the elimination of disease and infirmity and addresses their physical, mental, social well-being. Therefore attention must be given to the full range of human rights. It should rise above the provision of medical, nursing and related health services and contribute in many ways for the achievement and maintenance of health as defined by WHO.

Therefore, rights relevant to the promotion and protection of women's health also include:

- The right of women to be free from all forms of discrimination.

- Rights relating to women's freedom which include rights regarding survival, liberty and security, rights regarding family and private life and rights to education.
- Right to political participation.
- Rights regarding women's empowerment, including the access to income earning capacity.

Nevertheless "Health care" is one of the greater human rights of women and it is observed that apart from facing various gender inequalities, tribal women of Koraput district are deprived of basic health facilities. Their accessibility to professional standards of health is severely limited. Till now most deliveries take place at home by using primitive tools in unhygienic conditions. Women's choice in dealing with unwanted pregnancies is limited. Nutritional levels are low among tribal women. Anaemia rate is high among them.

Indicators of Health, Human Rights and Development in the District

A proper health and human rights conditions is the essential ingredient of overall integrated development. The following are some of the key indicator through which we can analyse the health, human rights conditions that prevail among the tribals of Koraput district.

Lack of Communication

Communication is the major problem particularly during monsoon seasons. Most of the areas are not connected by modern telecommunication facilities. During the monsoon seasons, the condition of roads makes travelling extremely difficult. Many tribal communities live in remote and inaccessible settlements. A large number of positions, especially those of specialists, are vacant in government institutions, which reduces accessibility to services. Moreover, transfers are frequent. ANMs are available at Sub-centres only for a day in a week because they keep travelling within the area for the rest of the week.

Diseases

Tribal communities suffer from several communicable diseases, many of which are seasonal. Some of the major diseases prevalent in the area are malaria, tuberculosis, and gastroenteritis. Malaria appears to be increasing more rapidly among children than adults, and is likely to contribute to higher levels of anaemia and malnutrition.

Malaria is more serious in the case of tribal communities that are living in remote hilly and forest areas. They are less aware of the disease and are less motivated to access the health services. Although local medical professionals are of the view that over a period of time, tribal people tend to develop immunity against malaria, children continue to remain the worst sufferers. Describing the drug availability situation, a doctor says, "We don't have the drugs that the patients need, and the drugs we have are not needed by the patients."

Fertility and Infant Mortality Rate (IMR)

Data on fertility and mortality for undivided Koraput (sample Research Survey and Census 1991) reveals that the crude birth rate (CBR) of Koraput district was 34.10 in 1991 which was even more than the state CBR rate (32.98). It had 3rd position in the entire state.

Orissa is one of the few states where the Infant mortality rate is high. The rate was 149 in 1979, 143 in 1980, and has declined to 125 in 1991 and further to 95 in 2002. In the case of Koraput district, IMR was 118 in 1991, 115 in 1993, and 97 in 1999 (Govt. of Orissa in 2002), which was higher than the state average.

The six major causes for infant mortality in Orissa are low birth weight and immaturity, fever, septicaemia, diarrhea, pneumonia, malnutrition, and birth injury. Apart from these, malaria has been one of the additional reasons for high IMR in the Koraput district.

Diagram-1
Crude Birth Rate of the District and State (1991CENSUS)

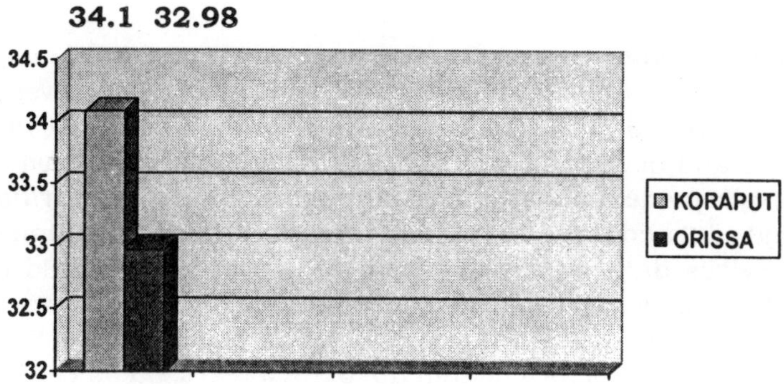

Diagram-2
Infant Mortality Rate of the District

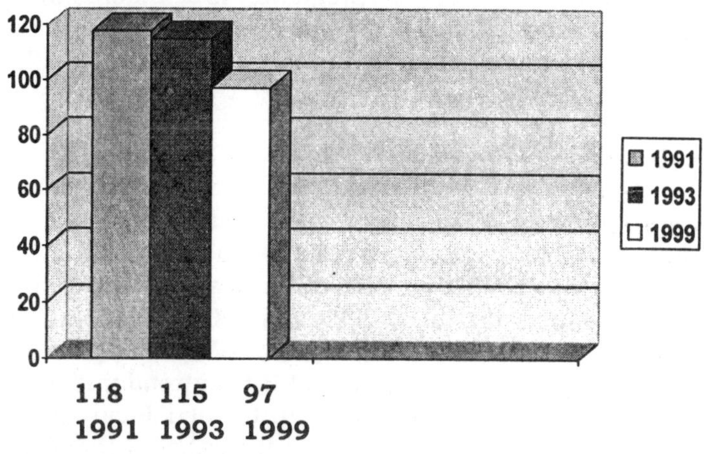

Maternal Mortality Rate (MMR)

The maternal mortality rates are also very high in Koraput district. In 1994, the maternal mortality ratio was at 74 per 1,00,000 live births in Orissa, and it was highest in the country. The case of Koraput is even worse than this. In 2002 the MMR has been reported as 95 for 1,00,000 births in Koraput.

Nutrition Rate

As manpower constitute the main source of power of a country, all emphasis has to be put for their proper health, food and development. Children under three years have to be given adequate attention in the field of health, nutrition and educational opportunities. Integrated child development services data on nutrition status of pre-school children (2003) shows that in the district, out of 97,322 children in the age group of 0-3 years, 94,367 (96.96) have been weighed. Out of the children up to three years, 63.55 percent are moderately mal-nourished and 1.85 per cent are severely mal-nourished (District Social Welfare Office, Koraput, 2003).

Early Marriage and Maternal Malnutrition

The age at marriage, especially among the tribal girls, is low. The mean age at marriage is 17.1 years (CDMO, Koraput, 2004) and teenage pregnancy is common. Poverty, communicable diseases, low food availability and hard physical labour by women have combined to produce high rates of maternal malnutrition and low birth weight.

Registration of Pregnancy

Among most of the tribals, the practice of self-delivery exists. Out of 24764 deliveries registered in 2002-2003, the number of the institutional deliveries was 11793 (47.62 per cent) and the number of home deliveries was 12971 (52.38 per cent). Out of the home deliveries 4308 cases (32.21 per cent) were attended by health staffs, 3886 cases (29.96 per cent) were attended by traditional Birth attendants *(Dhais)* and 4777 (36.83 per cent) by untrained local women. However it is evident that most of the tribal of the district go to these untrained local women. Among these 4777 deliveries, more than 80 per cent are belongs to tribal communities. It has been noted that, all pregnancies have not been registered in the district.

Most of the health delivery institutions are functioning under severe manpower constraints. A few women also go in for abortion in the event of an unwanted pregnancy. However, most of them prefer illegal institutions where practitioners are not qualified. The use of contraceptives is limited, and is restricted mostly to female sterilization. Vasectomies are still low.

Distribution of Work

Of all the workers in the district, 82 percent are "main" workers. But most of the tribal women are classified either as marginal workers or non-workers which does not take into account their contribution to household management and livelihood generation.

Diagram-3
Practice of Delivery

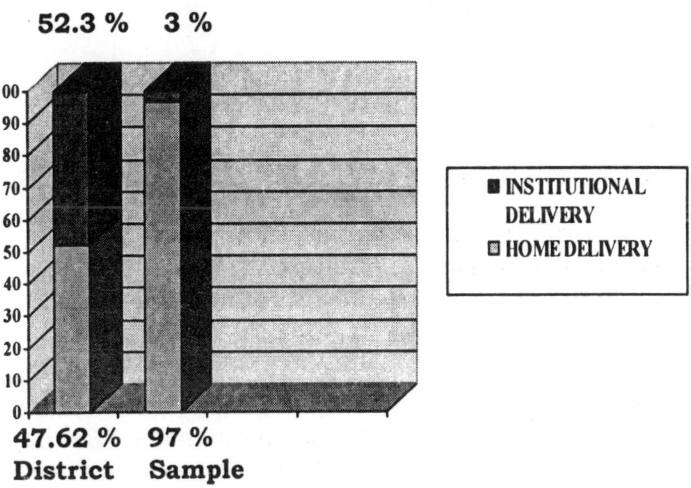

Diagram-4
Mode of Home Delivery in the District and Sample Area

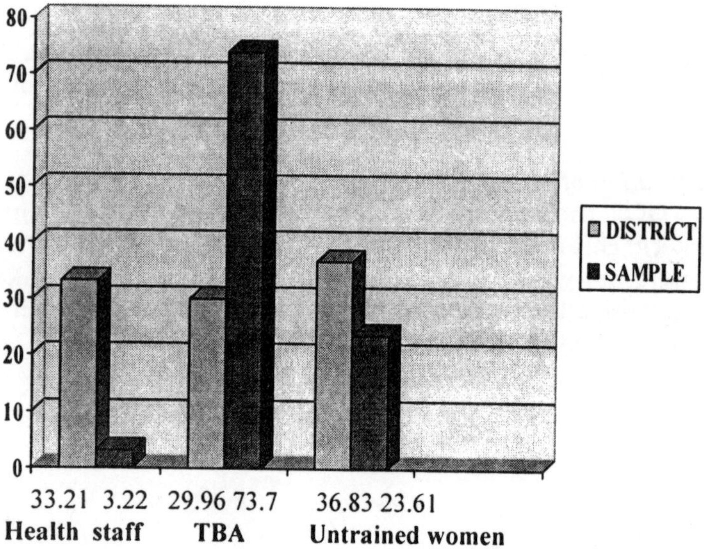

Economic Situation

A majority of the population i.e. 87 percent lives below poverty line i.e., income less that Rs.11,000 per annum [Statistical Handbook, 1993] and 50 per cent of the total BPL families are tribals.

Language and other Infrastructure Problem

Language is said to be a barriers between tribal and non-tribal people and sometimes prevents access to health services. For instance, most health personnel are unable to communicate in tribal dialects, or understand their values, though some health workers do learn tribal dialects in order to communicate better with tribal clients. There is little counselling and no use of communication aids. Post-operative and follow-up instructions are often inadequate.

There are many infrastructural problems exist in the district. Most primary health centres and sub-centres lack electricity or water, especially the ones located in tribal villages. The cost of services makes these unaffordable for the marginalized sections, especially tribals. The lack of specific laboratory tests in hospitals and primary health centres necessitates private lab testing, thereby increasing costs

Education

Poor socio-economic condition and lack of identification with school education are major reasons for the low enrolment and high drop-out rates in the rural and tribal areas. Access to education is denied more often to the girl child, reflected in the female literacy rate. The literacy rates in respect of Scheduled Tribes are still low.

Table-1

Educational Status of Tribal Women in the District

Year	*All classes*			*Schedule Tribe*		
	Male	*Female*	*Total*	*Male*	*Female*	*Total*
1991	39.99	15.15	24.64	14.61	02.14	08.34
2001	47.20	24.26	35.73	29.20	08.40	18.90

The undivided Koraput districts still occupy the lowest position in Orissa. According to 2001 census Koraput district ranks 28th among the 30th districts in Orissa. The tribal literary rate is only 8.34 per cent. It is 14.61 for male but just 2.14 for the tribal female, which indicates that tribal female well, lag behind their male counterparts (1991 census). In 2001 census it is 29.20 for tribal male but only 18.90 for females of tribal community.

Dropouts

There are problems relating to high dropout rates also. Various issues like inadequate school infrastructure, teacher absenteeism, large-scale teachers vacancies, inadequate teaching and learning materials, unsuitable timing of schools, unsuitable school atmosphere are responsible for the low educational status of tribal women. The dropout rate in respect of total tribals was 63.92 per cent. Among tribal boys it is 59.13 per cent but for tribal girls it is 70.55 per cent.

The National Policy on Education (NPE) has given great importance to Early Childhood Care and Education (ECCE). As a supportive programme for primary education, it provides a crucial input in the strategy of human development. It also provides support services for the working women of the disadvantaged section of the society. It includes care of mother during pregnancy, nutritional care of mother during lactation, and mother education in the childcare.

Mid-day Meal Scheme

The National Programme of Nutritional Support to Primary Education (NPNSPE), commonly known as Mid-day Meal Programme, was launched in the year 1995. It aims at giving a boost to universalisation of primary education by increasing enrolment, retention and attendance and at the same time improving the nutritional status of the students (including girl child) in primary level. The study conducted by operational Research Group in July, 1999 with the support of UNICEF has revealed that, even though this scheme has attracted SC/ST children, still it has a number of weaknesses such as:

(A) Non- provision of cooked meal.

(B) Enrolment which is to be provided by the states each year and on the basis of which food grains are allocated for 10 academic months is not available.

(C) Inability of the states to arrange the timely delivery of food grains.

(D) Lack of community participation in the implementation of this programme.

Crime against Women

Molestation of women appears to be a major crime in the district, accounting for 70 to 80 cases annually. On an average, about 30 cases of rape have been reported annually during the period between 1995 and 1997. It is observed that many incidents of rape within communities go unreported. In 1995, out of the 30 reported cases of rape, only13 of the accused persons were acquitted, and in 1996, four out of 22 accused men were acquitted. There are also dowry-related crimes against women.

Findings

The total populations of the 23 villages of the study area are 6417 with 3064 men and 3353 women, constituting the higher sex ratio of 1094 females per 1000 men.

Majority of the people are tribals and their annual family income is abysmally low. 1189 families out of 1701 families (69 per cent) have income of less than Rs.6000. This low economic condition is a great hurdle for the medication facility of tribal women.

Most of the houses built up with mud wall and thatched roofs. All most all the households have cattle sheds adjoining to the house, which give an inadequate picture of their sanitation system.

Health care facility is not adequate in these areas. In absence of adequate health care facilities, majority of the tribal women depends upon *Disaries* (Traditional Healers) and quacks.

Prevalence of early child marriage is high in the district. Generally the girls are getting married in the age group of 13-15 years. The early marriage and motherhood has badly affected the health and physical conditions of women.

The disease prevalence in the study area shows that malaria takes a heavy toll every year, followed by diarrhea, dysentery, measles, worm infection, typhoid, skin diseases, problem related dental care etc.

The disparities between tribal women with their male counterparts are visible. The available statistics reveals the gloomy picture of education and nutritional condition of tribal women.

Table-2 shows the education and nutrition status among the boys and girls in the sample area. 1650 persons are in the age group of 06-18 years, out of which 822 are boys and 828 are girls. 753 are school going children, out of which 62 per cent (470) are boys and 38 per cent (289) are girls. And out of total non school going children majority are girls (60 per cent) which is much higher in comparison to that of boys (40 per cent).

As far as education is concerned, there is a strong gender bias against girls. 3666 people are above age 15 years. Out of which 1780 are male and 1886 are female. 26.38 per cent of male are literate where as female literacy rate is only 06.67 per cent. There is only one girl studying intermediate, where as thirty seven male are studying intermediate.

The nutritional status among the boys and girls has calculated according to their weight and age. Out of 1287 children (0-6 years), 295 boys are having normal nutritional status but only 271 girls have nutritional status. 329 boys (nearly 25 per cent) are suffering from mal nutrition, where as there are 392 girls (more than 30 per cent) suffer from mal-nutrition.

In the study area, during the last three years there were 482 pregnant mothers out of them, 399 received T.T. Two incidence of maternal mortality also reported during the period. Only 133 pregnant women received antenatal care tests during the pregnancy period. Out of total 482 deliveries took place, 468 were delivered at home (97.09 per cent). Only 14 deliveries (2.90 per cent) are carried out at hospitals. While 341 deliveries (71.04 per cent) were assisted by Traditional Birth Attendant (TBA), 15 deliveries (3.12 per cent) assisted by ANM and 110 deliveries (22.82 per cent) were assisted by the family members or relatives of the women.

Table-2

Educational and Nutritional Status among the Boys and Girls in Sample Villages

a) Educational status at the age of 15 and above	*Boys*	*Percentage*	*Girls*	*Percentage*
Up to 5th Standard	221	12.41	58	3.07
6-7th Standard	119	6.68	47	2.49
8-10th Standard	93	5.22	20	1.06
10-12th Standard	33	1.85	1	0.05
Graduation	04	0.22	--	--
Total	470	26.38	126	6.67
b) Education In the Age group of 6-18				
School going	470	62	289	38
Non-School going	357	40	534	40
c) Nutritional status				
Normal	295	22.92	271	21.05
Mild	105	8.16	140	10.88
Moderate	102	7.93	104	8.08
Severe	122	9.48	148	11.51
Total	624	48.49	663	51.52

Source : Sample Survey.

Diagram-5

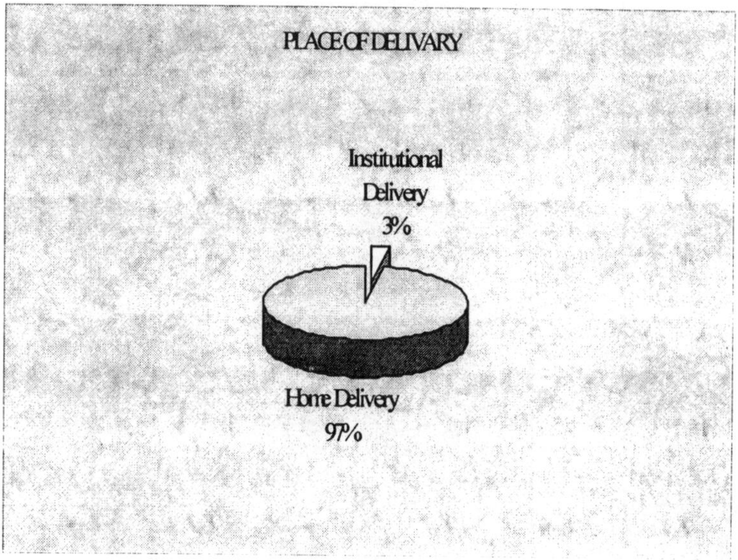

Status of Tribal Women in the District

The inferences collected from the sample villages can be safely taken as a generalization for the whole district. Most of the findings found in sample villages are almost same with the district. The following points summarises the above discussion.

- The Koraput district is a Scheduled Area.
- There is a high concentration of tribal population in the district. Nearly 50% of the total population belongs to tribal community and female constitutes 50.44% of the total tribal population (2001 Census).
- Neglect of women's health is pervasive, on grounds of both sex and their gender.
- The practice of self-delivery is very high among the tribal women. Out of 24764 deliveries registered in the district (2002-2003), the number of home deliveries was 12971 (52.38%). Out of total 482 deliveries took

place, 468 were delivered at home (97.09%). Only 14 deliveries (2.90%) are at hospitals.

- Malnutrition is a tragedy for tribal women in Koraput district. The nutritional status of the women is always related to the economic status of the family and here the poverty has played havoc on the health and nutrition condition of tribal women.
- The registrations of pregnant mother and antenatal care provided are not adequate. Due to their poverty and customary taboos the women are not taken to the hospital for delivery.
- It is a practice among some of the tribal communities that pregnant women work through out the day without rest. She has to resume her work within a day or two after delivery which clearly reflect the gender bias and exploitation of women in tribal society. However lack of education and awareness played a great role in it.
- The average age of tribal women at marriage is very low. The age at marriage among tribal girls is 13-15 years. Early marriage is a curse for tribal women. Ignorance, illiteracy, age-old practice and tradition etc. forces the women to marry at a younger age. They do not know why the children should not be married in a younger age and what harm it can cause to the girl child when she become pregnant in a very young age.
- Women suffer additional discrimination, because roles identified with female gender are not valued in social and economic terms. Those who perform domestic and child care work in their own homes are frequently regarded as "unemployed" and ineligible for monetary benefits.
- Everybody knows that educating a boy means a single man while educating a girl means educating a family but this is not in practice because the literacy among women is less than their counterpart which is evident from the census data. The literacy rate of district is 36.20% against the state average 63.61%, while the female literacy is only 24.81% (as per 2001 census).

- Education is the most important social input for the development of any society. However this is the most neglected side along with the health sector. In Koraput district the tribal literary rate is only 18.7%. It is 29.2% for male but just 8.4% for the tribal female, which indicates that tribal female well, lag behind their male counterparts (2001 census).
- The drop out among tribal girl is also very high. The dropout rate of the tribals is 63.92%. Among tribal boys it is 59.13 percent but for tribal girls it is very high i.e. 70.55%. Majority of tribal girls are out of school. They are either work in the field or take care of the child in their home. There are several factors that lead to the low enrolment and high drop out rates. They are such as less interest and knowledge of the parents, poverty, high absenteeism of teachers, lack of communication, poor infrastructure for education etc. However the illiteracy and high dropouts are responsible for the ignorance of tribal women, which has indirectly contributed for their low health status.
- Girl children have many disadvantages in education. Parents don't send them to school and usually they are instructed to take care of young children and assist mother in some domestic chores as carrying water, gathering fuel wood and preparing food. These girls gain no independent exposure either to education that can reveal alternative choices for their future or to knowledge of preventive health care and hygiene.
- Maternal mortality rate is highest among teenage mothers and risk is compounded by liability to repeated early pregnancy. Sexual abuse and economic pressures to engage in prostitution present adverse environments for adolescent health, including exposure to sexually transmitted diseases.
- Marriage or pregnancy prohibits the adolescent girls to continue school and the responsibilities of nursing and child care has decreased their attendance. It has resulted in poor health, inadequate education and limited opportunities for employment and earning.

- Tribal women work hard in their household from morning to night. Apart from this, they also carry heavy responsibility in employment outside the home. So they frequently bear a double burden. This aggravates the health strain that affects them and limits time for self-care and recuperation.
- Unskilled abortion procedures can endanger life, health and future fertility. Unwanted fertility often causes their poor health.
- Physical and psychological injuries caused by violence against women, including assaults by husband have been inadequately recognised, diagnosed and treated. Often in tribal communities physical force of husband is not considered a wrongful act and assaultive men do not face any stigma or condemnation.
- Most of the tribes of the district are forest dwellers. Forest plays a vital role in the life of these inhabitants. However in last five decades, a large amount of forest areas have been deforested. In 1956, 70% of the total geographical area constituted forest in undivided Koraput district. But in 1999, forest constituted only 23.8% and it is approximately 22% in 2001 (Forest Department, Orissa). Traditionally tribal women used to depend on forest for their medication purpose. With increasing deforestation the accessibility of tribal women to medication facilities has been reduced. On the one hand it has badly affected the health need of tribal women and the other hand the lack of communication facilities, lack of awareness and health care education, shyness among the tribal women etc. do not motivate them to avail modern health services.

Suggestions

There are many challenges in the attainment of the ultimate goals of "Health and Human Rights" for women. However the following are the some of the suggestion which will help to reduce the disparities that exist in the tribal communities:

- There is a real need at national, regional and international levels to improve the prevention, diagnosis and treatment of illnesses in women and to extend research on diseases and conditions that affect women.
- Health legislation has a great role to play in promoting public health and could be used more vigorously to promote women's health.
- The tribal women of the Koraput district need urgent action to improve their access to health.
- The wisdom and experience of traditional medicine man on the use of various herbals for cure of diseases are to be learnt by the service providers. The government should take maximum care for the development of herbal gardens. Due importance must be given for the documentation of traditional method of treatments.
- The traditional beliefs of tribal people that the cause of an ailment or a disease lies in the anger of the divine power or the ancestors need to be handled carefully.
- Community involvement, mutual interaction between the service provider and the beneficiaries, health consciousness of the tribal women etc. are some of the greatest challenges, which need to be effectively monitored and tackled.
- The Anganwadi workers, the Multi purpose Health workers, Voluntary Organizations, Primary School Teachers etc. can play vital role in the implementation of various health programmes. Proper motivation, practical training, and good incentives to these workers can definitely bring better results.
- The experience of tribal people towards the development functionaries is not pleasant. It is frequently alleged that they have been exploited, while receiving a benefit from the service providers. This perception has to be changed through honesty, commitment and involvement of the officials.

From exploitation to physical violence, women experience assault both inside and outside their homes. It badly affects their integrity, which deny them the sense of well-being, security and esteem that contributes to their health. Although women live longer than men on average, little attention has been paid to lessen the gender differences among the tribals with respect to quality of life. This is high time we should think about the overall development of this weaker sex of the weakest section of society.

References

Cook, R.J. 1994. *Women Health and Human Rights.* Switzerland: World Health Organization.

Das, Nirmal Chandra. 1997. *Tribal Demography.* Bhubaneswar: Sagar publications.

Directorate of Economics and Statistics. 2001. *District Statistical Hand Book of Koraput.* Bhubaneswar, Orissa.

Government of Orissa. 1991. *Tribal Sub-Plan 1992-97.* Bhubaneswar: H & TW Departments.

Mohapatra, P.C., Samal, J. and Pradhan, N.N. 2003 *Integrated Early Childhood Development Programme in Koraput District of Orissa.* Koraput: Council of Analytical Tribal Studies.

Nagda, B.L. 1999. 'Tribal Development in Rajasthan'. *Kurukshetra,* Vol. 47 (10).

Padhy, K.S. and Sathpathy, P.C. 1989. *Tribal India.* New Delhi: Ashish Publishing House.

Pal, Mahi. 2004. 'Social Development of Rural Women in India'. *Kurukshetra,* Vol. 52 (9).

Pati, R.N and Das, J. 2002 *Tribal and Indigenous People of India: Problems and prospectus.* New Delhi: A.P.H. Publishing Corporation.

Rout, Purna Chandra. 1989. *Tribal Education in Orissa.* Bhubaneswar: Eastern Graphics.

United Nations Population Fund (UNEPA). 1999. *Integrated population and Development Project Report.*

Vidyarthi, L.P. and Rai, B.K. 1985. *The Tribal Culture of Orissa.* New Delhi: Concept Publishing Company.

4

Gender, Property and Democracy in South Asian Tribal Societies: A Case Study in North-East India

R.A. Mangathai

The understanding of interplay of categories of impact in transitional societies is a matter of intense discourse. Analysis of pedagogical categories of modern thought - gender, property and democracy has provided conflicting and sometimes contradictory phenomena depending on the context, time and space of societies studied. It is not unfathomable to postulate therefore, that any universal pedagogical conclusions would not only be impossible to draw but would contribute to misunderstand the societies, thereby doing more harm to the scholarship and to the transitional societies. Therefore, it is appropriate to undertake disaggregated analysis of transitional societies, limited as it were, in terms of space, time and freedom to contribution to our epistemological enquiry on these societies.

The present study is about North-East India which is a geographical entity, comprising seven states with 3.88%

of population and 7.8% of total area of India. In terms of tribal population or indigenous people it is about 12.15% of India's population. The North Eastern States have other than geographical uniformity, predominantly tribal population with many languages, dialects, cultures, religions and histories. Each tribe claims to have its own culture, civilization and language or dialect. The seven states are Assam, Arunachal Pradesh, Meghalaya, Mizoram, Nagaland, Manipur and Tripura.

The region is said to consist of Tibeto Burmese groups in Arunachal, Nagaland, Manipur, Mizoram and parts of Meghalaya like Garos, Bodos, Katcharis in Assam. Indo-Aryan groups in the valley sections of Brahmaputra, Cachar and South Tripura plains. Monkhemer group in South of the Brahmaputra valley in Khasi and laintia hills.

Even after the annexation of the region by the British in 1826, except Brahmaputra and Cachar valley, many tribal groups could maintain exclusivity due to difficult terrain in the region and lack of common language British also followed the policy of relative noninterference in their way of life and imposed restrictions on outsider's settlement and interaction with tribal communities in the region.

Even in the post independent India also the British policy of relative isolation of tribes continued in this region due to a variety of reasons. In addition, regional autonomy, land rights and protection of customs and traditions were ensured through constitutional self-governance by declaring them as 6th Schedule areas. In the 6th Schedule areas choice was given to tribes to regulate land possession, residence, forest, customs, manage schools etc. This constitutional protection has ensured that tribes were given the freedom and informed choice to decide their terms of interaction, change and norms of behaviour. While this has prevented exploitation at the same time resulted in the isolation of the tribes from the so-called 'mainstream'

Status of Women in Tribal Societies

Each society has its own parameters to measure the status of women. To conclude women's status as high or low, through stereotyped criteria may be misleading. Ideal frame of reference is different from practical framework. So a broad spectrum of variables should be consulted for

The population of the seven sisters are per 1991 census is given in the Table-1

Table-1

Sl.	States	State Population (000) General	State Population (000) Tribal	Tribal Population as % of General Population
1.	Arunachal Pradesh	865	550	63.40
2.	Assam	22414	2874	12.80
3.	Manipur	1837	632	34.40
4.	Megalaya	1775	1518	85.50
5.	Mizoram	690	654	94.80
6.	Sikkim	406	91	22.4
7.	Tripura	2757	853	30.90
8.	Nagaland	1210	1061	87.70
*	Total North East	31354	8233	26.20
**	All India	846302	67758	08.00

assessing women's social status. Tribal societies in India do not maintain uniformity in terms of statuesque or change. They can be classified as traditional, transitional and transformed societies. This classification is not absolute. There may be overlap between two types of societies.

The presence and persistence of Gender inequality is explained in different ways. These approaches may be broadly classified under structural functional perspective and conflict perspective.

The structural functionalists consider inequality of sexes as a normal and hence a universal feature of society. They opine that Gender inequality through division of labour by sex is positively beneficial and functional for the society. This, according to them, contributes towards mutual' cooperation and dependence. They seek the difference in biology and culture as explanatory framework.

According to the biological explanation of the functional approach, men and women differ biologically and these differences in themselves are sufficient explanations for the origin- and practice of division of labour by sex or gender inequality. The functionalists consider social inequality, which include gender inequality, as a functional imperative. Any change in such division disturbs the normal structure, resulting in strain in the family relationships. The entry of women in to market is considered as undesirable, since it would lead to strain in marital relationship. Talcott Parsons (1964) the exponent of this theory holds the view that gender inequality/sex stratification is necessary in order to maintain the equilibrium within the conjugal family, which in turn contributes to the smooth functioning of the society.

The conflict analysis to women's question stems from the relations of production. Marx and Engel's viewed female sub ordination as a result of the emergence of the private property, in particular the private ownership of factors of production. The dialectical perspective believes that since the important goal of capitalists is accumulation of surplus value, they have an interest in keeping the workforce divided. The criterion of age, sex and race are used for such division. In consequence hierarchical division of society by sex impedes the tendency to organize themselves and confront the common enemy i.e. capitalist society. According to the diabolical or conflict thinkers in the ideal socialist state that rises from the ashes of the capitalists state, the society is uni-sex with equality as the guiding principle.

These explanations present a multidimensional view of the phenomena. One point needs to be made clear here. Where society locates the rationale for inequality in the sexual division is expressed in the strength of taboo / sanction against the fairer sex as the "cult of domesticity".

M. Papanek (1975) has rightly pointed out that in research on women in South Asia, the single most important aspect to be analyzed is social context. There is a great divergence in the treatment of women of tribal and non-tribal communities. Among the non-tribal communities the traditional norms have been neither very liberal used by the majority of the concerned population. However, in the case of the tribal communities on the other hand, women both at the ideal level and actual level have had more freedom and less reservations, constraints and impositions in various walks of life.

Lowie (1920-47) opined that "she is conceived as little better than a salve or beast of burden condemned to perform the hardest drudgery brought as a commodity") and without redress against her master's brutalities but the observation is true only partially as she is the undisputed mistress of the family, if not of the community as well. Majority of tribal women are enjoying a good deal of freedom and equality compared to the non-tribal societies.

Malinowski (1920: 20) correctly pointed out "a correct definition of status can be given only after taking into consideration all mutual duties between the sexes and safe guards provided for the protection of each sex against the high handedness of the other. Other criteria include equal opportunities at work, types of taboos, treatment of women and legal. status and contribution in the house economy".

But these factors cannot be applied in isolation from one another in the analysis of status. Equal opportunity for work does not necessarily mean equality. "Today women are debarred from ritual ceremonies and sacred deities but other wise treated kindly... on the other hand, in the religion-economic life of the tribal" (Majumdar 1944: 42). Lowie has further focused on the complexities when he opined that treatment of woman is one thing her legal status another.

Madan and Majumdar (1956: 146] have explained that "status of women in all types of societies, but particularly in patriarchic societies is determined by various types of taboos that are attached to women generally. These taboos might be protective, productive and preventive". A social policy analysis or a researcher should not approach the women of a society with a pre-set view that the status is either low or high. There can be many intermediate layers and there can be polarity through it my not be very striking.

Grigson (1938: 295) while writing about the Marias of Bestir felt that an average Maria woman is far freer that a Hindu woman. Even among the Serna Nagas, the position of women is that they enjoy a high social status, Hairnendarf (1943: 159) reveals that Chenchus of Andhra Pradesh divide even the household duties, including those that are generally assigned to women in other societies, equitably between sexes. He observed that "husband and wife are, for all practical purpose, partners with equal rights and their property is jointly owned".

The Lambada and Banjaras women of Andhra Pradesh are known not only as eqmi1 partners in the family life but also as bread winners contributing to the household budget. Among the patrilocal Tharus (Majumdar 1944: 164) woman's position is proverbially high, Both men and women own the property and the latter spend their income, if they wish without consulting their husbands.

Among the Khasis, the husband goes to live with his wife in her mother's house. Through this Matrarchical arrangement, the husband's authority is greatly curtailed. The Ho's have the problem of a high bride - price and the inability of the average Ho to afford it actually improves the status of the wife who is so difficult to get marriage.

Among the Bhils, Minas and Garasias (Mann and Mann, 1989: 9) a woman is considered important by these tribesman not only in the light of work and labour, which they do in and outside the house (the Bhils, Minas and Garasias are primarily agricultural tribes and their women have to share the labour required for various operations in agriculture), but also for the attainment of an experienced in each of these tribes.

Therefore in order to be more specific of the status of women in different tribals groups one would be required to make possible categories of tribes on the basis of major culture elements. With this brief description on the status of tribal women in general, we shall proceed to the discussion about the tribal women in North-East and particularly in Tripura.

The economic backbone of the North-East community is the tribal woman. Several studies in the North-East India reveal that they generally lead a life of excessive hardship and exposure. The shifting cultivation or jhooming is the main economic activity of these tribals. The women help looms. Women in addition to maintaining household chores are partners in every collective activity of the family either cultivation, or rearing pigs, goats, fowls etc. These tribal society of the North-East with the exception of Khasis and Garos of Meghalaya, follow the tradition of patriarchy. Even in Tripura, though the tribals follow the patriarchcal social organization, women are neither suppressed nor ill-treated. A Tripura woman or a Reang woman is active in both domestic and outside field. She used to enjoy the right to her father's property. There was practice of bride - price and marriage by service to prove his credibility, capability and morality.

In most of the tribal societies customary laws and practices, the regulatory self-governing systems are evolved to judge and control social behaviour of individual members and groups in the tribes. These are the norms followed by all the members of tribe for common good and to regulate deviance. The sanction to the customary laws and practices should be ritualistic traditions, taboos associated with defiance, religious fury and social segregation. Many tribes of North-East India still adhere however loosely, to the customary laws and refer to them as authoritative practices of history. Each tribe has its own self-regulatory governing systems, parallel to the modem jurisprudence. The 6th schedule to the constitution of India has also recognized the value and provided legal status to the codified laws. However many tribes within these areas are yet to evolve their customary practices legally.

The present analysis is, there fore, limited to only five tribes Dimasas and Patirabhas of Assam, Aos of Nagaland, Mizos of Mizoram and Thadou Kukis of Manipur. This analysis has the special purpose to analysis the gender status in personal law matters, inheritance of property and political participation.

Dimasas, Mizos and Thadou Kukis follow monogamy while Patirabhas and Aos are polygamous. The groom has to pay bride price in Patirabha, Dimasas, Mizo and Thadou Kukis. Among the Aos dowry is practiced, however, girls have choice of mate selection. In other tribes either it is mutual consent (Patirabha and Mizo) or parents choice (Thadou Kuki). In the matters of marriage the primus of bride is slowly replaced by groom's and mainstream Hindu traditions are gradually finding social acceptance.

While divorce can be initiated on the grounds socially accepted by all the tribes, no maintenance is allowed among, Dimasas, Aos and Thadou Kukis. In the case of Patirabhas, the party initiating the divorce has to pay compensation as decided by the elders of the village. But only among the Mizos the maintenance allowance is compulsory.

The descent among all the tribes is patrilineal. Even the Patirabha tribe that had matrilineal tendencies at the early stages also follows, now, patrilineal systems. After the marriage the bride has to go and stay with their husbands at their residences.

Property inheritance differs among the five tribes, though the common strand, gender inequality pervades. There are three types of property among the Dimasas - maternal, paternal and common property. Obviously maternal property (saris, vessels and ornaments) goes to daughter, paternal property (lands and valuables) goes to the sons and the common property earned by the parents, is shared among the sons and daughters.

Women among the Patirabhas used to inherit the property in the past but due to external influences this pattern has changed and there is no claim for women at all.

Entire property is equally shared among all the male members. Probably this has relation to the bride price among the Patirabhas. Since at the time of marriage a girls has to be paid bride price and hence there is no need further for paternal property. The eldest son inherits the headship of the family among the Aos and Thadou Kukis while the property is shared equally among all the children, even though dowry is prevalent in the tribe. In the case of Mizos, only the youngest son inherits property by share can be given to other sons. However this exception has become a norm now among the Mizos Political participation and empowerment of women in all the five tribes under analysis truly reflects the status of women. While women are not prevented to participate in the village/community meetings they are neither asked to attend also. They do not have any role in the forums of decision- making political or social apparatus. I have not come across any tribe having any woman as chief or sardar or even member of the traditional tribal bodies. Even in the 6th schedule areas, where modern democracy is practiced, women were never elected. Frankly women are shut out of both the traditional and elected institutions in the tribal societies.

In Tripura, now days, the practice of the rigidity of matriarchy is gradually breaking down and as a result, the females are going to the fold of male domination. There is a shift towards sanskritization. This collapse of matriarchical system is not the direct effect of sanskritization, but it is also accompanied by collapse of primitive tribal culture, decay of Jhum cultivation. The speedy introduction of plough agriculture (higher mode of production than the slash and burn cultivation) has strengthened the masculinity in family. Among the Baruas and Mogs of Tripura presently the girls do not have any share of their parental property. Bride price is being replaced by dowry system gradually.

Women's lives are circumscribed or characterized by patriarchy, productive resource access inadequacy, poverty and powerlessness. In these tribal societies, women enjoyed relatively more freedom when they were directly involved in subsistence activities. The more the women are moving away from the production activities the higher is the deprivation.

Historically land was common property and traditionally women had no individual right over land. The traditional system of property over land is not based on the principle of inequality while growth of private ownership shows a trend of segmentation in the tribal communities. This sense of private ownership spills over to the other domains of culture and it ultimately complicates gender relationship in the society.

While female literacy rates have shown greater increase than the males but differences still persists between the two sexes. The literacy rates of females however, do not reflect the profiles of tribes and space. Particular mention can be made of very abysmal rates of literacy of primitive tribe group, Reang, in Tripura which is continue to be one of the lowest, less than 9 per cent. Probably the nature of livelihood patterns has a determining effect on the attainment levels of literacy among them.

There have been various studies on the status of women relating to their socio-cultural problems: their economic rights, their access to education employment and health (K. Mann 1987; J.P. Singh, N.N. Vyas, and R.S. Mann, 1988; A. Chauhan 1940). It becomes important to perceive the problems of tribal women as they experience spatial differentiation owing to their geographical location, historical background and processes of social change. There is a greater need for undertaking area-specific study of the status and role of tribal women that alone can focus light to understand the social process and dynamics of change. In such a pursuit an attempt was made to understand the status of tribal women in Tripura. A study was conducted among the four major tribes of Tripura, i.e, Debbarma, Reang, Molson and Garo.

Tripura

Tripura is spread over an area of 10486 sq km with green valleys, forest and hills. This state is located between 26°56' and 24°32' North latitude and 91°10' and n02I' East longitude. On the north, west and south sides Tripura has a international boundary of 832 km with Bangladesh. On the other sides Assam and Mizoram bound it.

Tripura was a princely state for 1300 years ruled by Maharajs. This princely state formally acceded to the Union of India in October, 1949 as a part of category C states. It became a Union territory on 1st November, 1956 and a full-fledged state on 21st January, 1972.

The main tribes of Tripura are Puran Tripuri, Chakma, Jamatia, Reang, Halam and Noatia. Besides, there are Mogh, Kuki, Santals, Garo, Munda, Lushai, Oraon, tribes. Although before Independence they formed the majority, the ratio of tribal population to the total population has declined since the fifties. In 1951, the percentage of tribal population was 37, in 1961, 1971 and 1981 it declined to 31.5, 28.9 and 28.4 respectively. In absolute figures, however, the tribal population of the state increased from about 257,000 in 1941 to 583,920 in 1981. the principal reason for the relative decline in the tribal population of the state is that the socio-economic conditions and geographical contiguity attracted people in the territory from East Bengal, which almost encircles it. During pre-partition days, thousands of Bengalis were in fact the inhabitants of Chakla Roshanabad, the biggest zamindari estate of the Maharajas. With the partition of the country, that area went to the then East Pakistan and a large number of Hindus migrated to the state.

Moreover the Royal family wanted to maintain a close contact with Bengal for fostering education, trade and commerce in the State. Also administrative personnel of various sorts were also recruited from Bengal. Lastly the partition of the country forced thousands of people from the neighbouring districts to come and settle in Tripura.

The economy of the state had to undergo severe stress and strain as a result of unprecedented rise in population in the state during the fifties and sixties. The density of population is now 262 per sq k.m. second highest among the North Eastern States after Assam. There are two major racial elements, namely, the Indo-Aryans represented by the Bengalees and the Indo-Mongoloids represented by a few communities like the Tripura, the Reang, the Jamatias, the Noatias, the Kukis, the Halams, the Chakma, the Mogh and the Lushai. Besides these nine major tribes there are ten more tribes. All the nineteen tribes are classified as "Scheduled Tribes".

Objectives

- This study is an attempt to understand the phenomenon of democracy, property and equality in an ethnic society from a gender perspective. This encompasses the social, economic and political dimensions of the tribal community.
- To examine the validity of the common perception that gender relations in tribal societies are more egalitarian and less discriminative and that tribal women enjoy higher status than others.

Hypothesis

- Firstly, the property ownership and economic relation shape the gender relations in particular and social relations in general in a tribal community.
- Secondly, the status of women in the ethnic societies is more or less equal with men.
- Thirdly, participation of women in the non-domestic activities is higher and participation in collective political groups is encouraging.
- Fourthly, women in tribal societies have equal property rights of inheritance and distribution in the primary social unit, i.e., family.
- Fifthly, the Government acts as facilitator in encouraging participation of women in all spheres of social development.

Methodology

The study was conducted in four tribal villages namely, Bagmara (Garo), Abhiramchoudhurypara (Reang), Shibbari (Molsom) and Dhancherra (Debbarma) in Kamalpur Sub-Division of Dhalai District in Tripura. Here a tribal village refers to a census village, which is a cluster of households located in a compact area. These villages were selected through purposive sampling. From these villages 50 households of each tribe were selected for the study through random sampling method. A total of 200 households were studied for the present analysis.

The major concerns of the study are Gender, Democracy and Property. The economic or property relations determine the social equation in life. This social equation predominantly influences the popular participation in the community. The concept of property is used in the sense that it includes - rights of ownership, size of property, distribution of property and laws of inheritance. The concept democracy in the family and in the community has to be understood to comprehend how democratic are the gender relations in a tribal community. This includes division of labour, decision-making, and freedom in mate selection, participation in the traditional social institutions and participation in Local self-governments. An ideal social relation in these aspects of life leads to realizing the dream of democracy and equity. Gender is the common stream that flows in to both aspects of Democracy and property. An attempt to understand these dynamics in tribal societies is made here.

Reangs

The Reangs comprise about 14 per cent of the tribal population and 4 per cent of the total population of the state. They are settled predominantly in Amarpur, Belonia, Kamalpur and Dharmanagar Sub-Division. Reangs are categorized as one of the most primitive tribes in India. They are believed to have migrated from the neighbouring Chittagong hill tracts in the middle of the 15th century. The Reangs are, numerically speaking, the next most important tribal group in the State of Tripura. It is believed that being driven out by the Mugs, they migrated to the east of the Gomati River in Tripura from the neighbouring Chittagong Hill Tracts in the middle of the 15th century, during the reign of Ratna Manikya.

A disciplined community among the tribals of Tripura, the Reangs have very little feuds and dissension among them. A well-defined hierarchical institution governs the community, the chief in the hierarchical order enjoys the title Rai Next in the line of succession is called (in order) Chapia Khan and Chapin. It is not birth but the quality of leadership determines succession. A Chief Minister called

Raikachak aids the Rai in his internal administration. The personal staff consistent with the dignity of their high offices assists both the Rai and the Raikachak.

One of the strongest of the State's military forces during the royal regime the Reangs had a reputation for their martial quality. The Tripura rules could obtain the support and services of the Reang community by maintaining contact with these chieftains who had complete authority over them.

The Reangs are Hindus, and generally believes in the Sakti cult, although in recent years, some of them are turning to Vaishnavism and Christianity. Like other tribals, they also believe in animism- that all begins, animals, plants, rivers and mountains are endowed with a living spirit.

Among the Reangs both husband and wife participate in work. Both of them earn the livelihood equally. Nearly half of the respondents are daily labourers and the rest are cultivators, very few are Government Employees. Either as daily labourers or cultivators their earnings are Meagre. Hence both of them go to work. Except very few households (14 per cent) majority of the household (86 per cent) opined that "women have equal role in running the family and in decision making". The reason they cited was that as woman is also taking equal share in the family responsibilities, she should have equal hand in decision making "Two brains are always better than one" is their opinion. Those few (14 per cent) who opined that woman are not equal in decision making reasoned that women do not have enough experience or idea and also that she is not intelligent enough to do so.

In the process of decision-making children are not neglected. Children are also consulted on all-important family matters but whenever deviance is there the Reangs do not hesitate to punish the children. Democracy does not mean for them absolute freedom at the cost of the others freedom.

At the community level the Reangs have a local self-government body (tribal) elected democratically by them through direct vote (rising hands). This body in the Reang para consists of one 'Chowdari' and one 'Karbai' who was earlier known as Rai. The family disputes quarrels and litigations are the regular issues that are presented in this forum. The decision of this forum is final. Since it is a customary institution everybody respects the authority and they have a sense of belongingness. Every person has got equal chance to become the Choudhuri or Karbari/Raj ad each one is punishable under this body.

Reangs are nuclear, family-oriented patriarchic families characterized by monogamous marriages but still when questioned regarding the inheritance of property they feel that both son and daughter should have equal property rights. Since most (74 per cent) of them are land less they have answered that they accept at he idea that women should get equal share. It is at ideological level they opine that all are equal. A majority of them are asset less hence there is no harm in a noble idea. But in practice they are truly patriarchal. But in the case of those with property (26 per cent) majority are not willing to share with their women be it a mother/daughter or sister. Only 4 per cent of the respondents have given property (whole/share) to their daughter. So it shows what kind of relations the Reang society is heading for.

Men and women shared marketing and cooking. There is occasional but less wife beating. They feel that daughter is as important as the son. But not many (10 per cent) girls are sent to school. It is not just because they are girls but also because of the financial problems. Most of them revealed that son only would look after them in the old age. There is no dowry but bride price is prevalent. But slowly with the gradual changes, the concept of dowry is replacing the bride price either in the kind of girls or cash. In the case of mate selection the girls is given free choice. This gives a clear example of how a society with meager sources maintains noble ideas of equality at ideological level and keeps the traditional patriarchic values in the institutions alive in practice.

Tripuri

Tripuri or Debbarma is the major community among the tribals of Tripura. The Tripuris (also called Tripuas or Tipras), the original inhabitants of the State, constitute about a little over 16 per cent of the total and 57 per cent of the tribal population of the State. The former rules of the land emerged from this community, which is believed to be the descendants of the Kshatriya. In course of time, a section of this community came into close contact with the Bengalee settlers and was much influence by their language, culture and customs. Marital contacts followed and the result was the emergence of a new community now known as Natun (new Tripuris) a sort of breakaway group of the original (puran) Trpuris.

A few among the Tripuris who were close to the royal family (known as Thakur) and settled in and around Agartala are much unlike their counterparts in the hill areas, quite advanced in education and general enlightenment.

Tripuri, the language of the community, has no alphabet of its own, and is written both in Bengali and Roman alphabet. Most of the Tripuris, therefore, can speak and understand Bengali. Majority of them are animistic-Hindus and their religious rites and rituals are similar to those of other Hindu sects.

The economic status or the nature of occupation of this native Tripura did not change much over the decades. They practice jhooming (or shifting cultivation), fetch wood from the forests, sell vegetables and bamboos. The women help men in jhooming, weave cloth on their traditional loin looms and take care of pigs, fowl, etc. Partly because of their contact with the Bengales settlers and partly because of Government efforts of development, many among them are settling on the plain areas of the state and adopting settled cultivation.

Debbarmas position in these villages seem to be in a relatively better position, as there are 14 per cent Government employees among them and 80 per cent cultivations and negligent 6 per cent daily labourers. As many as 28 per cent of them have more than one hector land and 44 per cent possess 0.40 ha. to 1 ha. and only 8 per cent of the Debbarma are landless.

Most of the Debbarmas are cultivations (86 per cent). They cultivate their own land or work on others lands. Daily labourers are very few (6 per cent). The women are mostly housewives. They carry out daily chores at home, nourish children and fetch firewood. Non-strenuous jobs like weaving are also done. All their tasks are domestic in nature. Men go out to work and women stay at home. 33 per cent of the respondents feel that though women do not come in to non-domestic labour, she is equal to men in decision making either it is related to her family or general issues. Children are consulted in all the important decisions.

In the Debbarma community both son and daughter are considered equal. But on the issue of distribution of property their response is not so uniform. Half of them (50 per cent) consider that both son and daughter have equal share in the property. The other half opined that only son is the inheritor of the property. But again interestingly it is found that even among those 50 per cent who advocated equal rights of property, only 4 per cent had actually given equal share to girls and rest followed the practices of giving property to the sons only. They feel that sons only look after them in the old age and daughters will go to her husbands place after marriage. But majority of them are ready to help their daughters either married or unmarried if they are in need.

There was marriage by service and marriage by payment among the Debbarma. In the marriage by service, the bridegroom should do service at the brides house for a fixed period to prove his abilities. In marriage by payment, the bridegroom should pay bride to his would be father-in-law. This bride price can be either in cash or kind. But recently the present systems have tremendously changed. Dowry is being practiced vigorously among Debbarma community either in cash or kind like gifts, gold, furniture etc. This shows that an evident change in the equation from woman's favour to man's is occurring in the Debbama maitial system also.

In the mate selection, generally both the parents and the boy and girl have a free hand. Wife beating is common among the Debbarma. The wife does marketing and cooking regularly with occasional deviance. Girls are sent to school more or less equally with the boys till primary/secondary level but once they reach higher secondary they drop out very highly.

The tribal Panchayat or the local council is very effective in the tribe governance. All the respondents consider the community participation and community forum for the management of collective issues as important. Women participation is moderate in the meetings. They consider politics to be the male domain. But of late there is an increasing involvement and awareness among women in the management of the collective issues in their village. The Para Panchayats are more effective in matters like education of children, property related matters. In other areas the Para Panchayat plays major role in solving the Jhumia land disputes.

So as discussed here in education, property, marriage and village governance the Debbarma community has strong patriarchic leanings. Whatever equality preached by them is only conceptual here but not practical.

Molsom

Molsom are sub-tribe belonging to Kuki-Halam, which belongs to Tibeto-Burman group. They mostly resemble other tribal groups and do not have major distinguishing features culturally, linguistically or ethnically.

Molsom society practices a reasonable division of labour. Both men and women work on the land (Jhumia). Predominantly they follow jhum cultivation. Even as daily labourers both men and women go out to work. Women participate in the cultivation activities. Among Molsoms 58 per cent are land less and labourers. Rest of the 42 per cent is landholders of different sizes and cultivators. Even the household activities are shared between both husband and wife. Decision in the family is made after consultations among all the family members. The opinion of the wife on any matter is sought by the father/head of the family. Among the Molsom 84 per cent are literate or received primary education.

In spite of equal division of labour, good education, when it comes to the status of women they categorically denied equal status for man and woman. Being a partner in bread winning and running the family does not entitle her to have equal status in the society. This is because of patriarchic nature of Molsom society. The reasons they had given are many. They consider that women have very little experience of life or that they are not intelligent, 88 per cent of them were of the opinion that man and woman, wife and husband or daughter and son are never equal. There are no set laws regarding the distribution of property. But since the families are in a patriarchic set up the property goes to all the sons equally and the headship of the family goes to the eldest son in the family.

There is no practice of dowry or bride price among the Molsoms. Mate selection is the choice of girl or boy concerned. At the time of marriage, gifts are accepted from both the sides. Wife beating is non-prevalent. The women do marketing and cooking only like other tribes.

The Molsom community has a 'Sardar' who takes decisions regarding the tribe in consultation with members. There are three women members in the 15 members tribal council. But the attendance and participation is less. The major issues discussed in the tribal council are land disputes, litigations and divorce.

Though Molsoms are relatively better-education tribe with egalitarian economic division of labour here also we have to interact with the low social status of women. Thus the patriarchic nature of the society is determining the low social, political and economic status for women.

Garo

The story of Garos is very interesting. Garos were traditionally matriarchal, matrilineal societies. Female (mother) was the head of the family and daughter used to get the property. These societies were matri-local also. After the marriage the bridegroom should come and live with the bride's family. Only female children will inherit the property and the eldest daughter is the successor. There was the practice of bride price.

But now there has been tremendous change in the Garo society. Garo community is slowly transforming itself in to a patriarchic, patrilineal and patrilocal society. It does not mean that the traces of matriarchy have totally vanished. Even now women in some cases have rights to property along with her brothers. Wife and husband both take part in the livelihood earning activity. Among the Garos both men and women have to go for wood, as their financial position is not encouraging. About 60 per cent of the Garos are landless and the rest of the 40 per cent are small cultivators. No body owns land more than 5 kanis (1 ha). But, 10 per cent of the respondents are Government employees. Though major part of the respondents acquired primary education i.e. 88 per cent their conditions are better than the Molsoms where only 4 per cent are Government employees in spite of 84 per cent of them receiving primary education and 12 per cent studied up to secondary level.

The present day Garos, do not consider man and wife equal. Around 44 per cent opined that husband and wife are equal and they should have equal rights and the 56 per cent opined that men and women are not equal. The reason cited for this is that intellectually women are less capable and less experienced than men. In the case of treatment of son and daughter, 72 per cent of the respondents have replied that all the children are equal, only 28 per cent opined that son is more important that the daughter.

The property among the Garos is inherited generally by sons. There are some exceptions where the daughters are also given partial inheritance of property. This particular phenomenon can be traced to the influence of matriarchal value system once prevailed among them. The practice of bride price is slowly being replaced by dowry system. But dowry is not practiced is the strict sense of the term. It is given as gifts at the time of marriage according to their capability. Mate selection is done with the mutual consent of the boy or girl and parents. Wife beating is very uncommon. Both wife and husband share domestic responsibilities like cooking, marketing etc. education of the girls is given importance.

The group or community sense is very strong among

the Garos. All the Garos have expressed the opinion that major decisions pertaining to the tribe will have to be taken by the Sardar (head of the Panchayat). Participation of women at panchayat is not encouraged. Previously women used to be the head of the tribal Panchayat. The Panchayat discuss family feuds, land disputes and matters related to marriage and divorce.

Thus, Garos society is a mixed society undergoing transformation from a matriarchical to patriarchic society and adopting the values of that society. The details of the study are presented from Table-2 to 11.

Table-2 Age

Age range	*Tribes/ Nos. of persons*				
	Reang	*Debbarma*	*Molsom*	*Garo*	*Total*
25-40	28	22	27	25	102
45-90	22	28	23	25	98
Total	50	50	50	50	200

Table-3: Sex

Sex	*Tribes/ Nos. of persons*				
	Reang	*Debbarma*	*Molsom*	*Garo*	*Total*
Male	40	44	25	30	139
Female	10	6	25	20	61
Total	50	50	50	50	200

Table-4. Education

Education	Tribes/percentage				
	Reang	Debbarma	Molsom	Garo	Total
Primary	80	78	84	88	82.50
Secondary	20	18	16	12	16.50
Higher	0	4	0		1.00
Total	100	100	100	100	100.00

Table-5 . Occupation

Occupation	Tribes/ percentage				
	Reang	Debbarma	Molsom	Garo	Total
Labour	46	6	46	50	37.00
Cultivators	52	80	46	40	54.50
Govt. employee	2	14	8	10	8.50
Total	100	100	100	100	100.00

Table-6. Income

Range	Tribes/percentage				
Income	Rean	Debbarma	Molsom	Garo	Total
0-500	66	50	38	56	52.50
500-1000	28	24	50	30	33.00
1000-2000	6	8	12	8	8.50
2000-5000	0	16	0	6	5.50
5000-7000	0	2	0	0	0.50
Total	100	100	100	100	100.00

Table-7. Land Holdings

Size	Tribes/ Nos. of persons				
	Reang	*Debbarma*	*Molsom*	*Garo*	*Total*
Landless	38	4	28.	30	100
Upto 2.5 kanis	6	8	12	8	34
2.5 – 6 kanis	4	22	7	7	40
Above 6 kanis	2	14	3	5	24

Table-8. Equality of Son And Daughter

Son and Daughter are euqal	Tribes/ Nos. of persons				
	Reang	*Debbarma*	*Molsom*	*Garo*	*Total*
YES	30	35	6	36	107
NO	20	15	44	14	93

Table-9. Dowry

	Tribes/ percentage				
	Reang	*Debbarma*	*Molsom*	*Garo*	*Total*
Dowry	4	96	26	8	33.50
No dowry	96	4	74	92	66.50
Total	100	100	100	100	100

Table-10. Equality of Wife And Husband

Wife an husband are equal	*Tribes/ Nos. of persons*				
	Reang	*Debbarma*	*Molsom*	*Garo*	*Total*
YES	43	35	76	22	104
NO	7	17	44	28	96
Total	50	50	50		

Table-11. Property Given to Daughter

	Tribes/ Nos. of persons				
	Reang	*Debbarma*	*Molsom*	*Garo*	*Total*
Given	2	1	0	3	6
Not given	48	49	50	47	194

Conclusion

The perception that women in tribal societies enjoy higher status-social, political, economic spheres is a classical myth. Perpetuation of this myth reflects both the inadequate understanding of tribal social reality as well as defective tools of social methodology.

- Education among the tribals is restricted to primary level only. Secondly level education is rare and higher education is an exception. Access to education is limited due to lack of enabling environment and inaccessibility of schools. It also implies high drop out rates. High degree of requirement of time for food production is also a major hurdle. This is reflected in the low enrolment of girls and high dropout rates of their willingness to learn.

- Most of the respondents are either small cultivators or daily labourers. The number of Government employees is very less. Only Debbarma community has 14% as Government employees. However, there is not even a single woman employee among so many tribal households studied.
- The tribals are poor communities. 51 % of the total samples are living at Rs.500/- per month and another 33% "are living below Rs.I000/- per month. The livelihood opportunities and access to steady sources of income are highly constrained by primitive technological production systems and habitat constraints.
- Half of the tribals are land less. 37% of them are small cultivators. Only a meagre 13% posses land above 1 ha. Debbarma are the majority landowners, as 28% of them possess land more than 1 ha. The Reangs, a primitive tribal group, are the poorest among all the tribes in the study.
- The nature of all the tribes are patriarchic, patrilocal and patrilineal. The status of tribal women has worsened due to change in their terms and levels of interaction with non-tribals and aping of mainstream gender relations of the non-tribal communities. Even the matriarchal societies like Garos have also adopted patriarchic norms and values.
- Man and woman relations are characterized by male domination though 52% of the tribals consider wife and husband as equal. An equally large proportion of respondents considered the relation (48%) as unequal. They think women are less intelligent, less experienced therefore less capable. The equality and status of women is directly correlated to their participation in economic activities and earning capacity of women. With more tribes being modernized and mainstreamed, the women's economic value will decrease and consequently their status also.
- Son and daughter are considered as equal (53.5) by majority and an almost equal (46.5%) were of the opinion that son is more important than the daughter.

While the former represents the parental nature to treat the offspring equally but practice is to the contrary. Among the Molsom community only 12% were of the view that there should be equally, 78% were in favour of son's domination.

- In spite of advocating that wife and husband and son and daughter are equal, when it came to economic rights only a meager 3% gave a share to the daughters in property. The tribal societies denied their women equal property rights. 97% of the sample did not give any share to their daughters/sisters or wives. This portrays the social equations in practice in tribal societies.
- Women do marketing and cooking including other drudgery i.e. farm work in the shifting cultivation. Whatever is stage of development the basic "duties" are unchanged. Therefore, not many girls are sent ato school due to reasons like financial problem, lack of schools, gender bias etc.
- The system of dowry has not yet taken the villainous shape as it took in the non-tribal communities, but it has made its entry in to the tribal societies. All the four tribes have taken to the practice of dowry. 33.5% of the tribals have given or taken dowry. 61.5% of them have not taken/given dowry. Though dowry was not, established as a practice, some kind of gifts or the others were given to the boy at the time of the marriage.
- Wife beating is common among all the tribes. Husband beating is unheard of. Punishment to children who deviate from the normal ways of behaviour is accepted norm. Father as, usual, in most of the cases punishes children.
- Women in the family are consulted for taking all-important decisions. Daughters, with the consent of the parents, go for marriage. But the daughters have priority in mate selection. The traditional tribal societies in Tripura are less democratic than generally perceived. The decision of the head of the village is accepted more for social/economic reasons than for respect for associated spiritual superiority or for

democratic participation. The social capital of the tribal societies is eroded without substitution with any culturally acceptable set of values to foster community bonds and regulate social behaviour.

- Tribals have very few livelihood choices. Any change or deviation will have greater effect on their food security and culture.
- The tribal councillor Para panchayat is effective in solving the family disputes in marriage and land disputes. The participation of women in reasonable number is witnessed but the nature of participation is not encouraging. There has never been a woman head/ member of the tribal council. Modernity with all its encompassing values is only leading to gradual marginalisation of tribal women in social, economic, political and traditional forums.

Bibliography

Bose, A.B. 1970. 'Problems of education development of Scheduled Tribes'. *Man in India,* Vol. (1) pp. 26-51.

Census of India. 1991. New Delhi: Government of India Publication.

Chauhan, Abha 1990. *Tribal Women and social change in India.* A.C. Brothers, Etawah.

Gazette of Tripura. 1975.

Gogoi, J.K. 1990. 'Tribal' Demography in North-East India: some preliminary observations', in Ashish Bose, Tiplut Nanybri and Nikhlesh Kumar (Eds.) *Tribal Demography and Development in North-East India.* Delhi: B.R. Publishing Corporation.

Goswami M.C. 1982. *The customary Laws and Practices of the Pati Rabhas of Assam.* North-East Council, Shillong.

Goswami M.C. 1982. *The customary Laws and Practices of the Thadou Kukis of Manipur.* North-East Council, Shillong.

Grigson, W.V. 1938. *The Maria Gonds of Bastar.* Oxford.

Haimendorf, furer C. Von. 1943. *The Aboriginal Tribes of Hyderabad.* Macmillan: Landon.

Kar, P.C. 1982. *The Garos in Transition.* Cosmo Publications, New Delhi

Lowie R.H. 1920 *Primitive Society.* Nweyork Bani and Liverlight publishing.

Madan, T.N. 1951. 'Education of Tribal India'. *Eastern Anthropologist,* Vol. V (4): I79-82

Madan and Majumder D.N. 1956. *An Introduction to Social Carolina.* The University of North Carolina Press.

Malinowski 1920. *A Scientific Theory of Culture and other essay.* Carolina: The University of North Carolina Press.

Majumder D.N. 1944. *Fortunes of Primitive Tribes.* Lucknow University Press.

Mann, K. 1987. *Tribal Women in a changing Society.* Delhi: Mittal Publications.

Mann, R.S. and Mann K. 1989. *Tribal Culture an Change.* New Delhi: Mittal Publication.

Menon, Geeta 1987. 'Tribal Women victims of Development Process'. *Social Action,* Vol. 37.

5

Poverty Alleviation through Self Help Groups: Issues of Sustainability in Tripura

Jayanta Choudhury

Poverty is a common characteristic of people in rural areas of Tripura. As per the 55th round of NSS survey during 1999-2000, Tripura ranked third highest with its 40.04 per cent of rural population below poverty line, next to Orissa (48.01 per cent) and Bihar (44.30 per cent). But while we consider the overall situation of Tripura, it ranked fifth position with its 34.44 per cent of total population below poverty line. The average for the country was 27.09 per cent for the rural areas and 26.10 for rural and urban combined. It indicates that rural poverty in Tripura was higher than the national average. Thus, it is pertinent to point out that poverty ratio of rural and urban areas of all north-east states including Tripura was assumed identical with the poverty ratio of rural and urban areas of Assam. This assumption is questionable because factors responsible for poverty varies from states to states as socio-economic and geo-physical conditions differ. Another source to get an idea about the poverty scenario is the BPL survey by the states in 1997. According to this survey, 66.81 percent of rural households are below poverty line and the poverty scenario is almost uniform in all four districts of Tripura.

Table-1. District-wise Households below Poverty Line

Sl. No	*District*	*No. of Rural families*	*No.of BPL families*	*% of BPL families*
1.	South	148181	108214	73.02
2.	West	277294	1746	63.02
3.	Dhalai	65120	46487	71.38
4.	North	104302	68334	65.20
	Tripura	594897	397798	66.81

Source: Department of Rural Development, Govt. of Tripura.

The main factors for the prevalence of poverty in Tripura are low agricultural land holdings (90 percent of which are small and marginal holdings), mostly hilly area, communication bottleneck, geographically isolation, inadequate infrastructure, low rate of industrialization, over dependency on Government job of the youth and so on.

Poverty Alleviation through Self Help Groups

Poverty alleviation is the ultimate goal of all kinds of development programmes in India. The planners have taken up several approaches for combating poverty during different periods of time. While most of the programmes failed to deliver the expected results, certain innovative efforts hold out fresh hope. One such effort is the formation of Self Help Groups (hereafter SHGs) for enabling the poor to participate in the process of development in general and to come out from poverty in particular.

Figure-1

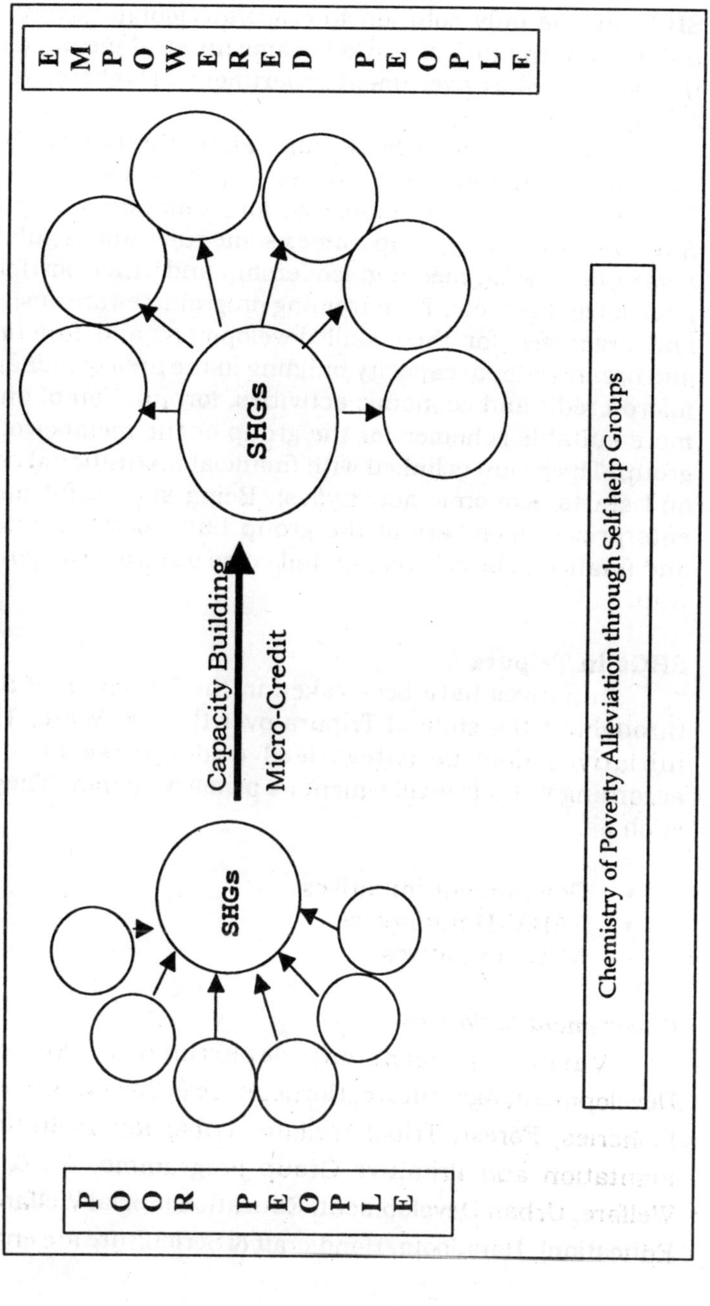

Chemistry of Poverty Alleviation through Self help Groups

Almost all the promoters of development have taken SHGs as the only solution to eradicate global poverty. In India too, formation of SHGs became an ideal means for all the agencies like Government departments, Bankers, NGOs, civil bodies.

The process of poverty alleviation through SHGs is explained in the Figure-1. In this approach few (generally 10-15) poor people are mobilized for formation of a group. After the formation, group frames some rules and regulation regarding saving, meeting, leadership and other portfolios, internal lending, etc. Then training programmes are designed and organized for their skill development and functional and organizational capacity building in the area of managing micro-credit and economic activities, formulation of one or more suitable schemes for the group or the member of the group. The group is linked with financial institutional credit and starts economic activity(ies). Being successful micro-enterprises, members of the group build both confidence and finance to be self-reliant and come out from the poverty trap.

SHGs in Tripura

Initiatives have been taken in the formation of SHGs throughout the state of Tripura over the last years. These initiatives may be categorised under three headings according to their involvement as primary agency. They are such as:

- Government initiatives
- NABARD initiatives
- NGOs initiatives

Government Initiatives

Various government departments like Rural Development, Agriculture, Horticulture & Soil Conservation, Fisheries, Forest, Tribal Welfare, Tribal Rehabilitation in Plantation and Primitive Group Programme, SC & OBC Welfare, Urban Development, Education (Social Welfare and Education), Handloom, Handicraft & Sericulture are engaged in implementation of various central government as well as State Government projects through formation of SHGs with specific objectives and targets. Among them the Department of Rural Development is successful in implementing Swarnajayanti Gram Swarojgar Yojana (SGSY), the single most programmes which directly links with poverty alleviation throughout the country.

Keeping in mind wide range of coverage, this paper will confine only to SHGs formed under SGSY.

Swarnajayanti Gram Swarojgar Yojana in Tripura

SGSY was launched through out the country on 1st April 1999 as a convergence of earlier Integrated Rural Development Programme (IRDP), Training of Rural Youth in Self-employment (TRYSEM), Development of Women and Children in Rural Areas (DWCRA), Supply of Improved Tool Kits to Rural Artisans (SITRA) and Million Wells Scheme (MWS). The primary objective of SGSY remains the same, that of lifting the BPL families up to join APL group. Group based approach has been given priority over individual approach.

Performance and Sustainability

Table-2 gives the picture about the progress and sustainability of the SHGs under SGSY in Tripura. Since its inception upto March 2004, more than thirteen thousands groups have been formed through out the state which is almost double of the cumulative target. But if we look at other components of a quality group, the results are not at all encouraging. Only 26.45 per cent SHGs were eligible for first gradation tests and only 16.74 per cent passed the first gradation and received revolving fund from the DRDA. Only 8.85 per cent opened CC account i.e. received fund from the banks. But most discouraging fact is that since inception only 1.05 percent SHGs (138 nos.) were able to pass second gradation and receive fund for income generation activities.

Table-2: Physical Performance upto March, 2004

Sl. No.		*West*	*North*	*South*	*Dhalai*	*Tripura*
1.	Cumulative target upto 2003-04	3110	1446	2071	1309	7936
2.	Total SHGs formed since inception	6621	1446	3918	1159	13144
	% Achievement over target	212.89%	100%	189.18%	88.54%	165.62%
3.	No.of group gradation test completed	1269 (19.17%)	419 (28.98%)	1478 (37.72%)	311 (26.83%)	3477 (26.45%)
4.	No.of SHGs recevied revolving fund	807 (12.19%)	261 (18.05%)	878 (22.41%)	254 (21.92%)	2200 (16.74%)
5.	No. of SHGs opened CC account	452 (06.83%)	146 (10.10%)	455 (11.61%)	110 (09.49%)	1163 (08.85%)
6.	No. of SHGs assisted for Economical Activites	48 (0.72%)	31 (02.14%)	01 (0.0003%)	60 (05.19%)	138 (01.05%)

Source: Department of Rural Development, Govt. of Tripura.

If we look at the district-wise performance of SHGs, the picture is not much different. The two districts- West and South- had achieved nearly twice their target, but the percentage of SHGs, which received fund for starting of income generation activities, was very poor. In these two districts only 0.72 per cent and 0.003 per cent respectively received funds for starting income generation activities. Interestingly, rest of the two districts i.e. North and Dhalai had achieved just 100 per cent and 88.54 per cent of their cumulative target but the percentage of SHGs, which received fund for starting of income generation activities were comparatively better than the other two districts of Tripura. These were 2.14 per cent and 5.19 per cent respectively.

Another important question is how many of all these groups, which received funds for micro enterprises will be successful. From this analysis we can conclude that mere achieving of target cannot ensure a quality and sustainable group.

Factors Hindering Sustainability of SHGs under SGSY

(a). *Identification of needy people* is a common most problem in SGSY. People who really want to help themselves should be incorporated into the groups.

(b). SGSY became a *target centric programme* like all other Government programmes. All the machineries involved in formation of SHGs, are just trying to achieve the given target.

(c). *Inadequate staffs in DRDAs* is also a major problem. All the four DRDAs in the state are suffering from acute shortage of staffs. Success of SHGs depends on continuous nurturing and nursing of the groups.

(d). *Lack of proper social mobilization process* is also hindering the group dynamics. The members are being mobilised to join the group to receive an immediate fund from the DRDAs and banks. But when they are fails in gradation tests and therefore do not receive the grant, they become reluctant to stay in the group.

Figure-2

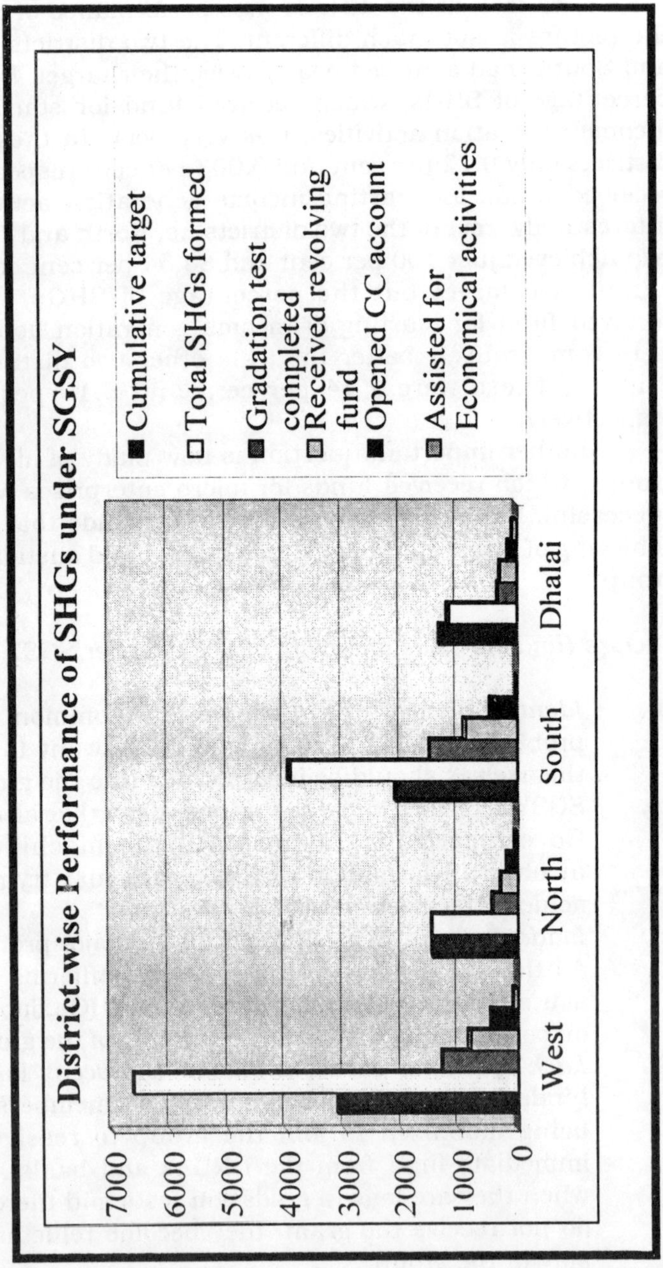
District-wise Performance of SHGs under SGSY
7000
6000
5000
4000
3000
2000
1000
0
West
North
South
Dhalai
Cumulative target
Total SHGs formed
Gradation test completed
Received revolving fund
Opened CC account
Assisted for Economical activities

(e). In this programme *hardly any NGOs are involved* in Tripura. It is a fact that throughout the country, NGOs are associated with various stages in SHGs particularly in social mobilization and capacity building process. Non-involvement of NGOs is also one of the factors behind poor performance of the SHGs under SGSY.

(f). Low investment and interest on capacity building / training is also one of the serious matters. It was seen that during the year 2003-2004, only 1.47 percent was spent on training. But as per the guidelines, 10 percent of the fund could be utilized for training.

(g). *Infrastructure development* is the basic requirement for sustainability of any programme. In case of SGSY also, proper infrastructure development is a prerequisite for creation of micro-enterprises. But it is frustrating to note that during the year 2003-2004, only 3.13 percent was utilized for creation of necessary infrastructure. As per the provision contained in the guidelines, the expenditure under infrastructure is permissible to the extent of 25 percent of available funds.

(h). Most of the SHGs are confined to some *monotonous* key activities for income generation. Over emphasis was given on animal resource based activities (51.03 percent) which is directly linked with quality of animal and service provided. No new and challenging activity was taken up.

(i). *Poor response from banks* is the biggest problem in sustainability of SHGs under SGSY. Major banks are not disbursing the loans timely to the SHGs. For example, since inception, 223 groups were sponsored to banks from South District of Tripura but till December 2004, only 17 SHGs i.e. 7.26 percent SHGs received bank loan.

(j). Due to the communication bottleneck, *non-availability of market* is one of the toughest problems for the SHGs. Purchase of necessary raw materials and selling of the products is a major challenge.

These activities form building block of micro-enterprises.

(II) *NABARD's Initiatives*

Since the year 1992, NABARD had taken initiative in financing the SHGs as a mainstream activity of the banks under their priority sector lending throughout the country. The banking system comprising public and private sector commercial banks, regional rural banks (RRBs) and cooperative banks have joined hands with several organizations in the formal and non-formal sectors to mainstream this informal delivery mechanism for providing financial services to a large number of poor. There are three models adopted by the NABARD through which SHGs are linked with formal banking system. These can be simplified in the Figure-3.

In Model-1, banks form and finance the SHGs and in Model-2, SHGs are formed by the NGOs but directly financed by the banks. In Model-3, NGOs work as financial intermediaries.

Performance and Sustainability

Through these three models in India, more than ten lakhs SHGs have been linked with formal banking systems. In Tripura upto March 2004, only 850 SHGs have been linked with the banks. If we see the cumulative progress of SHGs bank linkage in Tripura, we observe that it has started very late and its momentum is very low. The performance is not very good compared with other parts of the country.

Though the performance of bank linkage of SHGs is increasing very positively every year but sustainability of the SHGs is questionable. Table-4 gives a district wise picture of formation and bank linkage of SHGs. One can easily see that there is a big gap between formation and bank linkages of SHGs. During the year 2004-05, nearly 2350 SHGs have

Figure-3

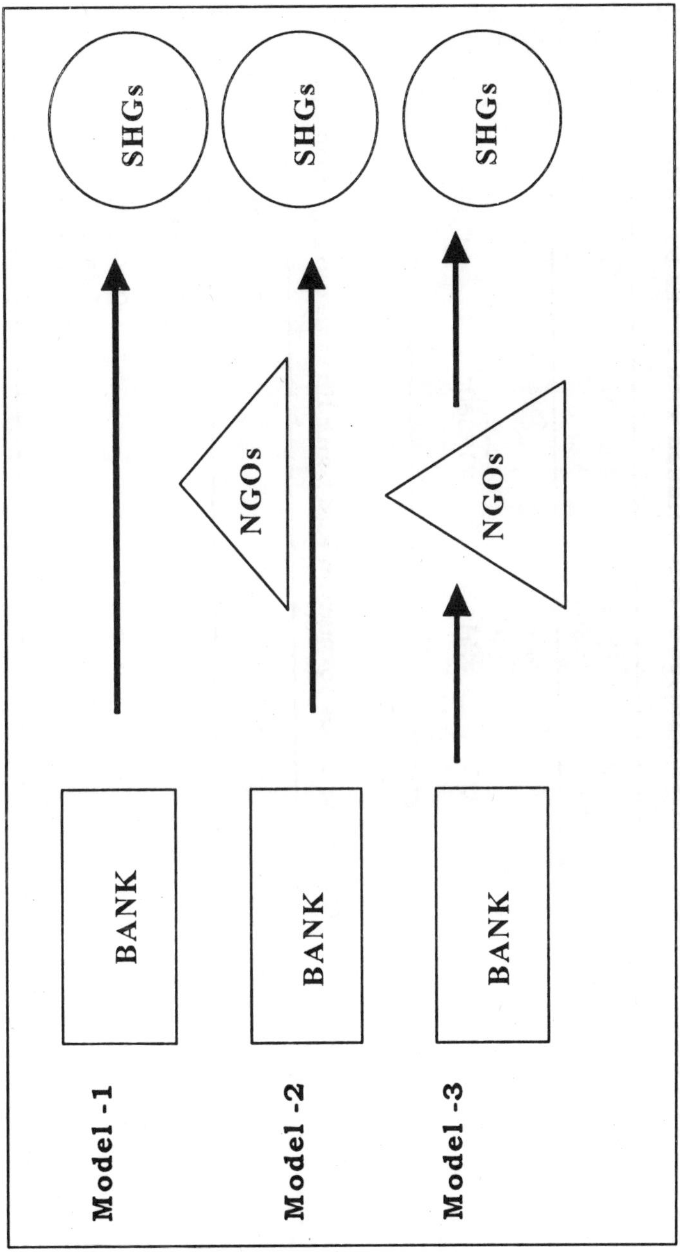
Model -1
BANK
SHGs
Model -2
BANK
NGOs
SHGs
Model -3
BANK
NGOs
SHGs

Table-3 Cumulative number of SHGs linked with banks by NABARD

Sl.No.	*March*	*Upto 31st March*	*Upto 31st March*	*Upto 31st March*	*Upto 31st*
1.	Tripura	5	7	104	850
2.	NER	477	1490	4069	11278
3.	India	263825	461478	717360	1079091

Table-4: Ditrict-wise SHGs formation and Bank linkage during 2004-05

Sl.No.	*Name of the Districts*	*Group Formed*	*Bank Linkage*
1	West	600	36 (0.06 %)
2	South	2750	75 (0.27 %)
3	Dhalai	500	03 (0.006 %)
4	North	500	10 (0.02 %)
	Total	2350	124 (0.053%)

Source : Progress of SHG-Bank linkage in India, 2003-04, NABARD, Mumbai

been formed but only 124 SHGs i.e. only 0.053 percent of total SHGs formed have been linked with different banks. This performance is almost similar for the all four districts of Tripura.

Factors Hindering Sustainability

(a). *Poor involvement of Tripura Cooperative Bank and Commercial banks* is one of the major factors responsible for poor performance. In other states, Cooperative banks are leading from the fronts but in Tripura the entire responsibly is handed over to the Tripura Grammeen Banks.

(b). NABARD models are *facing competition* from other SHGs related Government programmes. These programmes are subsidy oriented and as a result attract people easily. A person prefer those programmes to get a good amount of revolving fund within a short period whereas to receive the same amount it require longer period in the case of the NABARD models.

(c). *Non-availability of quality NGOs* is also a serious problem. In Tripura only two NGOs are associated in the SHGs-bank linkage models. Table-4 also supports this observation. While in India, a total of 80 percent SHGs are formed by the Model-2 and Model-3 where NGOs are mainly responsible for formation and financing of SHGs, in Tripura only 21.2 percent SHGs are formed by Model-2 and rest 78.8 percent SHGs are formed under Model-1.

(d). *Lack of Training Institute for Bankers* is also affecting sustainability of SHGs formed under various models of NABARD. Staffs of various banks, NGOs and SHGs members could not get proper training

Table-5: Performance of 3 Models in India and Tripura

SI.No.		M:1 (Formed and financed by Bank	M:2 (Formed by NGOs and Financed by Bank	M:3 (NGOs work as financial intermediates
1	India	20%	72%	8%
2	Tripura	78.8%	21.2%	0%

Source: Progress of SHG-Bank linkage in India, 2003-04, NABARD, Mumbai.

iii) *NGOs Initiatives*

Poverty alleviation through SHGs was initiated in different parts of India by various NGOs long before the Government's and NABARD's initiatives following the Grammen Bank concept of Bangladesh. In this approach NGOs act as Micro-finance Institutions (MFIs) by forming and financing the SHGs. They receive funds from various sources and channelise it to different small groups with a high rate of interest.

Figure-4

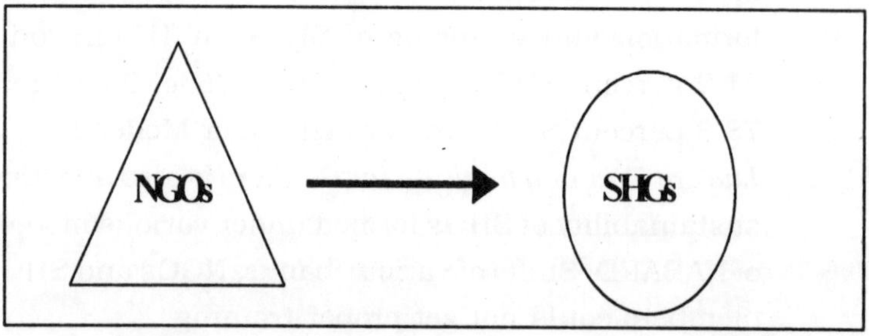

In Tripura only few NGOs namely ASHA, JUST, Dishari, Bandhan are following this approach. Detail data are not available in this area but nearly 500-750 SHGs are assisted by these NGOs.

Issues of Sustainability

Sustainability is difficult to achieve for following reasons:

(a) Very insignificant numbers of both NGOs and SHGs formed by them.

(b) High depends on external funds.

(c) Lack of quality / experienced staffs.

Issues and Policy Implication

- People who really want to help themselves and have entrepreneurial ability should be incorporated into the groups. For identification of such person in every village some benchmark participatory survey through group discussion etc. among different people is required. In this regard PRIs have to take more constructive role.
- Importance has to be given only on quality rather than quantity. Target should be reduced. Here we strongly recommend to declare one year as "No SHGs Formation Year". At least one year, let the DRDAs nurture properly their already formed groups which is already more than 12000. DRDAs should settle the entire backlog in gradation, bank linkage, training etc. for quality improvement of the already formed SHGs.
- NGOs should be involved in social mobilisation and capacity building process under SGSY.
- Marketing problem can be handled in different way. Till now, there is not a single activity cluster or federation for the SHGs. Immediately activity based cluster or federation should be developed including all the SHGs promoted by all the SHPIs. It may be GP wise or Block wise depends on the volume of the product or number of SHGs.

- SIPARD, (SIRD – Tripura) can play a very vital role in SHG movement in Tripura. It can fill the gap of quality training. For skilled based training also, master trainers can be organized on different specifically selected activities which have some demand and marketing potentiality. SIPARD and SWAVALAMBAN together can attach this problem and can arrange quality training both basic orientations as well as skilled training.
- Emphasis should be given on creation of rural infrastructure. Total fund available under SGSY should be properly utilized. It can solve lot of problems of SHGs.
- Continuous and quality research should be carried out in all blocks related to SHGs. It will help to explore further area for entrepreneurship development.
- Regular meeting with the bankers at various levels along with government is necessary. Government should take care about the recovery. PRIs can play very vital role in this regards. For better functioning and settle different bank cases, all the branches of all the banks should call any one day every week as "SHG Day".
- Some exposure visit for the officials of Cooperative and Commercial Banks can be made. It can bust up their confidence. As Bangladesh is very nearby and recently bus services had opened, exposure to Bangladesh where successful Grameen model is running could be a great help both economically and morally. NABARD can play a very effective role in this regards.
- Block wise Data bank related to SHGs must be created. It will help to check the duplication under various approaches and as a result will help in wider coverage. CICs in each bock can be effectively used in this regards.
- At least two years should be incumbency period for any officials who are associated with SHGs movement.

References

Bandopadhyay, D., B.N. Yugandhar and A. Mukherjee (2002). "Convergence of Programmes by Empowering SHGs and PRIs", *National Bank Review*, April-June, pp. 14-25.

Banking with Self-help Group, Resource and Research Centre, DHAN Foundation, 1998.

Bayadas, Mayada M., Douglas, H. Graham and Liza Valenzuela (1997). "Commercial Banks in Miocrofinance: New Actors in the Microfinance World", *Occasional Paper No.* 2372, *Rural Finance Program, Ohio State University.*

Berger, Marguerite (1989). "Giving Women Credit: The Strengths and Limitations of Credit as a Tool for Alleviating Poverty" *World Development,* Volume 17, Number 7.

Chakraborty, R. (2002) "The Indian Micro-finance Experience-: Accomplishments and Challenges" *mail rajeshchakraborty@ mgt.gatech.edu.*

Harper, M. (2002) "Promotion *of* SHGs under the SHG- Bank Linkage Programme in India". *Paper presented at the Seminar on SHG-Bank Linkage Programme, 25th and 26th November* 2002 *in New Delhi: published by Micro-credit Innovation, NABARD, Mumbai.*

Karmakar, K.G. (1999). "Rural Credit and Self Help Groups: Micro-finance Needs and Concepts in India", *Sage Publications,* India. -

Khandker, S.R., Khalily, B. and Khan Z. (1996). "Credit Programmes for the Poor: Household and Intrahousehold Impacts and Program Sustainability. Dhaka, Bangladesh": *Bangladesh Institute of Development Studies,* Volume 1.

Potential Linked Credit Plan, 2004-2005 by NABARD-Agartala Branch

6

Agro-Based Religion: A Case Study in Coastal Orissa

Niharranjan Mishra

Religion has exercised the most profound influence over man's thought since time immemorial. Religion has been regarded as the product of civilization until Tylor gave a convincing proof that primitive societies have their own version of religious activities, not very different from that of civilized societies. In all societies of simple technology, people believe that the process of nature and the success of human endeavour are under the control of entities outside the range cf everyday experience, whose intervention can change the course of events. In order to seek the blessings of these entities, human beings have developed and consolidated their faith in different gods and goddesses and have set aside certain days or periods of time for ritual celebrations.

Even today, when man has made tremendous progress especially in the quest of science and technology, he believes in his religion for getting some inspiration. In their study of religions, anthropologists are not concerned with the truth or error of specific beliefs. This is a question of theology and philosophy. Rather, they are interested in what these beliefs tell us about the people and their culture and how beliefs operate within the broader cultural system.

While defining religion, E. B. Tylor said, "...religion is nothing but belief in super natural being". According to Ronald L. Johnstone, "...religion is a system of beliefs and practices by which, a group of people interprets and responds to what they feel is supernatural and sacred" (1975: 20).

Ever since the history of the growth of human culture people have believed on different Gods and Goddesses. These Gods and Goddesses vary from one religion to another. The Gods and Goddesses in Hindu religion are numerous and vary from one state to another, from one religion to other and from one cast or tribal community to another. In spite of these varieties and variations, we may describe different levels of differentiation of these Gods and Goddesses.

Firstly, there are the *Pauranic* gods and goddesses, about whom myths are found more or less in a uniform manner all over India. The second level is concerned with certain Gods and Goddesses, especially sacred to certain regions, social communities or to a village. At the third level, we have deities, who are sacred specifically to an occupational group or a caste group or a tribal group.

The Hindu Gods - *Brahma, Vishnu, Maheswara,* have occupied their place in the first level. Throughout India, they are popularly known by these names. But some times, these Gods may appear in different incarnations at different places. Lord *Jagannatha* is considered as the incarnation of Lord *Krishna* and also of Lord *Vishnu.* Goddesses *Durga, Lakshmi, Kali* and *Dharitri* (Goddess Earth), etc is coming under this level. Centering on these Goddesses, a number of religious observances (*Osha* and *Vrata*) are being observed mostly by women in Orissa.

The various regional or local Gods and Goddesses of Orissa state culture like *Bhadrakali Chandi* of Bhadrak, *Balaramjue* in Kendraparha, *Kakatapur Mangala* in Kaktapur represent the second level. On the third level of differentiation, we find some Gods and Goddesses of all India adapted to the local context of the occupational or caste groups. For example, *Vishwakarma* is specifically sacred to the carpenters, smiths and in the present days to the engineers. Similarly, Goddess *Lakshmi is* specifically sacred to businessmen. But when Goddess *Lakshmi* is regarded as the Goddess of rice, 'She' is restricted to the farmers. When we think of the Gods and Goddesses belonging to the folk society or village, we invariably think of the last two levels in addition to those of the first level that is all India level.

Beliefs in gods and goddesses, and worshiping idols have also become inseparable parts of the socio-cultural life of the people of Orissa. At the centre of idol-worship is the practice of honouring gods and goddesses in their various forms, and observance of numerous festivals on different agricultural, religious or social occasions or events to invoke or appease them. It is no wonder that most of the rituals or festivals that the people of Orissa observe are basically agro-centric as the society revolves around agriculture. In the period from the advent of sowing to the ripening of crops and harvesting, different rituals are celebrated in rural Orissa with the agricultural cycle as well as with the renewal of seasons (Mohanty 1992). Ritual observances for the propitiation of deities at the time of seasonal renewals are primarily to reduce or evade the evil influences caused by such cyclic changes of nature. The food grains harvested seasonally are also offered symbolically to the presiding gods and goddesses through various harvesting festivals. For instance, on *manabasa* days, in the month of *Margashira* (December-January), paddy is harvested, and the Oriya housewives worship goddess Lakshmi, the goddess of wealth, and offer the newly harvested crop to the deity, praying and hoping that the same wealth and prosperity may prevail forever in their families.

In Western Orissa, *nuakhia* or the first eating of the newly harvested rice is observed as an important festival with much fun and frolic. Patnaik (1982), emphasizing on the fact that the festivals of Orissa as agro-based maintains that, Orissa which is a land of festivals is mostly the country of farmers. Even today about 80% of the total population depends on farming. So the festivals and rituals celebrated here not only reflect the religious attitude of farmers but also their way of life. Sahoo (1980) has a similar opinion, when he says that the food grains harvested seasonally are offered symbolically to the different gods and goddesses to reduce the evil influences caused by cyclic changes of nature.

Satpathy (1996), emphasizing on the belief systems, has mentioned that the villagers in Orissa used to worship the goddess Durga as *Sakambari,* who saves them from draught and famine providing abundant crops. Citing many different secondary and primary sources, Mishra (2003) reveals that the villagers have even structured the hierarchy among the gods and goddesses considering different roles played by them in agriculture, which reinforces the views regarding the nexus between agriculture and religious beliefs and practices in rural Orissa.

The present paper is a modest attempt in analysing empirically the agro-based religion in rural Orissa. The interface between changing agricultural practices and agro-based religion, among other socio-cultural phenomena, is considered as very important due to the fact that for the people of rural Orissa agriculture is not merely construed as a means of livelihood but also a way of life.

Methodology

This study is based on the data collected from the village Jagdalpur in Bhadrak district of Orissa during the year 2003, when the author spent considerable time of the year in the village to collect primary data on agro-based religion and rituals using standard anthropological tools and techniques. Quantitative information with regard to technological modernization in agriculture, land holding, village demography, cropping pattern, irrigation system, etc. were collected by using household schedules and district statistical hand books. Relevant secondary sources, such as published and unpublished materials were also used to see the picture of agro-based religion in the village.

The Village and its People

Jagdalpur is situated in the Jagdalpur Panchayat of Bhadrak block in Bhadrak district; about 10 km from the district headquarters (see Map of Bhadrak). It is a multi-*jati* village inhabited by 10 *jatis*. 2 of these *jatis* - the Brahman and the Khandayat (traditionally engaged as farmers in peace times and as –warriors in the local royal army in war times) - belong to the forward *jati* category. 6 of the *jatis*, such as the Gouda (milkmen), Kumbhar (potters), Kamar (blacksmiths), Bania (goldsmiths), Barik (barbers), and Tanti (weavers) are considered as the backward *jatis* by the villagers. The remaining 2 belongs to the category of untouchables that include the Dhoba (washermen) and Pana (ritual drum beaters). Although the Panas are numerically highest among the 10 *jatis* in the village, the Khandayats play a dominant role, both economically and politically because they own most of the land in the village.

The village has 102 households with a total population of 639. Out of 102 households, 72 (70.5%) own land. Among the landless *jatis*, 63.33% belongs to the pana *jati*. Most of the landowners own land between 1 and 5 acres. Whereas 33 households have less than 3 acres of land, 9 households enjoy the status of owning more than 10 acres of land. The Brahman and the Khandayat together constitute 27% of the total population in the village and acquire 58.2% of the total land. The panas that constitute 25% the total population posseses only 3.5% of the total land, which confirms positive correlation between the *jati* status and land ownership in Jagdalpur as it is the case in other Indian villages (*cf* Srinivas 2000).

The village is one of the agriculturally advanced villages of Bhadrak district served by the Salandi canal as the main source of irrigation. The main crops traditionally grown are paddy (*dhana*), mustard (*sorisa*), black gram (*biri*) and green gram (*muga*). Along with water availability and utilization, the use of HYV seeds, chemical fertilizers, and ploughing machines have accelerated the desire of the villagers to cultivate more and more cash crops in place of subsistence crops. There are 2 tractors, 2 power tillers, 20 water pumps, 25 wooden ploughs, 30 sprayers, 59 pairs of bullocks and 68 threshing machines, out of which 30 are electric machines and the remaining are operated manually. The locational advantage of the village being closer to the district headquarters helps the villagers in marketing of their agricultural produce easily compared to other remote villages in the district.

Agricultural Calendar and Agro-Based Religion in Jagdalpur

The villagers observe a number of festivals cyclically starting from the stage of field preparation to harvesting. These festivals are organized both at the individual as well as community levels to propitiate the supernatural beings. The material requirements in various festivals are standardized. The site is cleared and purified with earth and cow dung and is then decorated with banana leaves, mango twigs and flowers. All the rituals require turmeric powder, vermilion, incense sticks, flowers, and earthen lamps.

The rituals associated with agriculture of the study village can be classified as follows:

- There are some rituals, which are basically family oriented and are observed according to the convenience of the individual families. Such rituals do not take place on a fixed date but held in a particular month.
- There are certain other family oriented rituals, which take place on the same date through out the village.
- Some rituals are purely community based. These rituals are performed on a fixed date or according to the convenience of all the villagers as a whole.

The rituals like Halasutra, Raja Parba, Akhi Trutiya, Dusahara, Gamha Purnima, Garvana Sankranti, Aghira Purnami, Mana Basa, etc. are observed by the villagers of Jagdalpur, which reinforce their relationship with agriculture as a way of life. In many cases the ritual observances find expressions in their proverbs and folk songs as well. The villagers used to worship different Gods and Goddesses during these festivals. Since the beginning of cultivation they start observing these festivals. A number of Gods, Goddesses are worshiped by them.

In the present study, the villagers used to revere a number of Gods and Goddesses for the fulfilment of different needs. Out of these Gods and Goddesses, a few have captured the role for the fulfilment of agricultural needs.

they are Lord *Jagannatha, Siva, Indra,* Goddess *Lakshmi* and *Grama Devati Kharakhai* (village deity). Although all these five Gods and Goddesses are venerated by the villagers for the fulfilment of agricultural needs, based on their role in agriculture, Goddess *Lakshmi* occupies the first and foremost place, followed by Lord *Jagannatha, Indra, Grama Devati and, Siva.* Even there is not a single agro-based festival, when the villagers do not worship Goddess *Lakshmi.*

The culture of Orissa is known as *Jaganatha* culture and Lord *Jagannatha,* the husband of Goddess *Lakshmi,* is worshipped in each and every corner of Orissa for the fulfilment of different desires, but whenever the question of agriculture comes, the name of Goddess *Lakshmi* immediately comes to the mind of the villagers. Although the people of Orissa in general consider Lord *Jagannatha* as a superior God, the villagers have always argued in favour of *Lakshmi.* For this, they refer a mythological story from *Lakshmi Purana,* where Lord *Jagannatha* surrenders Himself to *Lakshmi* for the fulfilment of His hunger. The story has been described as follows: *Shriya Chanduluni,* an untouchable woman worshipped Goddess *Lakshmi* by observing this festival. Being moved by her devotion, *Lakshmi* left 'Her' permanent abode, the temple, which is situated inside the campus of the temple Lord *Jagannath* and visited *Shreeya's* home. When Lord *Balabhadra,* the elder brother of Lord *Jagannath* came to know about this, she was declared defiled, and was not allowed to come back into the temple. *Lakshmi* was deeply hurt and went to her father *Sagara.* When *Lakshmi* went out of the temple, all the wealth in the temple started vanishing immediately. Later, the God *Balabhadra* and *Jagannath* could not find food to sustain. They came out of the temple in the guise of Brahmin beggars in search of food. Ultimately, they landed at the door of the Goddess *Lakshmi. Balabhadra* apologized for the mistake and all of them returned to the temple. The *purana* ultimately teaches all to pay extreme regards to Goddess *Lakshmi* and the person who disregards 'Her' is sure to fall onto the evil days.

In order to convey their gratitude to *Lakshmi* for her benevolence, the farmer's wife organizes the *Manabasa* festival throughout the month of *Margasira* (December - January). On each Thursday, the houses are smeared with cow dung the floors are decorated with beautiful flora designs drawn with rice paste called *Jhoti.* Footmarks are printed from doorstep to the place of worship, as if Goddess *Lakshmi* has entered. The roofs are decorated with *dhana menta* (festoon woven out of paddy stalks). There is a belief among the farmers' wives that on this day, Goddess *Lakshmi* comes from the Heaven to visit their houses. Therefore, they make all these decorations.

After having a bath in the early morning, the housewives put some special variety of whitish paddies in a *Mana* (grain measurer). Then they put three betel nuts on the paddy kept on *Mana,* and on the betel nut, they fix a *dhana menta* and also a piece of sugarcane and radish. At last they decorate this *Mana* as a woman with a piece of cotton (chita). Then they start worshipping Goddess *Lakshmi* offering 'Her' favourite flowers such as jàsmine, gomphrena, mist rose, gardenia, etc. No body uses China rose, red water lily, Sacharam and *Tamala* flower in 'Her' *puja*, as there is a belief among the villagers that Goddess *Lakshmi* dislikes these flowers. So, if they offer these to 'Her', then 'She' will get angry. As a result, the next year production could be lessened. According to the *Lakshmi Purana (Patheon of Lakshmi),* different varieties of rice cakes and *khiri* are prepared by every household and offered to the deities. On the first Thursday, they offer rice pudding and *khechidi,* on the second Thursday, *Chitau pitha* and curd-rice water, on the third Thursday, cheese, greens and lolley toffee and on the fourth or last Thursday, sandwich. The concluding festivities of the last Thursday of the month are the most elaborate. The lady of the house has to fast to worship the Goddess on all these four Thursdays. In order to make "Her" please, they keep their house clean. Only members of the family (the married daughters who have changed their *gotra* in marriage, and have their own separate households are excluded) can partake of the oblations, otherwise, Goddess *Lakshmi* may leave the household of the worshiper.

After Goddess *Lakshmi,* Lord *Jagannatha* has also occupied the major place in the field of agriculture. In most of the agricultural festivals, the farmers of the study village pay their obeisance to Lord *Jagannatha,* as an incarnation of Lord *Vishnu.* There is a belief among the farmers that *Ekadasi* is a day particularly sacred to Lord *Vishnu.* So, to respect Lord *Jagannatha,* an incarnation of *Vishnu,* farmers of the village observe *Ekadasi* as a ritual prohibition of ploughing land on this day. They do not plough their land on *Sayan Ekadasi* (the eleventh lunar day of the light fortnight in the month of *Asadha* when Vishnu is said to go to sleep for four months), *parsva Eka dasi* (the eleventh lunar day of the light fortnight of *Bhadra* when, Vishnu is believed to turn upon his side), *Utthara Ekadasi* (the eleventh lunar day of the light fortnight in the month of *Kartik,* when Vishnu is believed to awake up from His sleep).

Lord *Jagannatha* is believed to be the family deity, who protects the villagers from each and every suffering whether it is agricultural or anything else. So, they prohibit ploughing in these days as a respect to Lord *Jagannatha.* In order to make Lord *Jagannatha* pleased, the farmers use to offer the newly harvested fruits and paddy to Him before giving it to anybody else. They offer the rice pudding made from the newly harvested paddy. They offer them along with certain flowers such as: oleander, night jasmine, lotus, white tulip, champak, etc.

Lord *Siva* has also occupied an *important* place in the field of agro-based religion. During the time of *Halasutra* festival, the farmers plough for two and half furrows without any break, as they believe that Lord *Siva* who had started *Halasutra* near the *Subarnarekha* River had made two and half furrows. Most of the farmers in the study village revealed that Lord *Siva* is the incarnation of Lord *Balarama,* who is considered as the inventor of plough and methods of agriculture. For this reason, most of the farmers pay their obeisance in village *Siva* temple, during the time of *Gahma Purnami* (the full-moon day of *Shravan,* July-August). The farmers always try to please Lord *Siva* by offering different flowers like stramoni flower, night jasmine, oleander, china rose, mist rose, dhak flower, balsam, white lotus, etc. and fruits like banana, apple, etc. Sometimes the individual farmer's household organises *Panchanana Mela* to please the Lord *Siva*. The farmer's belief that if they do not perform these rituals, Lord Siva will get angry with them. As a result, their plough may break down while ploughing, which will create problem for them.

When the irrigation system of the study village was not so developed, the villagers were performing various rites and rituals through ages for receiving rain at the time of drought. It is viewed that the time of difficulties, when there was drought, the villagers used to collectively arrange for the worship of the village deities to bring rainfall. The *Pandit* worshiped the deities. The belief is that if the *Pandit* performs the practice in a proper way, then rainfall will inevitably occur while, the worship is held. The *Pandit* did not leave his *Asana* (seat) until it rains. As we have asked some farmers of the study village, whether they have performed any rites to bring about rain, they have reported to have done it before, but they could not mention any such particular rite. The present study did not find any performances of *Indra Puja* being held by the villagers. When the villagers were asked whether this *Puja* is still going on or not, they immediately said that it used to be held earlier, when there was no development in irrigation facilities and people were fully dependent on rain fall.

Although the practice of *Indra Puja* is completely vanished from the study village, their practice of starting all-agricultural operations from *Isan* (North-East) corner reveals that this is nothing but a respect to Lord *Indra*. As the farmers believe that Lord *Indra* is the protector of Northeast corner, if they do not start the agricultural operation from this *Isan* corner, then there could be flood or drought, which cannot be protected by any developmental mechanism.

The *Grama Devati* (*Khara Khai*) plays an important role in each and every sphere of life of the villagers. In the study village, Goddess *Khara Khai* is represented by a piece of stone, which is restored under an old Banyan tree. It is smeared with a thick layer of vermilion and surrounded by a large collection of earthen houses and elephants. There is a belief among the villagers that the *Khara Khai Takurani* helps people to take crisis at home, in cultivation or in the outbreak of epidemics and drought. For this reason, *Khara Khai Takurani* is presented with flowers and fruits before human beings use them. The farmers believe that this presentation to God or Goddess would bring in more flowers and fruit. Usually, a ritual is organised by the villagers during *Pana Sankranti* in honcur of the *Grama Devati.* On this occasion, the villagers sacrifice cocks to propitiate the *Grama Devati.* It is viewed that Goddess *Grama Devati* visits the cornfield during the harvesting period. At the time of drought, *Grama Devati* is worshipped in expectation of rain.

During different agro-based festivals these above mentioned Gods and Goddesses used to be worshiped by the villagers. While the Goddess Lakshmi is being worshiped in all the festivals, the Lord Siva during *Halasutra,* Lord Indra in *Akhi Trutiya,* Balabhadra in *Gamha Purnami,* etc.

But, in course of time, a lot of change has been taken place in peoples' belief system. The modernization in agriculture has brought an indirect effect on it. Due to developed irrigation system, they are not praying Lord *Indra* to get rain during the drought period. This modernization of agriculture has raised their confidence. No more animal sacrifices near village deities are done today.

Conclusion

From the foregoing analyses, it is observed that there is a rich tradition binding with the agro-based religion in Orissa. It proves that the culture of Orissa is no doubt the culture of agriculture. Though the Goddess Lakshmi has occupied the important place in each and every agro-based festival, other Gods and Goddesses have also possessed their respective places.

No doubt, the advent of modernization of agriculture has brought a change in traditional religion, rites and rituals. But these changes are not so rapid. These rites and rituals offer resistance in some cases to such intended changes. The advent of new technology in agriculture has affected to some extent in the belief system of people. The development of irrigation system has raised the people's confidence on themselves. As a result, people have lost the importance to worship the Lord *Indra* at the time of drought. But the ritual of *Indra Puja* is still performed by the farmers today in northeast direction, while starting the agricultural rituals in the field, because *Indra* is considered as the protector of this direction.

References

Bhattacharya, S.K. 1976. *Farmers Rituals and Modernization*, Calcutta: Minerva Associates Publications Pvt.Ltd.

Chakrabarty, F. 1987. "Agricultural Rituals of the Santals of Ajodhya Hills: Techno-ecological Perspective". *Man in India*, 67(2), 99-123.

Das, K. 1991. *Folklore of Orissa*, Bhubaneswar: Orissa Sahitya Academy.

Das, K and L. K. Mahapatra. 1993. *Folklore of Orissa*, New Delhi: National Book Trust of India.

Deva,I. 1989. *Folk Culture and Peasant Society in India*, Jaipur: Rawat Publication.

Dube,S.C.1993. *Understanding Change: Anthropological and Sociological Perspectives*, New Delhi: Vikas Publishing House Pvt Ltd.

Foster, G.M. 1973. *Traditional Society and Technological Change*, New Delhi: Allied Publishers Private Limited.

Frazer, J. 1976. The *Golden Bough*, Part-V, Vol.-II, London: The Macmillan Press Ltd.

Hobsbawm, E and T. Ranger. 2002. *The Invention of Tradition*, Cambridge: Cambridge University Press.

Kani, Takhe. 1993. *Agricultural Festival of Arunachal Pradesh*, Itanagar: IPACL.

Mishra, P.K. (ed). 1997. *Comprehensive History and Culture of Orissa*, Vol.2, Part 2, New Delhi: Kaveri Books.

Mishra, N.2003. Changing Agricultural Practices and Their impact on Rural Institutions in Orissa, Unpublished M.Phil Dissertation, University of Hyderabad, Department of Anthropology.

Mishra, N.2005, Technological Changes in Orissan Agriculture, *Vision*, Vol. XXV No-1-2.

Mishra, N.2005, Farmers Festivals: A Case from Eastern Orissa, *Journal* of *Indian Anthropological Society*, Vol-40, No-2.

Mishra, N. (fourth coming, 2006), New Agro-Technology and Traditional Family and Rural Power Structure: A Case from Coastal Orissa, *Man and Life.*

Misra, K. K & Nihar Mishra. 2005, Agricultural Modernization and Agrarian Relations: A Study of Changing Jajmani Relations in Rural Orissa, *Journal of Humankind*, Vol-1, No-1.

Mahapatra, K. ed. 1978. *Folk Culture and the Great Tradition*, Vol. V, Cuttack: Council of Growth and Cultural Relations and Institute of Orientational And Orissa Studies.

Patnaik, D. 1982. *Festivals of Orissa*, Bhubaneswar: Orissa Sahitya Academy.

Singh, Y. 1986. *Modernization of Indian Tradition*, Jaipur: Rawat Publications.

BOOKS AND JOURNALS IN ORIYA

Das, K. 1954. *Palligeeti Sanchayana*, Part-I, Shantiniketan: Visvabarati University Publication.

Das, K. 1973. *Lokabani Sanchayan*, Part-I, Cuttack.

Satpathy N. 1996. "Lakshmi Myth and Balaramanka Lakshmi Purana", *Jhankara*, 53(3).

Mishra, P. K. 1981. *Purba Bharatara Hindu Lokamyth Oddissa*, Cuttack: Orissa Book Store.

Mohanty, B and Mohanty, S. 1991. *Oddissara Sanskrutika Parampara*, Cuttack: Utkal Pathaka Sansada, Vol-II.

Mohanty, B and Mohanty, S. 1998. *Oddissara Parbaparbani Osabrata Janijatra*, Cuttack: Utkal Pathak Sansad.

Mohanty, B and Mohanty, S. 1989. *Oddissara Sanskrutika Parampara,* Cuttack: Utkal Pathaka Sansada, Vol-I.

Mohapatra, C. 1939. *Utkalara Gaunligita,* Cuttack: Cuttack Publishing Press.

Mohapatra, C. 1960. *Oriya Gramyageeti,* Bhubaneswar: Orissa Sahitya Academy.

Sahoo, B 1980. *Prachina Bharatara Krusi,* Bhubaneswar: The Orissa State Bureau of Text book Preparation and Production.

Satpathy N. 1996a. "Lakshmi Myth and Balaramanka Lakshmi Purana", *Jhankara,* 53(3).

Satpathy, N. 1996b. "Durgati Nasini Debi Durga", *Utkal Prasanga,* Septmber-October.

Map of Orissa

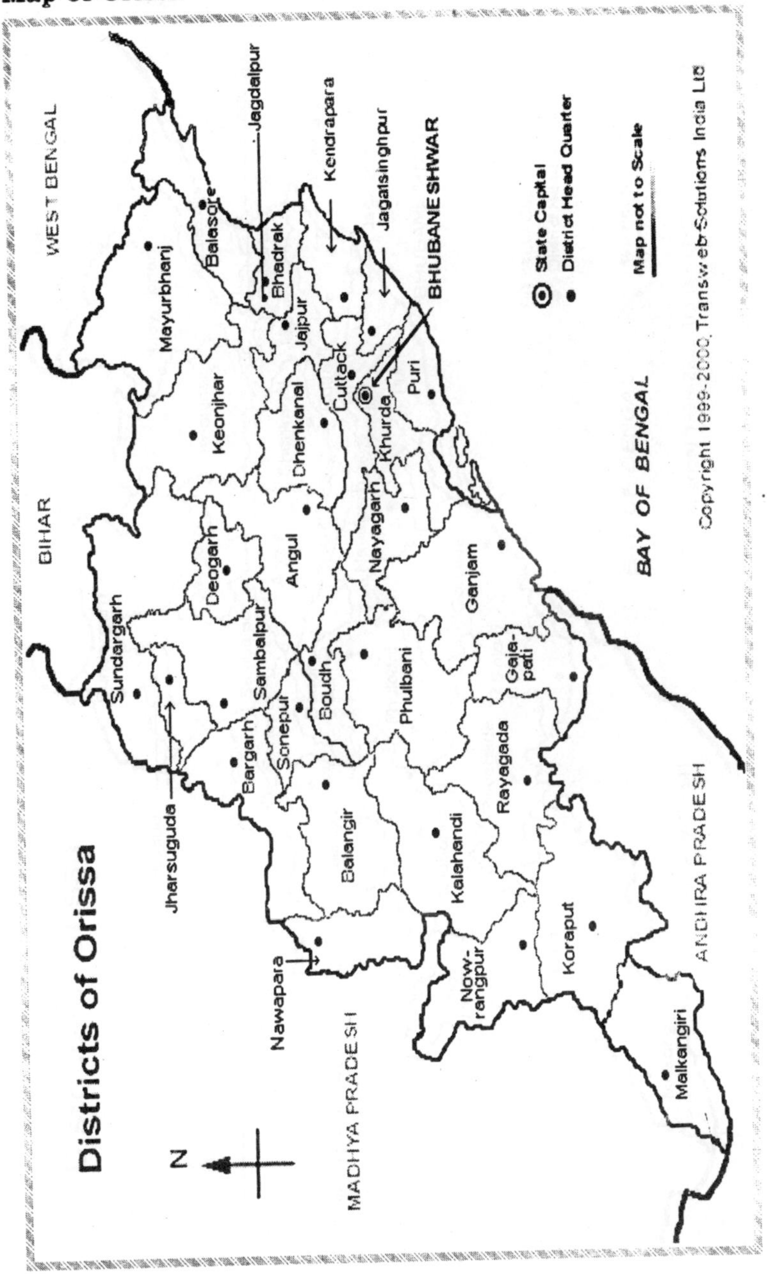

7

Rural Health and Disease: A Case Study of Gurdaspur District of Punjab

N.R. Kahlon

Concept of "positive health" is popularized by the World Health Organization (WHO). According to WHO, health is a state of complete, physical, mental and social well-being and not merely the absence of disease or infirmity (Mead, 1953). But, health has a social value attached to it and is often judged in terms of a host of social factors. These factors vary from society to society but the fact remains that they are held in high esteem in almost every society.

Disease usually refers to a deviation in the normal functioning of the body, which produces discomfort or adversely affects the individuals' future health status (Mechanic: 1962). Every society has certain norms, values and ideals in regard to health and disease, a deviation from which is treated as an aberration or a disease. Disease can also be explained in terms of an invasion of an organism by germs, bacteria or other pathogenic agents, which disturb the homeostatic balance and results in some form of malfunctioning (Najman, 1980). The perception of disease and its cure, assumes different dimensions in different societies. Cultural patterns and typical ways of life, give substance to the manner, in which, illness is perceived, expressed and reached to.

In each human society health and disease co-exist. Society changes and adapts itself to the varying needs of its individuals. In a man's life, there are some disruptive forces that tend to paralyse him. These forces are external and internal. The external disruptive forces could be environmental or socio-cultural. The internal disruptive forces could be personal-social (such as employment), personal-psychological (such as mental aberrations) and personal-physiological (such as diseases) (Pokarana, 1994).

Normalcy of health is man's precious possession. It influences all his activities and shapes his daily routine. In ancient Greece as well as in India, health was conceived as a cherished goal. But the fact of disease, injury and health is also a universal fact of human life in every human society. No society or individual is free from these happenings, although its nature, frequency and degree vary from man to man and from society to society. Every society has developed a system to cope with diseases according to its beliefs and values. In other words, every human society has created a "pharmacopoeia and a therapeutic system, be it magico-religious, secular or scientific" (Castiglioni, 1947).

India still lives in villages and agriculture is the main source of livelihood of villagers. Even after many technological, economic and social developments the rural sector is still underdeveloped. Every side of human life in rural community is governed by traditional norms and practical values. The injunction settled by the community governs human life. The main emphasis lies on health and disease. Notion of disease depends rather on decision of society than on the objective facts (Hyman, 1968). In the rural areas, disease has been attributed to extra biological reason such as man's disobedience of natural and religious laws. It has been attributed to the sins and crimes committed by a person in the present life or in previous lives. Some diseases have been attributed to the wrath of gods and goddesses. This notion about the disease resulted in the acceptance of many irrational practices. To get rid of disease and to have good health, villagers worship the gods or goddesses or sought the services of the sainas or magicians or went to saints, to find out how best they could make deities or evil spirits happy. Appeasements of deities are the common practices. Thus, in India, the approach towards disease and its curative aspects have been inextricable linked to religious and cultural norms and practices (Hasan, 1967, Pokrana, 1994).

Ideal health conditions, however, always remain elusive because of the rapid changes in the society, which foster conditions that are conductive to the health of a person. Good health is a relative concept having no fixed standards for what is considered normal in one person may be abnormal in another. For example, a newborn baby weighs 2.8 kg on an average in India as compared to 3.5 kg in developed countries and yet they are considered healthy. It is generally observed, that even normal healthy people show signs of heart murmurs, enlarged tonsils and other diseases. Yet, they are not considered to be in bad health. Health is hence a relative concept and its standard varies from person to person and from society to society (Basu, 1977).

In rural community, people hardly talk about health. They reserve their comments until they are forced to say something, because for them disease and health are coincidental. They still believe that disease; birth, marriage and death etc, the so-called crises of the life are recognized to be settled by God.

The present study has covered the concept of sociology of health and focused attention on the understanding of the social realities of health systems in the rural setting. It has been assumed, that perception of the villagers regarding health and illness is traditional and is governed by extra medication (traditional faith healing) norms. These irrational beliefs and practices regarding, health and disease tend to make the task of health care quite difficult.

Methodology

The study was carried out in the villages of Kalanaur Community Development Block of Gurdaspur district of Punjab. After having necessary discussions with the district level officers, the universe of the study was selected. Block wise list of villages along with households was obtained from the Block Development Officer. Purposive random sampling technique was used. Data was collected from a sample of hundred community members through structured and unstructured interviews and case studies. These respondents were suffering from surgical pain, skin diseases, fractures, problem of eyes, and arthritis etc.

Major Findings

Table -1. Distribution of Respondents According to their Perception of Etiology of Disease

Etiology of disease	*Number of Respondents*	*Percentage*
Due to Impurity in eatables	31	31.00
Due to un-availability of expertise in rural health Centres	16	16.00
Due to watch of God/Goddesses or Faultrs (Dosha)	53	53.00
Total	100	100

Instead of scientific basis regarding the etiology of disease, villagers are still influenced by social psychological and cultural factors. They believed disease to be a sign of wrath of God and goddesses or supernatural beings and because of disobedience of religions and ritual norms. Table-1 indicates that more than fifty percent of respondents believed that the disease was due to the wrath of God and Goddess is associated with the sins committed in the previous or in the present life. Sinful acts not only bring miseries or sufferings upon oneself but also on the members of the family. As many as, thirty one percent reported that it was due to impurities in eatables, while sixteen percent believed that disease was aggravated due to unavailability of specialists in the rural health centres. Following case study can prove the above given findings.

> A.S., is suffering from asthmatic and breathing problem. He was totally in bed for last ten days, but his disease becomes chronic just because of his past deeds.

> B.S., age fifty years, living in village Dostpur, nearly 20 Kms. away from Kalanaur reported that generally these diseases are due to impurities in eatable and drinks. So I don't like to eat anything from the market.

Concept of Health

What do the community members understand by health and whom do they believe to be healthy? All the respondents of the present study reported, that they consider those persons to be healthy, who can eat and digest the healthy food. Those who have good muscles and are able to do all the hard physical labours demand of them. They maintain, that it is necessary to be carefree and tension free, to have good health. Thus, health was considered as functional concept.

Generally villagers are less worried about health. Due to pollution free environment and easy availabilities of natural facilities, villagers believe that health will become good automatically. The matters they usually discuss are; legal battles or court cases, village or State politics and tensions etc., and rarely talk about health issues. In the initial stage of disease or sickness they never consult the doctor. If, they ever have to consult the physician they prefer to consult the ojhas or the traditional healers who give folk medicines to the patients. In the light of above observations, the respondents were asked to give their view about health.

Table 2. - Distribution of Respondents According to their Health Beliefs
N=100*

Sl. No	*Beliefs*	*Number of Respondents*	*Percentage*
1.	Village life is better than urban life	55	55.00
2.	Intake of nutritious diet and regular exercise	65	35.00
3.	Good health is result of God's grace	80	80.00

*Multiple resources.

Table 2: reveals that majority of the respondents (80 percent) believed that good health is result of God's grace. Two third reported that the intakes of nutritious diet and a regular exercise is a pre-condition of good health. More than fifty percent have considered village life as better than the urban life. This is just because of the clean environment of villages, where one gets open spaces, fresh air, adequate sunlight and use of clean and fresh water and verdure which foster good health. This finding indicates that the rural people are also aware of the harmful effects of pollution, a common feature of city life.

Belief in Spiritual Medication or Traditional Faith Healing

Punjabi idea about health and sickness correspond in several respects to those of 'Indians' as pointed out by Adams (1957) and to those of 'Ladino' as expressed by Gonzales (1966). Punjabis curative measures, as our study indicates, involved not in the use on magical medicines to correct bodily conditions, but also spiritual or religious practices to do away with the basic cause of illness. Since, treatment depended both on herbs and magical devices; many a time, elaborate rites were performed to effectively deal with 'internal' and 'external' conditions (Kakar, 1977). Villagers worship gods and goddesses, recite religious verses and try to make evil spirit happy to get rid of their disease. The Punjabis, also considered illness as a misfortunate, which may or may not be due to the fault of a family member; in fact, it may be due to the wrath of gods/goddesses against the whole family. Malevolent spirits of dead ancestors or jealous living relatives may also cause illness. Thus, in order to avoid evil doings, they wore charms, made offerings to the saints and ancestors and even avoid visiting such sports in the villages where spirits believed to reside. In the light of all the factors, the respondents were asked about their perception of traditional faith healing practices.

Table 3: - Distribution of Respondent as per their Perception of Traditional Faith Healing Measures

SI.No	*Traditional faith healing measures*	*Positive (%)*	*Negative (%)*	*Total (%)*
1	To visit religious places and take bath in holy water tank (Sarovar)	64 (64.0)	36 (36.0)	100 (100.0)
2	To perform religious functions	62 (62.0)	38 (38.0)	100 (100.0)
3	To get the blessings of Saints or sainas	60 (60.0)	40 (40.0)	100 (100.0)
4	To follow the instructions and precautions of sianas or saints	69 (69.0)	31 (31.0)	100 (100.0)

Most of the respondents stressed on traditional faith healing practices to remedies disease and for the physical welfare of the patients (see Table-3). Nearly two thirds reported that the patient must visit religious places like Gurudwara or

Mandir. Mazars of Muslims pir (Saint) and if possible they should take bath in holy water tank (Sarover). As many as sixty two percent reported that the patient should try to make gods/goddesses happy by organizing religious meetings etc., to have their blessings. Despite the best efforts, one may not always succeed in getting total cure from the disease. In order to deal with these situations, saints or sianas are still considered indispensable by rural community. Sixty percent believed that the patient should try to get the blessings of the saints. Sixty nine percent stated that after getting the blessings of the saints or sianas, the patient should also follow the instructions and prescriptions of these religious persons, because it is the sianas who know what curative measures are required to remove the basic cause of the disease. These measures ranged from a mere utterance of a magical formula, to the performance of elaborate rites. So, as modem medication techniques are there in the primary health centre and in a nearby town/city, even then rural community is very religious and traditional. To fight with their disease, they are fully influenced by these traditional faith healings norms.

The following selected case studies highlight certain important aspects of etiology, diagnosis and therapy.

> M.S., was Majbi Sikh by caste, living in village Barilla district Gurdaspur, illiterate and making his both ends meet by doing agriculture labour. Total members in his family were seven, including his wife and five children. While viewing etiology, diagnosis and therapy, he told one incident that once his son was suffering from measles. When he went to consult an allopathic doctor in a nearby village he diagnosed that his son was suffering from measles. He gave some medicines to our son, but my wife and other elderly ladies of the villages said that administration of drugs may be harmful and

asked me to observe certain taboos like everyone in the family; eat pure vegetarian food and avoid the consumption of onion and garlic for good medication and worship goddess Shitla. We strictly followed these rules. After some days my son was totally cured from such dreaded disease. So M.S. preferred traditional faith healing practices in comparison to modem scientific medication.

S.K was Jat Sikh by caste, illiterate, her husband was farmer. She had narrated the story of her son. He had fever and frequent episodes of diaerhoea and dysentery. He was diagnosed with marasmus, locally known as 'Soka'. Nearly two months of treatment and feeding him on breast milk did not bring about any significant improvement in his condition. Yet, in the face of all failures she did not lose heart and approached other physicians. At the same time, she was advised to take him for a ritual bath at Gurdwara Achal Saheb's sarovar which was located near Batala, on dark moon night (at least five dark moon nights). The medicines given by the doctor were also given due importance. Still she believes that her son's recovery from maramus was more due to religious practices instead of doctor's treatment.

R.S. Jat Sikh by caste is a literate and also a landlord. He narrated his own story of snakebite. He stated that, one night when he was coming back from his fields something pricked his feet. Due to the dark night he himself couldn't see the snake. But within few minutes he started feeling drowsiness. His son immediately took him to a nearby snakebites curer, very religious and blessed

> with the skill for curing snakebites. He recited some 'mantras' and gave him holy water to drink. After drinking the holy water he felt total relief from the severe pain. For curing the wound, he gave them a recipe of 'Gur da-Karah' prepared with mustard oil. His wound was completely healed within seven days. He believed that, had his son ever taken him to the doctor, he would have died of medication. Snakebite could be cured only with the blessings of snakebite curers as well as with their home remedies.

Conclusion

The study clearly indicates that the modern health care delivery system has not made much headway in the rural areas and that the traditional faith healing practices continue to play a predominant role in the treatment of diseases. In rural areas, health and disease are more influenced by traditional norms and values. Diseases are still believed to be caused by sins or wraths of gods/goddesses and are considered as an outcome of physical conditions as well as supernatural deistic beliefs. Both physical and supernatural therapies are tried and whatever improvement they observed, it is attributed predominantly to traditional faith healing practices or supernatural therapy. They are not willing to abandon their faith in these practices, at any cost. The study highlights the need to find ways and means for making use of traditional beliefs and practices, as a launching pad to initiate culturally acceptable methods of treatment of diseases and promotion of health. The findings of the paper call for the expansion of education and development of scientific attitudes and beliefs to counter the magico-religious interpretation of health and disease. The role of traditional faith healers as primary health care providers, also needs to be studied, who with some training can provide useful services to the rural community.

References

Adam: Cultural Surveys of Panama, Nicarggua, Guatemala, EI Salvador, Honduras, Pan-American union scientific Publication, Washington, No. 33, 1957.

Basu, S.C: Handbook of preventive and social Medicine, current book International, Calcutta, 1977.

Castigilion: A History of Medicine, Routedge and Kegan Paul Ltd., London, 1947.

Gonzales, S.N. : Health behaviour in Cross Cultural perspective: A Guatemalan example, Human Organization, V 01.25, summer 1966.

Hagan, K.A.: The cultural frontier and Health in a village India, Manktalas, Bombay, 1967.

Hyman, Martin D.: 'Medicine' In 'The uses of Sociology', Lazarsfeld, Paul, F. et al., (eds.), Weidenfeld and Nicolson, London 1968.

Mehanic, D.: Medical Sociology, The free press, New York, 1962.

Najman, J. M: "Theories of Disease causation and the concept General Susceptibility: A Review", Social Science and Medicine, 14 A, 231, 1980.

Pokarna, K.L: Social Beliefs, Cultural Practices in Health and Disease; Rawat Publications, New Delhi: 1994.

8

Development of *Sugalis*: An Empirical Study in Andhra Pradesh

Eswarappa Kasi
and
R. Siva Prasad

Introduction

The paper examines the impact of developmental efforts made by the government and non-government agencies to bring desired socio-economic changes in the lives of marginalized tribal communities in Andhra Pradesh. Till the emergence of new economic policy of Government of India and consequently liberalization of economic policies it is felt that the responsibilities of a welfare state must be not only as regulator but also provider of infrastructure so that the poor get freed themselves from the cycle of poverty (Gupta, 2004:1-5). Third World countries have tried to attempt and to extricate themselves from the immense burden of international debts and from internal economic morass, by way of adapting new strategies, of development aping the developed countries seeking loans from the World Bank, International Monetary Fund (IMF) and other agencies. As a part of structural adjustment they had to adapt new economic policies in which the state had to shake off its primary responsibilities of providing welfare measures to the poor (Eswarappa and Siva Prasad, 2005). This new development opened floodgates for the entry of local, international non-government organizations (NGOs) as benefactors to the poor alongside the state. Meanwhile the meaning of the concept of development also changed. It is in this context the present paper attempts to understand the impact of developmental efforts made by an NGO called Social Education Development Society (SEDS) and various government departments on Sugalis, a nomadic Tribe, in a village called *Adadakulapalle* in Anantapur District of Andhra Pradesh.

The present paper has been organised into four sections. The first section briefly explains the general background of development; the second section deals with the profile of the village; the third section explores the macro and micro analysis of development intervention of public and private agencies and final section draws the conclusions.

I

General Background of Development

There are two dominant theoretical formulations that have greatly influenced the concept of socio-economic development through planned change. These are the approaches of Karl Marx and Max Weber (ibid).

Marx proceeds from economic change to cultural change and strongly feels that the social philosophy conforms to the economic set up. Whenever a society changes its methods of production, it also changes its whole social outlook. Economic structure supplies a basis upon which the legal and political superstructure is raised and corresponding to it are certain social forms, which depend upon the public conscience (Gide and Rist, 1959). Cole (cited in Jain, 2004), in the context of post industrial revolution in Britain found that economic change itself brought considerable change in cultural patterns, beliefs, and other aspects of life. A development in economic sphere causes various changes in value system and norms of life.

On the other hand Max Weber establishes a reverse causality. Veblen, Spengler, Williamson and Buttricks and Parson (cited in Jain, 2004) treat non-economic factors of paramount importance in understanding the process of economic change. Theodore Schultz (1968) stresses the supreme importance of investment in human capital as a motivating force for economic change. Changes in the structure of demand for products are associated with factors like size and composition of population, level and pattern of distribution of income, aspirations, and institutional and organisational arrangements as felt by Clark (1951).

Some social scientists emphasize on the need of bringing economic change first which will eventually bring changes in social, cultural, and in the political spheres. However, other groups like UNRISD (1972) and UNDP (1990) feel that economic change should take place along with other factors of life. While this debate still remains alive there are quite a few Marxists and Liberals who view that development is related to the relative participation of the deprived groups, who are the marginalized and powerless groups in a society, in the socio-political process. Thus, development is expected to free these sections from all forms of dependency - social, cultural and political – in order that their full potentials as human beings are fully brought out for their blossoming. Thus mobilization of the poor and their participation in socio-political process becomes an important feature of development (quoted in Eswarappa, 2001).

From the above discussion it may be said that development is both a cause and a consequence of change. Change implies physical, technological, economic, social, cultural, attitudinal, and organisational change. A change may be either positive (development), or negative (retrogression). Jan Drewnowski (1996: 2-3) as rightly pointed out that "Development is a process of qualitative change and quantitative growth of the social and economic reality which we call either society or economy. Because of the close interrelation of economic and social elements no purely social or purely economic development is possible. Consequently, it is better not to speak of social development separately. It is a single process which is best called simply development".

In this perspective the term development may be defined as a process of developing and utilizing natural and human resources, technologies, infrastructural facilities, institutions and organizations, and government policies and programmes. In a nutshell, the process of development must represent the entire gamut of changes by which a social system moves away from a state of life perceived as unsatisfactory towards a materially and spiritually better conditions of life. While anthropologists in their understanding or evaluation of various development programmes either as advisors or as action anthropologists have more or less agreed to the above explanation of development. So far as Anthropological contribution to understand the developmental process is to analyse micro and macro processes which play significant role in the overall development of a community as conceptualised above. With this background, the paper analyses development processes in *Adadakulapalle* village, inhabited by *Sugali* tribal group in Anantapur district of Andhra Pradesh.

II

Profile of the Village

The Village under study is situated in the Penukonda Mandal in Anantapur district and is about 10 kilometres away from Penukonda, the Mandal headquarters. *Adadakulapalle* is a multi-caste village consisting of 439 households of which 155 (35.6 %) households belong to *Sugali* a Scheduled Tribe, who form a separate constituent of the village. The habitations of *Sugali* are called as *Thandas*, which locate *Thandas* a little away from the main multi-caste villages are identified as the *Thandas* of the villages. Anthropologists are familiar with these multi-caste villages by the writings of M.N. Srinivas, Mckim Marriot and others. However, there are multi-castes villages, which incorporate the tribal populations also (S.C. Dube) and *Adadakulapalle* is one of such villages.

The *Thanda* under study is included in *Adadakulapalle* village Panchayat of Penukonda Mandal. The *Sugalis* are divided into two *thandas* and known as *Jalapalle*

Table 1
Distribution of Households by Caste/ Community*

SI.No.	Type of House	Type of Castes (No. of Households)				
		Scheduled Tribe	Scheduled Caste	Backward Castes	Other Castes	Total
1.	Stone Houses	98	46	113	75	332
2.	Mud Houses	28	10	21	----	59
3.	Huts	29	04	15	-----	48
Total		155	60	149	75	439

**Source : SEDS Office, Mekalapalle.*

Thanda or *Patha Thanda* (old *Thanda*) and *Kothapalle Thanda* (new *Thanda*) and two members represent one each from these wards in the *Adadakulapalle* Panchayat. *Adadakulapalle* Panchayat is reserved for *Sugalis*. *Kothapalle Thanda* is a new colony of houses built during the earlier Congress rule during 1989-94 in the same old *Thanda* area.

Infrastructure facilities

There is only one seven-seater auto that runs on the 10km metal road that connects *Adadakulapalle* and Penukonda. It is only means of transport communication for the people of the village. There is no public telephone facility in the entire village. However, one Sugali who is presently Sarpanch of the village Panchayat has a private telephone connection in his house. The village has post office facility located in the middle of the village. It also has a ration shop under the public distribution system (PDS) to supply the necessary commodities to the residents at concessional rates. There is primary school with four teachers in the main village. For upper primary education they have to go to Penukonda, the Mandal headquarter. One of the reasons for the drop out of children after the primary schooling is the difficulty of travelling the distance of 10 kms every day. It is observed from the field that very often girls are badly affected due to non-availability of upper primary school in the village. PHC is located in Penukonda, and therefore they have to go to mandal headquarters to avail the medical facilities. ANM also comes from Mandal headquarters and PHC personnel rarely visit the village for health check up. Protected drinking water is available to all the people of *Adadakulapalle* under Rural Water Supply scheme. Each lane has taps and there are hand pumps within the village, which provide water for through out the year.

In *Adadakulapalle* the majority of *Sugalis* are small and marginal farmers. The type of land available in the village is dry land and only one *Sugali* farmer has a tube (bore) well in his land as against 90 borewells owned other castes in the village and the rest of the Sugalis depend upon monsoon. The major crops cultivated are groundnut, ragi and paddy.

Ragi and Paddy are the staple crops and they constitute the staple diet of the farmers and agricultural labourers.

Table 2
Available Livelihoods in the Village*

SI.No.	*Type of Livelihoods*	*Total Households in the villages*	*Scheduled Tribe (Sugalis)*	*% of ST's in the total*
1.	Wage Labourers/ Land less People	237	124	52.32
2.	Agriculture	225	80	35.55
3.	Petty Business	25	10	40.00
4.	Others (Dependents)	25	10	40.00

* *Source:* SEDS Office, *Mekalapalle*

The above table indicates the available livelihoods of the *Sugalis* as well as other communities in the village. It may be observed that the households depending on wage labour are more among *Sugalis* because they consist of more landless people and wage labourers. It also observed from the table that the total numbers of households in the village and among *Sugalis* are more than the rest of the inhabitants. It is due to the involvement of *Sugalis* in more than one activity to earn their livelihood. Though majority of the wage labourers own small plots of land, the land is unsuitable for cultivation.

The livelihoods activities of *Sugalis* are cultivation, followed by daily wage works, and petty business (running own and rented autos and *kirana* (provisions) shop and hotel (tea and tiffin stall). Majority of them depend on agricultural labour, construction or repair works in and outside the village. Since the type of land available is dry land, they have to depend upon monsoon for their cultivation. Frequent failure of the monsoons made the people to migrate to other areas. People from the *Thanda* explained that seasonal migration is high in the area as majority of them are marginal farmers and landless agricultural labourers. Almost half of the households in the *Thanda* migrate to towns in the off-season, according to the Gram Panchayat Sarpanch. One informant stated that they are helpless and there is no other way except to migrate to other areas. Some of them have settled in the towns leaving their old in the *Thanda* and support by their remittances. Younger people migrate to towns in the off seasons and come back to *Thanda* during rainy season, to cultivate land or work as farm labourers. Agriculture is their main source of livelihood followed by agricultural labour and seasonal migration. Cattle, goat, and sheep are the major livestock in the area.

Since five years they did not have one good crop due to drought in the area and their lives and livelihoods have been threatened. Even when they get any yields, they are low and are further affected by the vagaries of the market. It further aggravates their poverty situation in the village.

People who suffer most from crop failures have no option but to migrate leaving women, children and the old in the village. Sometimes they do not get even a square meal in a day. Women face severe stress due to the migration of male members of the family. They have to take care of children as well as older people, in addition to cattle. As stated by some of the elderly *Sugalis*, some of the youth, who are educated, remain idle at home without any work. They hesitate to go for wage works available in the area and have become a burden to their parents.

Ration: The issue of ration cards indicate the economic status of a household as those who are under below poverty line (BPL), are eligible to get the ration under PDS Scheme. It is observed from the PDS records that 110 households from Sugalis have the ration cards. Thus, while 71 percent of the *Sugali* live below the poverty only 27.8 percent of others are in this category (See Table1). Though majority of the people depend on Public Distribution System (PDS), the dealer has not been supplying the ration regularly to the people in the village.

Poverty in the Village: As indicated above, among the landless labourers in the village, (Table No.2), 52.3 percent of them are *Sugali* and among the *Sugali,* they constitutes 55 percent. This category forms only 46 percent in the entire village, which speaks very clearly and more than half the *Sugali* are landless labourers. About 36.8 percent *Sugali* live in either in hut or mud houses (Eswarappa and Siva Prasad, 2005). Even in the possession of livestock they remain at the margin. The resultant of poverty in the village is migration. Since the male members migrate to the towns, women are the major sufferers, as they have to take care of their families. The conditions of women are very poor in the village. *Sugalis* though maintains good physique they have no cloth to wear due to their poverty. Due to poor sanitation they frequently affected of diseases and more people are prone to ill health.

III

Analysis of the Schemes at Macro level

Given the precarious conditions, the government and NGO made several efforts to ameliorate the conditions of the *Sugalis* in the village. The approach of the government though holistic in nature, the conceptualization and implementation of the schemes as popularly known as 'top down' approach. The NGO's approach is though from 'bottom to top'; the focus is mainly on economic improvement. These two approaches appear to be following the broad theoretical formulations of development discussed earlier in the paper. While NGO's emphasize on the economic improvement, it is implied that economic change will lead to other social and cultural changes favoring for faster development of Sugalis. The government programmes are aimed to bring over all socio-economic development of the people.

The following development programmes have been implemented in the village for the last few years: Deepam, Food for Work Programme, Housing programme, Watershed programme, Public Distribution System (PDS), and Development of Women and Children in Rural Areas (DWCRA) etc. Some of these programmes have been discussed below.

Deepam Scheme: The government of Andhra Pradesh has launched Deepam Scheme in the 1999 with the objective of providing 10 lakh domestic LPG connections to women members of the BPL families in the rural areas. The scheme was intended to provide a number of benefits to these families, which include reduced dependence on forest firewood, saved time from cooking that can be used for productive purposes and improved health status of women due to reduced physical stress and strain. Beneficiaries under the scheme are members from DWACA groups that are in existence for one ear or above, since June 1999.

Housing Programme: The Government of India is implementing Indira Awaas Yojana (IAY) since the year 1985-86 with an objective of providing dwelling units free of cost to the members of Scheduled Castes, Scheduled Tribes and free bonded labourers living below the poverty line in rural areas. From the year 1993-94, its scope has been extended to cover non-scheduled caste and non-scheduled tribe rural poor, subject to the condition that the benefits to non SCs/STs shall not be more than 40 percent of IAY allocation. Benefits of the scheme have also been extended to the families of ex-servicemen of the armed and paramilitary forces killed in action. Three percent of the houses are reserved for the below poverty line disabled persons living in rural areas.

Public Distribution System (PDS): The Government of Andhra Pradesh introduced the subsidized rise scheme in early 80s to improve the consumption levels of the weaker sections of the society. Since August 1996, a poor household is entitled to 5 kgs of rice per person per month subject to a ceiling of 20 kgs at Rs.3.50 per kg. Besides rice, they are entitled to sugar and kerosene on subsidized rates.

Food for Work Programme: Food for Work Programme was initiated in September 2001 with the objective of removing hunger in villages and rural areas by providing them with work against wages in kind and cash. Under this programme construction of metal link roads were be taken up and each and every one who is in need of work were be provided with employment. The workers were be provided with 5 kg rice and Rs 30 cash having a total cash value of Rs 56. Thus, the scheme successfully addresses the issue of lack of food at the same time developing infrastructure in villages.

Development of Women and Children in Rural Areas (DWCRA): The issues of economic upliftment of women and their empowerment were also included in the Integrated Rural Development Programme and Jawahar Rojgar Yojana, aiming to provide durable assets and employment generation during the lean periods. In practice however, participation of women in all these schemes remained very low. Keeping this in view the government conceived of Development of Women and Children in Rural Areas (DWCRA). The long term objective of DWCRA programme is to improve the survival of young children and women and the quality of their lives, and to achieve a significant growth in the income of poor women through appropriate interventions and to organize women in groups to create a demand pull on the existing delivery system along with creation of awareness to strengthen their bargaining capabilities.

Besides the above, the government has been keen to bring development in the areas of education, health, economy, and political participation and so on through five-year plans implemented through various schemes and programmes. As detailed earlier, a primary school in the village and an upper primary school at a distance of 10kms were established to bring the educational development among the Sugalis. Similarly, primary health centre was also established at the mandal headquarters and health functionaries were to periodically visit the *Sugali Thandas* to extend health facilities. Thus, the approach of government towards development has been comprehensive and holistic in nature. Here no effort has been made to critically examine the policies, implementation processes and draw backs in the schemes as several scholars have discussed these issues at length in various forums.

NGO Intervention in the *Thanda*

An NGO by name Social Education Development Society (SEDS) has been working in the area for the last twenty-five years. It was started in the year 1980 and its head office is located in *Mekalapalle* village, which is 15 kilometres away from the Mandal headquarters. SEDS facilitates government-sponsored programmes and they also have their own programmes in the villages. Initially, they were working in two Mandals and now their coverage has risen to five Mandals (Penukonda, Somandepalle, Goranla, Roddam, and Chilamathur) covering 209 villages.

According to the Manager of SEDS, their main concentration is on Scheduled Tribes, Scheduled Castes and other weaker sections in all the villages. In each village they have a community level organizer who is based in the village and looks after their works. Likewise, *Adadakulapalle* is one of their mainly focussed villages in the area. SEDS has vocational training centre in Penukonda, the mandal headquarters. They select young people and give them training on welding, motor repairing, scooter repairing and television repairing. They provide accommodation in their hostel located in Penukonda.

Now, the major activities of the NGO are Land Development Programmes, School Development programmes (where they construct toilets and plant trees in the school surroundings), Horticulture programmes, Women Empowerment through the formation of Self Help groups (SHGs), Water harvesting schemes and to provide minimum wage works to assist the marginal people and landless agricultural labourers. They have initiated a Village Organisation with all SHGs in the village. Village Organisation was started with two people from each SHG in the village. At preset, the total strength of the Village Organisation is 36 in the village. Village Organisation acts as a nodal agency in the village and undertakes all the developmental works. SEDS concentration is more on wasteland plantation, Horticulture, water conservation and land development programmes. It can be noted from the above that the SEDS working in this area has been focusing mainly on the economic development of the schemes by involving particularly youth, women and poor and marginal farmers. As there are functionaries of this NGO at the grass root level to organize local communities in the village there is a possibility of effective implementation of the schemes. More over it deals with the primary concerns of the people-food and clothing. To make people self-reliant and the NGO plans to slowly withdraw, so that dependency of the people on external agencies may be minimized which is sound objective for the real development of the local communities.

Microanalysis of the schemes

In the following an attempt is made to analyse the implementation of the above schemes and their outcomes in *Adadakulapalle Sugali Thanda.* It will be seen that there have been several problems in implementing the schemes. Thus, the objectives of the schemes have partially met.

Deepam Scheme: There are 13 households who have been benefited from the scheme in the *Thanda.* It is said that they got the scheme after the long waiting for three months, and initially appreciated it as it saved lot of their time. But the initial euphoria lasted only for few days as purchase of gas was beyond their reach. Therefore a majority of them have sold away their cylinders to other caste people in the village whereas the others are just keeping the connection with them without any use. There are also criticisms on the selection of the beneficiaries as only one section of the DWCRA members was given the connection in the *Thanda.* Other section of DWCRA members has complained that officials did not entertain their applications since they did not belong to the Telugu Desam party.

Housing Programme: Under Indira Aawas Yojana Scheme 50 houses were sanctioned to the *Sugalis* during the previous congress government (1989-1994) and were named as *Kothapalle Thanda.* Instead of assistance in the form of cash they were supplied with materials such as 550 cement bricks, 24 stone plates of one and a half square feet (locally called *bandalu*), 6 bags of cement, 2 windows and 12 *tati teerulu* (Palm beams), etc. and the financial need was to be met from their own resources. Out of 50 beneficiaries only 20 were able to construct their houses with the material, whereas the rest were not able to bear the remaining cost and therefore did not construct their houses so far. They are not aware of the Member of Legislative Assembly (MLA) and Member of Parliament (MP) housing schemes where they may have grant for the programme.

Public Distribution System (PDS): A total of 115 families have been issued ration cards in the *Thanda* as stated before. It is observed that though the PDS shop is reserved for the Scheduled Tribe, they are not running the shop. According to the *Sugali* headman the ration shop was originally sanctioned to one Shivaji Naik but was taken over later by a local dominant caste member who wields enormous economic, political and muscle power. All the people of the *Thanda* have complained about the increase in the prices of ration items like kerosene, rice, and sugar. They also complained about the quantity of items, which have reduced drastically over a period of time. It is because of the frequent change of norms by the government as well as problem in weighing machine of the dealer.

Food for Work Programme (FFW): Under this programme construction of metal link roads have taken up in the *Thanda* and every one who is in need of work have been provided with employment. This programme was discontinued since May 2004 due to non-availability of funds in the new regime. As a result the works initiated in this programmes were discontinued which adversely affected the Sugalis of the village.

SEDS (NGO) Activities in the *Thanda*

Land Development Programme (LDP): Under this programme, wastelands have been converted into agricultural fields through soil conservation. Soil conservation works include Stone Bunding, Gully checks, Spill ways, Woodlots, fire tracing, ploughing, and trenching activities. All these works are being undertaken in the summer season, which provides some wage works to the people of the village. Collecting some contribution from the beneficiaries carries some of the works like stone bunding, ploughing, fire tracing, and trenching. The share is like this: NGO's share is 75% and the beneficiary has to bear 25% of the total costs incurred for the works. The following table shows the details of the implementation of the scheme.

Table 3
NGO undertaken works in the Village during 2001-2005*

Name of the Activity	*Total Area*
Horticulture	100 Acres
Wasteland Plantation	250 Acres
Water Ponds	68
Fire Tracing	32988.80 sq m
Check Dams Desilting	4
Gully Checks	25
Soil Bunding	50 Acres
Seed Dibbling	50 kgs
Avenue Plantation	4kms

* *Source: SEDS Office, Mekalapalle.*

The land development programme has benefited to the *Sugalis* in the *Thanda*, to a certain extent only. The implementation of the programme was initiated in the year 2001 and some benefits were derived in the following year. Subsequently, due to failure of monsoons, the programme did not take off. Moreover, as mentioned before majority of the *Sugalis* are landless this programme has not been of much relevance to them.

Women Empowerment: There are 4 SHGs functioning in the *Thanda*. The women were attracted to the benefits such as savings, availability of loans for purchase of sheep, buffalo and other cattle. After the formation of one group people realized the importance of such groups and slowly new groups emerged. The group members meet regularly and decide the future course of action. In these meetings the SEDS functionaries educate them about savings, health etc. Due to regular meetings and Gram sabhas conducted by SEDS their awareness level has increased enormously about their health, children's education and, most importantly, savings. As savings accumulated women members are able to withdraw money during emergency situation. According to Radha Bai, 42 years, before the formation of the groups, if anybody was ill in the family, they had to rush to moneylender for help. Whereas now, there are SHGs to help them. They borrow money from the group. The lending of money one's own or children's is decided on the severity or necessity of the person or demand, which they feel urgent, such as health, or children's school fee or any other urgent need.

Till recently due to lack of work and consequently no wages they used to spend sleepless nights. They used to migrate to other areas for wage labour. Wages were also very less and working hours were more. They were not aware of their health, children's education, sanitation, savings, etc. Earlier they also felt that for women there was no role to play in the family or household decision-making process except to nod her head to the mothers- in-law and the husband's opinion. Women were not aware of the programmes like *Balika samriddi Yojana* (Girl Child Development Programme), mother and children's protection, etc. After the entry of SEDS, works such as pebble bunding and contour bundings have become regular. Another important feature is that there is no difference in wage rates for men and women. Women felt very happy that there is no gender discrimination in the rates of wages. Their saving levels, according to them, have improved enormously due to the efforts of the SEDS. Majority of the women are sending their children to schools as they have realised about the significance of education. They also have plans to contest and win the elections in the village and thus participate in the village administration and policymaking process.

In-spite of the above-mentioned efforts of both Government as well as NGO, Sugalis position in the *Thanda* has not changed significantly. One dominant reason for such static conditions inspite of efforts made to effect change is obviously as in any other part of the country due to the apathy of the government functionaries at different levels. Local conditions such as poor infrustructural development, failure of monsoons, interests of the communities are also to some extent responsible for the inertia.

It is contended that even the NGO does not perform its function objectively. It is believed that the NGO is favouring one section of the Sugalis in the *Thanda* and delivers all its services to the same section of the *Sugalis* and deliberately neglecting the other. This is due to the party politics prevalent in the village. The NGO manager, who is based in the *Thanda,* has resigned from his post to put his supporter as Telugu Desam party candidate in the last Local Body elections. Some of the youth from the *Thanda* openly opposed to the NGO's stand but it was of no use. The manager accepted the role-played by him in the last elections and said that there was no other way for him except to support Telugu Desam party for their survival and existence in the area. Thus, the party politics have a direct bearing on the development efforts, either by NGO or government machinery.

The levels of interaction of *Sugalis* with both the government officials and NGO can be seen in terms of their involvement in the party politics and factions. Ruling party is always ahead in the factional politics in the village and Sugalis have to take sides with one of the party's or factions. Present Sarpanch was elected on Telugu Desam party ticket twice and his group is representing one section of the Sugalis in the village. The NGO is also supporting this group in the village at the cost of the other section.

The above-described macro and microanalysis perspective revealed the nature of development processes in the *Adadakulapalle Thanda.* Even though there is no significant socio-economic change of the Sugalis compare to the non-*Sugali* population in the village, it cannot be denied some qualitative change in the lives of the Sugalis. In terms of quantity that is the number of households who cross the below poverty line due to the efforts of the government and the SEDS, there is initiation of change among Sugalis which may take some time to yield perceptible results. Some micro level changes, which are qualitative in nature likely to produce results, have been noticed in the study. It shall now be attempted to understand these changes.

It has been noted earlier that non-economic factors are paramount important in understanding the process of economic change. These factors are related to three basic elements of economy such as a) those favouring availability of savings, b) those favouring the utilisation of resources and c) those favouring the availability of labour (Williamson and Buttricks, 1964). In the present case as described and analysed above the NGO seem to have successfully brought the awareness and institutional means of savings among the Sugalis. Though the government provided the conceptual framework, it is NGO, which completed the process for a success. Though the banking institutions existed in the country even before independence, they never reached to the marginalized communities' inspite of several reformations and change of regulations and massive expansion of banking system in the country. The new forms of organised savings through informal transactions are met the needs of the poor participants (SHGs). In order to keep the savings sustainable some efforts were made to increase the income by making wage labour available to the Sugalis.

The resources available in the village primarily are human resource and land resource. The SEDS recognised the availability of youth who could be used for capacity building purposes. This programme is successful as the youth though a small number were able to make their own living better than those who depended entirely on the wage labour and small farming. Otherwise this could have been migrant labour in other states to eke out their living as semi-skilled labourers. The NGO also successfully exploited women resource, which is culturally potential, as men are tending to be spendthrift and women being conserver of material sources in the interest of the family maintenance. In this respect the organisation of Self Help Groups played vital role in the savings of money and NGO made use of these formally organised groups to educate, to bring awareness and to inspire women to actively participate in the various development activities. As a result of these efforts many children are being sent to school as they are the future human resource for the development of the village. Attempts have been made to help the Sugalis who live on agriculture

(35.8 percent) for developing their lands through land development scheme. Unfortunately, natural conditions did not cooperate for yielding perceptible results for *Sugalis* in the *Thanda*. Lastly, in all these efforts, there has been no dearth of labour to participate and also to derive the benefits. In other words these programmes are locally relevant for economic change.

It is no doubt that the government approach has been integrative but there is poor coordination of various departments for various reasons. The holistic development has been conceived but due to weakness in delivery systems the end results is pathetically obtusely stagnant. But, consistent efforts made, with all inherent problems focusing on economic change while consciously taking care of supportive cultural capital, has yielded some positive results. As the village is part of the wider political system it cannot escape from the good and bad aspects of the system. Some negative effects are visible hampering the development of the local population, which requires solution at different levels beyond the village.

IV

Conclusion

There are two active players, government and NGO, in bringing planned social and economic change leading to development of a marginal community, *Sugali* tribe, inhabiting in *Adadakulapalle* village. The dry land farming, drought situation and factional politics that grip the village for a long time left most of them orphans. The *Sugalis* have been poverty-stricken, which is observed in the *Thanda*, largely remained wage labourers and migrants to different towns and cities needed the intervention of government and NGO for being rescued from their deplorable conditions.

In order to understand the impact of the interventions of the above agencies to bring socio-economic development, the study has taken anthropological perspective of analysing development process at macro and micro levels. The development programmes and schemes at macro level are broad encompassing various issues, integrative and ideal efforts to stamp out poverty by creating infrastructures and offering support to individuals and individual households. At the micro level, the programmes are beset with problems relating to coordination of various elements that necessarily intervene and intersect the areas of operation. These include human elements – discharging the duties of the functionaries, location of the institutions, power politics and natural local conditions. There is a complex relationship of these elements. For success of any programme, proper configuration, manipulation and exploitation of these elements for advantage become necessary. Whoever, either an individual or agency, is able to handle judiciously and overcome these problems will be a successful player. To some extent in this case NGO played better than that of the government. Economic focus ensuring support of cultural elements seems to yield desired result, as can be thinly drawn from this study.

References

Clark, Colin. 1951. *Conditions of Economic Progress.* London: Macmillan, 2nd Edition.

Drewnowski, Jan. 1966. *Social and Economic Factors in Development.* Geneva: UNRISD, Paper No.3.

Eswarappa Kasi & R. Siva Prasad .2005. *Development and Change among Sugalis: An Ethnographic Evidence from a NGO Based Village,* presented in the 37th World Congress of International Institute of Sociology (IIS), Stockholm, Sweden, July, 5-9, 2005.

Eswarappa Kasi. 2001. *Development and Change due to Sericulture – A Village Study* in Chittoor District, (An unpublished M.Phil Dissertation Submitted to University of Hyderabad, Hyderabad).

Gide, C. and C. Rist. 1959. *History of Economic Doctrines.* Translated by Richards, George G. Harrap and CO.

Gupta, Dipankar 2004, *Meeting "Felt Aspirations": Globalization and Equity from an Anthropological Perspective.* www.anthrosource.net/doi/abs/10.1525/Gupta.2004/pdf

Jain, Hans. 2004. *Scheduled Tribes - Changes in Socio-Economic Conditions.* New Delhi: Classical Publishing Company.

Schultz, Theodore Walter. 1968. *Economic Growth and Agriculture.* Bombay: Tata-Mcgraw Hill.

UNDP. 1990. *Human Development Report,* Oxford University Press, New York.

UNRISD. 1972. *Contents and Measurements* by Mr. D.U. McGraham C. Richard Proust, N.V. Sovani and M. Subramanyam, Praeger Publishers, New York.

Weidner E.W. 1970. The Elements of Development Administration. In Weidner, E.W. (ed.), *Development Administration in Asia.* Durham, N.C.: Duke University Press.

Williamson and Bricks. 1964. Economic Development, Principles and Patterns. New Delhi: Prentice Hall.

9

Business Process Outsourcing-IT Enabled Services: Consolidation and Beyond

Taruna Upadhyaya

Business Process Outsourcing [hereafter BPO] has been the latest mantra in India today. IT services companies are making a quick entry into the BPO sector on the strength of their existing set of clients. Even companies are now moving their non-core business processes to outsource providers. BPO saves precious management time and resources while building upon core competencies. It results in increasing shareholder value. In the present context, where outsourcing by overseas companies is becoming the need of the hour, India's prospects in this emerging opportunity segment are getting brighter.

The BPO sector in India has evolved in three phases. The first phase was led by *captive players* like GE, DELL, HP, and HSBC to name a few. It then went on and later led by *venture backed companies* like Customer Asset, daksh, First Ring, transworks etc. Most of them have consolidated, either by way of an acquisition or a merger. Then *IT Services players* and *large corporate houses* like the Aditya Birla group came as the third wave. During the same time there emerged companies like Progeon, backed by Infosys, Nipuna backed by Satyam, Spectramind that was acquired by Wipro. The *fourth wave* is witnessing a lot of traction from *international players* who are aggressively building their domestic presence coupled with Indian players, who are strengthening their domestic presence.

The country's unmatched value proposition for customers—based on the factors such as cost savings, productivity gains and quality improvements have given India an edge in the global ITES-BPO marketplace. India is taking the lead in this field on account of the following factors:

- Abundant, skilled, English-speaking manpower, which is being harnessed even by ITES hubs such as Singapore and Ireland.
- Improving telecom and other infrastructure which is matching global standards.
- Strong quality orientation among players and their focus on measuring and monitoring quality targets.
- Fast turnaround times and the ability to offer 24x7 services based on the country's unique geographic location that allows for leveraging time zone differences.
- Proactive and positive policy environment which encourages ITES-BPO investments and simplifies rules and procedures.
- A friendly income tax structure, which places the ITES-BPO industry on par with IT services companies.

BPO conceptually allows an enterprise to just focus on its core competency and by outsourcing all the other support based facets that generally consumes a substantial amount of a firm's time and energy. A firm's energy should be highly focused around its core competency which is what ensures it a place in the market, earns revenue for it and keeps it going.

Figure-1
Diverse Outsourcing Agreements

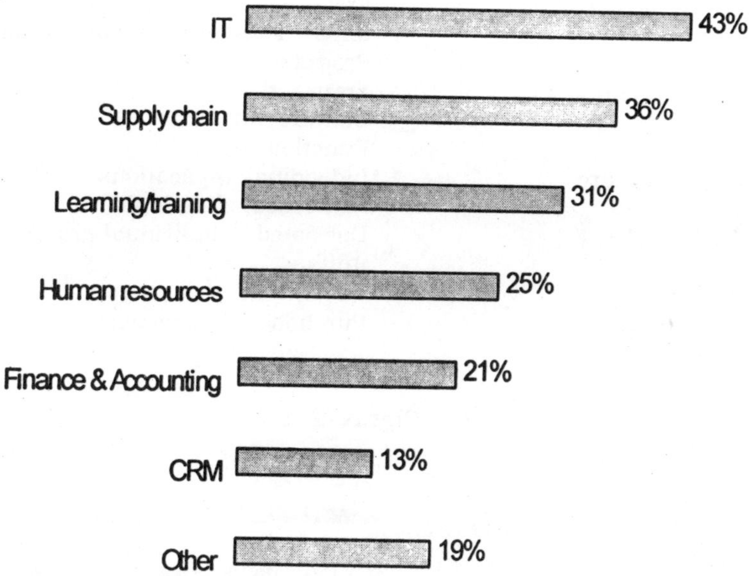

The ITES-BPO industry in India is a relatively young and nascent sector, barely over five years old. It is a broad based business platform backed by leading Indian IT software and services organizations and other third party providers. According to NASSCOM report, there are over 200 companies participating in the ITES-BPO segment and the numbers are growing every year. The ITES-BPO market today is characterized by the presence of companies such as Dell, HP, EXL, WNS, Sitel, HSBC, the Standard Chartered Bank, Convergys, Wipro Spectramind, AOL, Daksh, MsourcE, among others

Table-1

BPO is	*BPO is not*
Business discipline	Procurement routine
Long-term	Single developments/consulting Projects
Relationship	Transaction
Enabled	Contract out
Process	Function, tasks
Infrastructure	Individiual applications
Maintained	As needed, situational
High level	Delegated to individual process units
Mutual	Buyer-seller deal
Collaboration	Purchase and payment

Figure-2

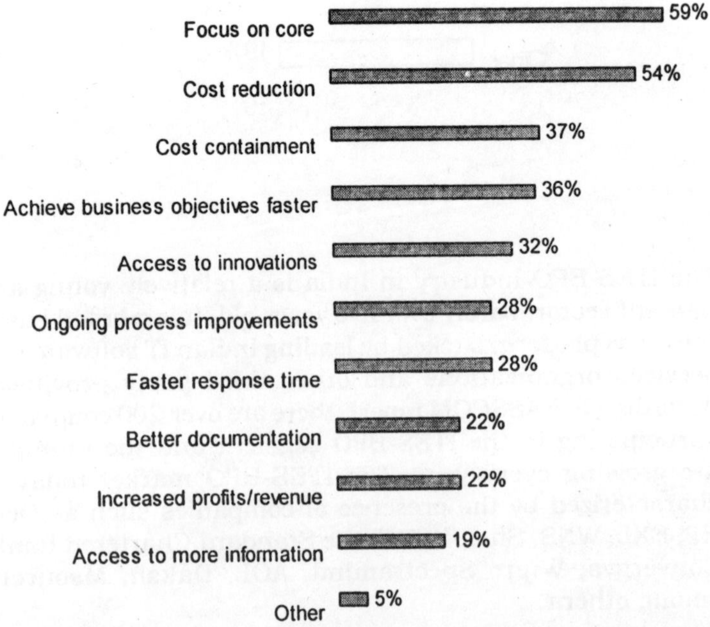

Global Delivery Model (GDM): The World Scenario

What is the effect of outsourcing on global economy? How does it help an economy that is in a state of flux? In a way outsourcing is driving the global economy, helping in the faster introduction of products, it builds communication and interactivity across borders, and underlying all this is the spread of Information Technology. Outsourcing itself is a huge economic engineer and an important economic contributor; creates jobs, increases opportunities for shareholders and investors. And secondly, it helps the customers of outsourcing to grow and shrink businesses, provides more flexibility and allows the service provider to target more customers across industries. It also acts as a 'shock absorber' for the highs and lows of businesses, in turn providing more stability.

Wal-Mart: it is outstanding at what it does and outstanding also in what it has others do. Wal-Mart's key suppliers manage what goods are on its shelves and how they get there; Wal-Mart manages relationships and service for the customers who buy those goods. Nike was one of the first to embody the concept of the "virtual" firm by concentrating on design and sourcing every other key capability from outside. It was a manufacturer that manufactured nothing, but who made sure that "its" manufacturing processes were the best.

Toyota made its supply chain collaboration the core of its production system, reflects BPO strategies: the percent of value-added benefit in each car that came from in-house manufacturing and supplies versus from outside. For GM the figure was well over twice that of Toyota. For every single automotive firm that has survived the competitive shakeout, cutting out in-house manufacturing and shifting to outsourced logistics were strategic necessities. Outsourcing required collaboration with suppliers to ensure highest quality and tight links with product planning and production. Any process can be outsourced creatively to add capabilities rather than get rid of tasks.

British Petroleum (BP) in the 1980s was a massive firm with thousands of staff in its head office, majestically named Britannic House. BP rebuilt itself, with process outsourcing a significant lever that helped to turn the tanker into a powerboat. BP is skilled in oil exploration. It outsourced financial accounting and general ledger processes, data center operations and tax reporting processes to equally skilled specialists in these areas. BP retained in house the processes that link to the outsourced

Figure-3

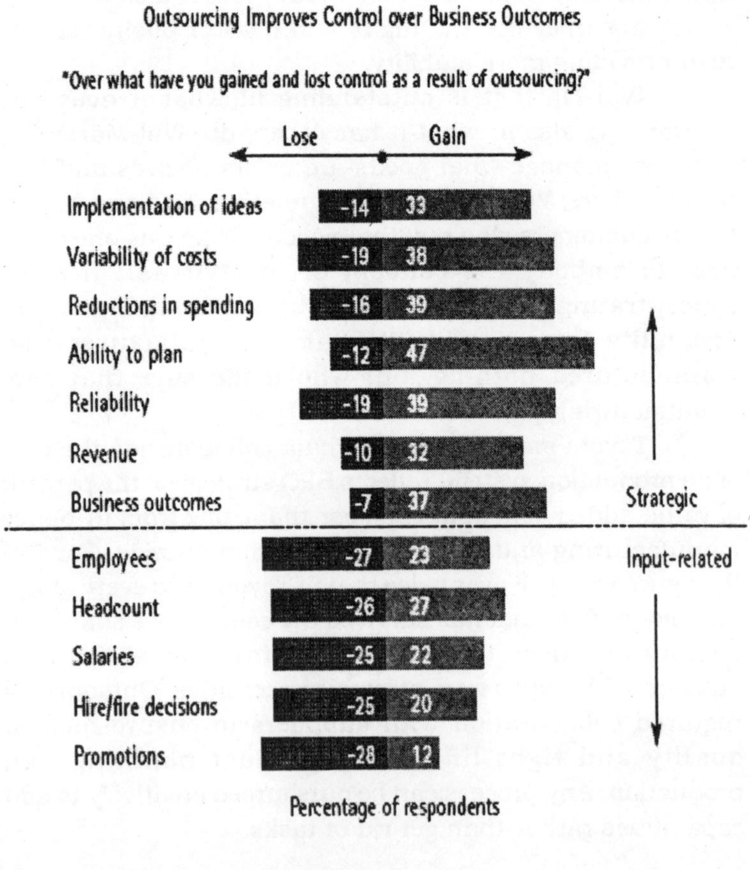

ones: Management reporting and planning link to financial accounting, information analysis and communications link to data center operations, and tax planning links to tax reporting.

Global Delivery Model (GDM): The Indian Scenario

GDM is increasingly becoming popular among pure-play call centres in India as this would help industry to move up the value chain by cashing in on various factors, including cost arbitrage and back-up advantage, and also to build confidence and comfort levels among European clients.

Many BPO clients are demanding GDM. Such a model will help call centres get an additional share of work which non-English speaking clients used to hold back so far. In addition to customer comfort, GDM will facilitate business continuity, multi-lingual capability and better workflow. In case of any eventuality, it also gives clients the assurance that the data is safe. GDM is more important for BPO businesses that impact large number of multilingual customers. Although locations like Ireland, Hungary, Mauritius are slightly expensive compared to India, they are much cheaper than the customer countries.

Table-2

Number of Seats In Call Centers

Country	2003	2004
Australia	1,35,000	1,46,000
India	96,000	1,58,000
China	38,000	54,000
Philippiness	20,000	40,000
New Zealand	12,000	13,500
Thailand	11,000	13,000
Singapore	10,000	10,100
Hong Kong	10,000	10,700
Total	3,32,000	4,45,300

The BPO Opportunity

BPO is considered a business discipline because it is centered on optimizing a firm's process portfolio. That demands skills and methods to:

- Maximize the company's capabilities via best practice processes, both built in house and handled through BPO. These capabilities rest on the three pillars of 1) sustainable competitive advantage 2) customer relationships as capital assets; 3) knowledge mobilization and intellectual capital; and the organizational "triangle" of a) culture, b) technology and c) process working together.
- Leverage and sustain the firm's core competencies and competitive differentiators by focusing on and freeing up organizational resources, simplifying the organization and concentrating on innovation and change management.
- Maximize financial performance by freeing up capital, improving capital efficiency per unit of revenue, maximizes revenue per employee and minimizing overhead.
- Brand the end-to-end customer relationship via end-to-end process excellence sourced to provide best practice.
- Make today's environment of uncertainty and constant change the company's ally, not a threat, by maximizing organizational flexibility, speed of response and the ability to scale operations up or down.

BPO marks the convergence of three well-established and major long-term historical forces that have increasingly affected business for over a decade. It is the coming together of these forces that is new and news. BPO is their integrator and enhanced enabler. The three forces are:

1. The transformation of corporate financial management and the move toward capital efficiency and shareholder value rather than earnings per share

as the metric of performance; this historical shift makes BPO a massive source of economic leverage because it helps maximize cash flow while minimizing capital deployment.

2. The maturation of information technology as a business resource, which makes online process sourcing and integration practical. Companies with well-integrated technology platforms can exploit the many new tools of software, telecommunications and the Internet to link their own processes, applications and information resources to a BPO provider "seamlessly" and on demand, in response to business innovation opportunities, operational needs and business scaling.
3. The evolution of process understanding and methods, which makes BPO a natural extension of such process movements as TQM (total quality management), BPR (business process reengineering) and supply chain management. In addition, it builds on and extends best practice trends in outsourcing of technology operations.

BPO leverages process-driven opportunities in four ways:

1. Operational excellence
2. Financial efficiency
3. Branding and customer relationships
4. Organizational responsiveness.

Outsourcing: The U.S. and India Venture

The Bush administration has acknowledged that outsourcing is a positive link between India and the US with the potential to bring both countries closer. India is "becoming a nursery of high-technology". Outsourcing allows companies to operate on an around-the-clock, 24/7 production cycle, further adding to productivity, political benefits reaped from outsourcing, as the United States seeks to win friends and influence events in South Asia and elsewhere, it would be hard to find a more naturally pro-American enclave than the Indian high-tech sector.

Outsourcing has enabled thousands of college graduates in cities like Bangalore, Hyderabad, Kolkata and New Delhi to "reap the fruits of middle-class life" that Americans take for granted. It would be "terribly short-sighted" to disrupt America's growing, mutually beneficial trade and security relationship with the world's most populous democracy to save a relatively small number of jobs that are not among the more well-paying in the US. Far more Americans lose their jobs to technology, domestic competition, and changing consumer tastes than to foreign outsourcing or other forms of international competition. The recent job losses in IT have not been driven mainly by foreign outsourcing. Hence, instead of blaming IT providers in India, displaced high-tech workers should blame the bursting of the dotcom and telecom bubbles, the subsequent plunge in the Nasdaq, the recession and decline of business investment, the September 11 terrorist attacks and the uncertainty that followed, corporate scandals, and slow growth abroad.

Mackinac Centre quotes that "the number of US jobs outsourced abroad will increase from an estimated cumulative total of 315,000 in 2003 to 3.4 million by 2015. That would mean an average of 257,000 additional jobs outsourced each year". However, these losses as "just a few drops in the big bucket of a $11 trillion economy that employs 138 million people and creates and destroys millions of jobs every month". If US, its companies and its workers are to remain leaders in the global economy, offshoring must remain a tool available to our corporations.

Security Factor

According to Information Technology Association of America (ITAA), the main issue is protection of privacy and security. ITAA is the US equivalent of India's National Association for Software and Service Companies (NASSCOM), and is engaged in formulating IT policies and liaisoning with the government. Moving jobs to developing nations would raise a security issue as financial and health data of Americans would be processed halfway across the world. Cyber security is a global challenge, which has to be addressed on a war-footing.

Indian Companies offering BPO Services from India

For the local consumer with all for the big Indian players like Reliance, Tata, Bharti, Wipro and MNCs like Accenture and IBM Global Services too eyeing the local pie. And the burst of acceleration comes in the form the recent DoT ruling that permits the use of common infrastructure for domestic, as well as international call centres. Market buzz is that arch rivals Reliance and Bharti are betting big on this. The Tata group too has joined domestic call centre pushcart with its recently launched Pune based firm offering call centre services to Indian customers and will soon be expanding to overseas clients. The company is offering customer care services to all Tata group companies and is looking at acquiring global customers.

Meanwhile, there is a spectacular growth in the domestic market. Telecom, financial services are today at the top of the list. Interestingly, Accenture which is providing IT infrastructure services to large Indian corporates like Indorama is also handling a pure play outsourced call centre for an Indian client. Sources in Wipro Spectramind reveal that it is also interested in the local market.

Indian IT Firms: Beyond Metro Cities

Faced with overcrowding and crumbling infrastructure in metros, Indian software makers and outsourcing firms are likely to queue up before smaller cities that offer better prospects. Backed by large pool of human resource, infrastructure and policy support, smaller cities are attracting IT firms like never before (source: NASSCOM, KPMG) location-wise attractiveness are encouraging technology firms to target cities like Jaipur, Pune, Mohali, Ahmedabad, Vizag and Kochi.

The framework used for assessment includes human resources, infrastructure, focus on IT enabled services (ITES), support group presence, and geographic location. The government's move to set up an IT park closer to the main city and favorable power situation with ITES-BPO companies being charged lower rates also makes it an attractive destination for companies. Wipro, listed on the

Table -3

IT Landscape of key Indian cities

City	*Focus*	*Prominent firms*	*Employees*
Delhi (includes Gurgaon and Noida)	Call centres, transaction processing, chip design, software	GE, American Express, STMicroelectronics, Wipro Spectramind, Convergys, Daksh, ExL	73,000
Mumbai	Financial research, back office, software	TCS, MphasiS, i -flex, Morgan Stanley, Citigroup	62,050
Bangalore	Chip design, software, bio - informatics, call centres, IT consulting, tax processing	Infosys, Wipro, Intel, IBM, SAP, SAS, Dell, Tisco, TI, Motorola, HP, Oracle, AOL, E & Y, Accenture	109,500
Hyderabad	Software, back office, product design	HSBC, Satyam, Microsoft	36,500
Chennai	Software, transaction processing, animation	Cognizant, World Bank, Standard Chartered, Polaris, EDS, Pentamedia	51,100
Kolkata	Consulting, software	PwC, IBM, ITC Infotech, TCS	7,300
Pune	Call centres, chip design, embedded software	MsourcE, C -DAC, Persistent Systems, Zensar	7,300

New York Stock Exchange, is set to unveil a development centre in Kolkata in the current month that would house 5,000 professionals.

Infosys Technologies, India's largest listed software exporter, reportedly plans to set up a 2,400-person centre at the 111-acre software technology park in Chandigarh.

Economic Side

India's export earnings from business process outsourcing is likely to reach $21-24 billion by 2008 with an increased marketshare of 4.8 per cent, according to a study by IDCAssocham. India's BPO revenues will increase to $12.2 billion by 2006. It is observed that the global BPO industry is growing at a pace of 60-70 per cent and is estimated to be between "$150 billion and $700 billion". Out of this, only five per cent of the processes are currently being outsourced.

The burgeoning growth in the BPO industry increased the size of the ancillary industry in India, like catering, security and transportation sectors to an estimated amount of $1.15 billion. The growth in BPO industry has also generated over one lakh employment and will employ over a million in a little over five years. McKinsey & Co. predicts global market for IT-enabled services to be over $140 billion by 2008.

Table-4

These $142 Billion can be broken up and shown as below:

Customer Interaction Services	33.0
Finance and Accounting Services	15.0
Translation, Transcription and Localization	2.0
Engineering and Design	1.2
HR Services	5.0
Data Search, Integration and Management	44.0
Remote Education	18.0
Networking Consulting and Management	15.0
Website Services	5.0
Market Research	3.0
Total	141.2

Source: *NASSCOM McKinsey Study - India IT Strategies. In that the opportunity for India will be $ 17 Billion.*

Indian ITES industry employed more than 100,000 people in 2001-2002. This industry clocked approximately 70% growth last year is expected to grow similarly in 2002-2003.

Global Market size estimates of BPO

- $712 billion in 2001
- Gartner/Dataquest: $ 544 billion in 2004
- Gartner: $173 billion in 2007, of which $24.23 billion would be outsourced to offshore contractors
- IDC: $300 billion in 2004
- IDC: $1.2 trillion in 2006

How UNITED NATIONS Looks at OUTSOURCING?

Multinational companies are on the brink of shifting more services to cheaper locations abroad as the trend towards "offshoring" in the sector reaches a "tipping point," a UN report said.

The UN Conference on Trade and Development (UNCTAD) warned the predominantly industrialized countries which are the source of Foreign Direct Investment (FDI) that it would be "short-sighted" to resist the trend by forcing corporate service jobs to stay at home. "It may well mark the next stage in the evolution of the international division of labour," the agency's 2004 World Investment Report said.

The report pointed out that economists regard the offshore provision of services, such as locating western airline reservation centres or computing services in India, as "the cutting edge of the shift in global economic activity." However, UNCTAD estimated that investment in offshore "business processing" would expand from 1.3 billion dollars in 2002 to 24 billion dollars by 2007, although it would not necessarily all flow to developing countries. "This is essentially a north-north phenomenon. There is a myth that essentially offshoring is done to developing countries, this is not true," said Carlos Fortin, the agency's deputy secretary general.

"India is also an important location, but it is the only one in the developing world," Fortin added. Fifty percent of telephone call centres shifted abroad - went to developing countries during 2002 and 2003, the report said. Overall investment in offshore industrial plants and services accounted for only 32 billion dollars of the global total of 720 billion dollars in foreign direct investment, UNCTAD said.

BPO Vs IT: Language Wars

IT services firms are now looking for people with excellent command over English to fill positions that demand increased customer/end-user interface or product understanding.

Like in the case of BPO, IT industry too gauges candidates on four-main yardsticks: Voice clarity, neutral accent, fluency and grammar. This is a fresh trend. Today IT companies are keen to get people with excellent communication skills in addition to technical qualification.

India to Focus on Attrition

Crucial issues like high attrition rate and growing merger and acquisition deals, training, information security, infrastructure, real estate and telecom, operational excellence and strategies for the industry to sustain and further improve its competitiveness in the global economy are the challenges that BPO industry is facing these days. Indian ITES-BPO industry has a high attrition rate of 30-35 percent. Experts warn if the companies fail to check the spiralling turnout rate it will badly affect the growth of the booming industry.

The industry, which has helped India emerge as an electronic housekeeper to global firms like GE, British Airways, and Citibank is expected to grow seven fold by the end of 2008 generating revenue of $21 billion, up from $3.5 billion now.

Areas that Indian BPO Service Providers Need to Improve

Quality is the No.1 issue. The delivery of a service/ product has to improve. There are too many instances of long transition periods. Another is integrating and strategic planning along with the customer. One has to align work processes along customers' needs and business and aim to become a seamless partner. The other issues would be Security, IP and Privacy. Some of this is being tackled, but India does require legislation on Privacy.

Table-5 Skills Required

Segments	*Skills*
Call center	Good communication and language skills, accent understanding team leadership, basic computing skills
Remote customer interaction	Language and accent understanding
Date search, Integration	Computing, language and analytical skills
Human Resource Services	Country specific HR policies, rules and regulations
Remote education	Subject knowledge, computing and language skills
Engineering and design	Technical and engineering design and computing skills
Translation, medical transcription and Localisation	Language understanding, basic computing (wordprocessing knowledge) and understanding of various medical terminologies
Animation	Drawing and creative skills, computer graphic skills
Finance and accounting	International/ country specific accounting rules

(Contd.)

(Contd.. Table-5)

Segments	*Skills*
Market Research	Understanding statistical sales and marketing concepts
Network Consultancy and management	Understanding different network configurations and support equipment, technical/ computing skills

SWOT Analysis on Indian ITES Sector

Strengths

- Highly skilled, English-speaking workforce.
- Cheaper workforce than their Western counterparts. According to NASSCOM, the wage difference is as high as 70-80 percent when compared to their Western counterparts.
- Lower attrition rates than in the West.
- Dedicated workforce aiming at making a long-term career in the field.
- Round-the-clock advantage for Western companies due to the huge time difference.
- Lower response time with efficient and effective service.

Weaknesses

- Recent months have seen a rise in the level of attrition rates among ITES workers who are quitting their jobs to pursue higher studies. Of late workers have shown a tendency not to pursue ITES as a full-time career.
- The cost of telecom and network infrastructure is much higher in India than in the US.

Opportunities

- To work closely with associations like NASSCOM to portray India as the most favoured ITES destination in the world.
- Indian ITES companies should work closely with Western governments and assuage their concerns and issues.
- India can be branded as a quality ITES destination rather than a low-cost destination.

Threats

- The anti-outsourcing legislation in the US state of New Jersey. Three more states in the United States are planning legislation against outsourcing Connecticut, Missouri and Wisconsin.
- Workers in British Telecom have protested against outsourcing of work to Indian BPO companies.
- Other ITES destinations such as China, Philippines and South Africa could have an edge on the cost factor.

State-level Incentives for the ITES Industry

Getting enablers (decision making bodies, policies, institutions, IT architecture) in place, defining thrust areas, catalyzing the creation of infrastructure, leveraging private sector initiatives, accelerating the development of a knowledge hub and providing the right social environment are some of the key factors state governments have taken into consideration when designing a policy for the IT/ITES sector.Indian states Governments have taken the following steps to boost the growth of the ITES/BPO industry within their domains. These include the following:

- A majority of the states have either promulgated a government order or a notification permitting all establishments in the respective jurisdictions engaged in IT-enabled services (including call centers) to: work on National Holidays; allow women to work in night shifts; and offices to function 24 hours a day, all through the year (i.e. 24*7*365).

- IT policies that seek to create (through focused HRD programs), a trained pool of manpower with the skills and aptitudes appropriate for the ITES industry requirements
- Most of the states in India have Software Technology Parks (STPs) and Export Processing Zones (EPZs) offering world-class infrastructure with reliable data communication facilities.
- Further, to leverage private sector investments, the state governments have proactively come out with several special incentives

Growing demand in the ITES-BPO Sector and the Future

The U.S. is expected to be the largest source market for the ITES accounting for nearly 60 per cent of the market. The share of the offshore component is expected to increase to 23 per cent of the total spending by 2007. Europe is expected to be the second largest market for the ITES sector, accounting for 22 per cent of total spending which is expected to reach Euro 129 billion by 2008. U.K and Ireland being the main markets for BPO in Europe are likely to account for about 45 per cent of the European market followed by countries like Germany, Switzerland and Austria with a 20 per cent share. The fastest growth expected within the European market is in the U.K and Ireland with a CAGR of 14 per cent. However the maximum growth is expected n the Asia-Pacific region, with ITES-BPO spending to grow at 14.7 per cent for the next two years. Japan's second largest car maker, Nissan, is joining the bandwagon of multinational firms outsourcing IT- related jobs to India. Nissan has announced that IT is increasingly become an ideal hub for sourcing low-priced components.

Conclusion

As far as IT staffs are concerned, outsourcing breaks up the traditional budget patterns wherein a company had direct control over 80 per cent of IT spending. IT outsourcing is seen as a threat to the status quo and to the custodianship of custom-made systems. IT staffs now have to compete with outsiders. Systems designs that locked in costly corporate-specific solutions now have to become open to standard and even commodity solutions. Nevertheless, IT outsourcing is here to stay and will continue to grow with the rise in global commerce.

References

Business Process Outsourcing by John K. Halvey, Barbara Murphy Melby

Outsourcing by Steven M. Bragg

Strategic Outsourcing by Maurice F. Greaver

www.accenture.com
www.outsourcing.com
www.timesofindia.indiatimes.com
www.pwcglobal.com
www.wipro.com

10

Socio-Economic Dimensions of Indian Diaspora in the Globalisation Era

V. Basil Hans

> The pastor, an exile and resident alien, reached out to offer the strong hand of fellowship to a flock of refugees. This group spoke a language he knew. Others later would speak different ones, but all shared the condition of having been uprooted from home and everything familiar. The young man remembered that from his own experience. Thankful to have been received into this community, these new exiles asked for prayers for the friends they had left far way, and help for themselves...
>
> - *Bishop Gustav Bolcskei: 2005*

Indian society is not static. It has been changing fast. The changes have been more rapid in the last one and half decade, popularly known as the period of economic reforms unleashed by way of liberalisation, privatisation and globalisation (LPG, for short). In this context it is interesting to note that India is changing for its people who are not only in India but also outside India, the latter referred to as the diasporic Indians. These changes have been analysed by economists as well as sociologists. The changes are related to various aspects of the social, political and economic life of Indians. They include education, industry, entrepreneurship, citizenship etc.[1]

In 1947 free India was born after a very long battle that was not just political, but economic and social as well.[2] It also gave rise to a new constitution, a new republic and a citizenship to Indians that was strictly and legally 'territorial' (Mitra, et.al.: 2005).[3] With LPG new ramifications of 'territory', 'citizen' (netizen?), 'sovereignty' have emerged. New economic contours encompassing new capital, new investments, new technology, new enterprises and new cultural culinary comprise the content of the contemporary globality. Understanding the contemporary globality and the role of Indian Diaspora is the need of the hour. It is required that the socio-economic dimensions of this content be fully and carefully examined. The social and economic contents have to be examined not merely as consequences or implications of the core globalising process, but as central to the meaning of globality itself.[4] The present paper seeks answer(s) to a moot question: What is the direction of diasporic change in today's civil society? In a flux society this may be a big question. But it is worth answering because both Indians and Non Resident Indians (NRIs) want to know what, if anything, state can do to promote economic production and social protection in an era of growing economic interdependence (Weiss, 2003). The on-going debate[5] hinges on wealth creation and welfare augmentation and the nexus between the two. In trying to find the answers it becomes necessary to identify the trends of Indian Diaspora itself. Three major trends can be identified:

(1) increasing economic open-ness of Indian economy to the influence of the diaspora;

(2) rapid transformation of Indian Diaspora from a traditional to a modern one;

(3) transition followed by introduction of new technology and new economic and public policies; and

(4) emergence of various associations and institutions having intra diasporic and inter diasporic linkages.

There have been some benefits from the diasporic changes, but as any change is not one-sided there have been some negative spill-over too. But the fact remains that the diasporic Indians as a whole have developed. It is also interesting to know that a new (social) class of Indians has emerged. This class consists mainly of the big industrialists, technocrats and elites of academicians and political personalities. The main focus of this paper is to trace the development of Indian Diaspora in the context of globalisation, while examining the text of globalisation itself.

The main objectives of this paper are:

(i) to examine the factors influencing the changes in Indian Diaspora – post globalisation – and its impact on the Indian economy;
(ii) to analyse the pulls and pressures of globalisation in the expanse of Indian Diaspora;
(iii) to know the intransigent and aporetic war between globalisation and localisation vis-à-vis the Indian Diaspora. (Lai:2002), and
(iv) to refurbish the reciprocity index of Indians in India and Indians Abroad.

Indian Diaspora: The Concept[6]

Conceptualising the Indian Diaspora helps us in placing it in the globalisation framework and in assessing its capacity. There are four well-known diasporas in the world: the Jewish, the British, the Chinese and the Indian, (not necessarily in that order). In terms of numbers the Indian Diaspora is smaller than that of the Chinese and the Jewish but perhaps the oldest and the most widespread amongst them all. Beginning from the ancient maritime adventurists, 'gurus' and missionaries to the most prosperous businessmen, technocrats and professionals, Indian Diaspora is made up of five generations of migrants.

Currently this number is estimated at 24 million in over 100 countries. In this the PIOs make two-thirds of the total. The remaining are the NRIs (See Table-1 for NRI figures).[7] Arguably this is the largest on-going migration in the world and it makes (economic) sense to say that this is not only an export advantage and not merely an expatriate advantage.

Statistical information on Indian Diaspora reveal that the largest part of the NRIs are nearer home, namely in various countries of Asia, followed by Africa and the Middle East. The smallest figure is in Europe. Within Asia, the number ranges from 4,000,000 in Nepal to 25,000 in Hong Kong. The ranges for Oceania, Latin America, North America, Europe, Africa and Middle East are 350,000 (Fiji)-70,000 (New Zealand), 315,000 (Guyana), 5000 (Panama), 1,500,000 (UK), 1,200,000 (Zimbabwe) and 1,200,000 (UAE), 100,000 (Yemen), respectively. As far as PIO is concerned, one of the largest groups is in USA which is about 1.7 million. In UK the census figure of April 2001 shows that 4.73 per cent of its population are Asians (covering Indians, Pakistanis and Bangladeshis). In Malaysia not less than 10 per cent of the people are those with Indian origin. The large number for Asia can be attributed to the nature of first military, then religious expeditions and later labour migration to this territory. For instance, even today Nepal, Indonesia etc., have a very strong influence of Indian culture. Large emigration to the Middle East is attributed to the Oil boom of the seventies. The pattern of migration is significant both from historical and economic perspectives. In the earlier times it was a massive importation of workers engaged under contracts of indentured servitude to work sites (say the tea and rubber plantations) in the British colonies. After independence in 1947, the pattern of emigration naturally changed. At first Indians sought better fortune mainly in UK, but later North America, especially the USA), became the favoured destination after change in Indian emigration law that made this possible. Some displaced PIOs in Africa (especially under Idi Amin in Uganda) and the Caribbean also reached the UK. Smaller numbers of Indians have also emigrated to the English-speaking countries like Australia and New Zealand.

Today the Indian Diaspora is more diverse. For instance, in US the Indian Americans are well represented in all walks of life, but particularly so in academia, information technology and medicine.

There were over 4000 PIO professors and 33,000 Indian-born students in American universities in 1997-98. The American Association of the Physicians of Indian Origin boasts a membership of 35,000 billion. In UK stereotypes about Indians have now moved from their being bus-conductors, waiters, and small shopkeepers to their being doctors, lawyers, accountants and successful businesspeople. In the Middle East, most Indians took to work as labourers and clerks. However, a significant minority are either employed in the highest echelons of major banks and corporations or have prospered greatly through conducting business in the region. Globally, today the range of activities of Indians Abroad is from running hotels and taxis to hi-tech companies.

Indian Diaspora is also known for its wanderlust, expertise, and enterprising qualities as well. Indians living abroad have an annual income of $160 billion that happens to be a third of India's GDP (Kalyani, 2003). This indicates how much India can gain by way of NRI remittances and deposits. This apart, Indian Diaspora has retained its emotional, cultural and spiritual links with the Motherland. There is a reciprocal chord in the hearts of people of India. This symbiotic relationship needs nurturing for mutual advantage.

The past decade has witnessed the growth of diasporic Indians in politics, administration and academics too. At present there are at least three Prime Ministers, about 300 parliamentarians and 28 ministers of Indian origin. While some had left India for greener pastures in the 19th century today it is the third generation which is seeking its roots in the Indian soil. In some countries like the US it is the second generation which is flourishing. Some have even hired researchers to find their moorings. The NRIs are also getting slowly organised. The fag end of the last century saw the vibrant face of Indian Diaspora be it in the United States, United Kingdom or in other countries. They have become more organised and understand their influence even as these countries too recognise their worth. Thus, Indian Diaspora is significant from social and economic angles. It is a force to reckon with.

Indian Diaspora and Globalisation: The Inter-connectedness

With globalisation there is a renewed focus on Indian Diaspora. This has two significant ramifications: one, the need to address issues of discriminations against the Persons of Indian Origins (PIOs) in some parts of the globe; Second, policy initiatives to collaborate with the NRIs and PIOs in the process of India's economic development. Obviously increasing attention is being given to the NRIs and PIOs by the academicians, administrators and the media. In the metros like Bangalore (Silicon Valley, for the computer savvy), the overseas Indian has become the toast of the town. Mumbai's Bollywood is churning film after film primarily to cater to these audiences. The 'Mulk' and the 'Watan' have once again become catchy words to emotionally bind the far-away Indians to a shared geographical space. The diaspora has carved a Bollystan[8] out of the Bollywood. Yet the cultural transmission model is rapidly transforming from a one-way street, in which the Motherland gives and the diaspora receives, to a two-way street, in which the diaspora is as confidently Indian, sometimes more so, than India itself. Bollystan ('Bolly-' for Bollywood, and 'Stan', the Persian suffix for 'land' comprise this term) is a 'neologism' which recognises this changing balance of power between the home country and its diaspora. Technology has enabled the diaspora to manufacture 'Indian-ness' as competently as their home-bound relatives through film, dance, music and even religious practices. These externally produced symbols of Indian-ness have in many ways become the primary representation of India in the West and around the world.

The Government in its turn is facilitating networks of PIOs as advocacy groups to influence policy in the countries of their residence. The labourer, the trader, the business and the professional, are getting one incentive or/

after other from the side of the Government. A few policy measures to provide incentives are listed below:

- 100 per cent Scheme for High Priority Industries
- 51 per cent Subscription Scheme for New Issues
- 100 per cent Investment in Housing and Real Estate Development
- 100 per cent Equity Participation in Air Taxi Operations
- 100 per cent Investment on Revival of Sick Units
- Gift Tax Benefits
- Wealth Tax Benefits
- Permission to Returning Indians for retaining Foreign Currency Accounts
- Allowing the NRIs to purchase immovable property for residential use in India
- General Permission to purchase Shares of Public Sector Enterprises.

The latest bogey in the train is the policy of dual citizenship.[9] So India finally discovered the Overseas Indian. He was (almost) elevated to the position of saviour of bankrupt India in 1991.[10]

In the light of borderless trade via market integration, shrinking space and time, and widening networks of culture and communication, the social and economic relationships between Indians far and near have undergone vast changes. One such change is the immense possibilities for persistent interaction and exchanges across distances and time, which is more often than not, sans physical contact. This is the new interconnectedness.[11] The economic gain out of this interconnectedness is crystal clear. Post-liberalisation a consensual economic reforms package has been formulated and this has led to India becoming a truly globalised economy. This spirit is well reflected in active participation of the Indian Diaspora. The near-around 10 per cent growth rate of the economy, the bouncing back of the agricultural sector (specifically through its transformation in agribusiness), revival of the manufacturing sector, rising levels of foreign reserves and current account surplus – all speak volumes for the new vibrancy in the economy, made possible by an upsurge in investment and trade. In all these achievements there is a significant contribution of the Indian Diaspora, financially, and intellectually. By their sheer confidence, high spirit and hard work, they along with the resident Indians, made India engage economically and build a new paradigm of development.

Efforts are being devoted to the mobilisation of the global NRI/PIO communities and resources for political, social and economic goals including developmental, philanthropic and educational activities of the NRI/PIO communities as well as India. Inder Singh, President of the Global Organisation of People of Indian Origin (GOPIO) [12]says,

> "We at GOPIO believe that the NRIs/PIOs have contributed significantly to the countries of their adoption as well as to India, and have added a special glitter to the resurgence of India." (Indolink)

The resurgent India now comprises of richer people at home and away from home. A study has shown that Indian American households are richer than other households in US. A calculation based on a 5 per cent sample of people in the 2000 census showed that the median income of the Indian American household was substantially higher than that of White or African-American population. The White households of the US had a median income of about $ 44,500, the African-American households had a median income of $29,000 and the Indian-American households had a median income of about $63,500. With good education, good jobs, and high incomes Indian Americans look like a privileged lot in America. What is more, these Indian elite have both the means and the desire to support the economic liberalisation of India. Their commitment to bharatiyatha (Indian-ness) is boon for India. This can go a long way in global *garibi hatao* provided strategies with effective links between diasporic communities on the one hand and between diasporas and people at home are devised.

Of late, the help sought from resourceful Indian Diaspora is found in every quarter in India. The increasing role of Indian Diaspora in the arena of economic development, in recent times, is clearly visible. Investment in primary health care in Rural India is a strong point in the case. Charities Aid Foundation, Naandi Foundation, and several Telugu associations, for instance, have come forward to collaborate with organisations in India, to aid health care programmes, including access to safe drinking water. What they are asking from us here in India is an assurance of proper utilisation of funds. Accountability, after all, is not a heavy price to pay for trust-building.

Undoubtedly, the globalisation era has witnessed a phenomenal dynamism among the diasporic communities, made possible by the rapid advancement in technologies for travel, transport ad communication. The emerging social formation from the fusion of real and virtual communities is essentially transnational in nature. Alejandro Portes opines that there are two features in this transnationalism: *one*, the emergence of transnational communities is tied to the logic of capitalism itself; and *two*, the distinct phenomenon that these communities represent is fuelled by the dynamics of globalisation itself, and hence has greater potential (Bhat and Sahoo, 2003). A clear achievement under globalisation banner for India lies in making its labour relatively more mobile, spatially and occupationally, horizontally as well as vertically in the 'new' societies. Other South Asians have not been so fortunate, caught as they are on the wrong end of a new international division of labour, in a country that doesn't care. (Laxmi Narayan, 2005).

The NRIs command sizeable resources in terms of finance apart from the technical know-how. The NRI direct investment has been more on repatriation than on non-repatriation basis. The former is about 80 per cent of the total direct investment by the NRIs. The NRI direct investment rose from 3 per cent in 1982-83 to over 10 per cent in the following decade. The total Foreign Direct

Investment (FDI) also went up substantially.[13] Today by any count India is not a back-office. The NRIs are a bastion by themselves. Economic compulsions may have driven them abroad to earn name and fame but now India recognises their economic contributions. The picture of Indian Diaspora has changed from the so-called export fatalism to the present import capitalism. The resourceful Indian Diaspora has shown its keenness and capacity to the striking of a balance between its 'brick economy' and 'click economy'. With every contribution made by the NRIs and the PIO, the economic role of Indian Diaspora is building up, so do the expectations. The significant changes taking place in global politics, trade etc will, hopefully, convince the authorities in India that there is more to the Indian Diaspora than mere sloganeering or rewording. The onward journey, therefore, has to be a joint one for state and civil society.

Diasporic Changes – A Factor Analysis

Indian Diaspora is, thus, changing for its own advantage and of its homeland. Various factors such as culture, religion, education, finance and technology have determined the influence, image, and identity of the far-away Indians. The strong points of India in this regard are its vast geographical area in a peninsular topography, a very old civilisation, a rich cultural heritage (including culinary arts), and a 'never-say die' entrepreneurial attitude.

Indian Diaspora is a unique part of Indian History. Moving-on-out is our cultural history. Migration is still a potent force changing social and economic life of Indians. Indians have gone in search of fruits in different parts of the world, but their roots are in India. This is quite sentimental too. In many cases it has been a no-return journey. What began as an aspect of mere presence has culminated in permanence. (That way international migration is one of the central directions of globalisation. For the trends in international migration from Sixties to 2000, see Table-2).[14]

The role played by various institutions in the strengthening of the base and bonds between India and its diaspora also need to be highlighted. The erstwhile Indian

Investment Centre (IIC), the Foreign Investment Promotion Board (FIPB), the Federation of Indian Chamber of Commerce and Industry (FICCI), and the more recent Ministry of Overseas Indian Affairs (MOIA), have all contributed their mite in this regard.

Education (add distance) is another key factor for the growing strength and stability of the Indian Diaspora. It is a fact that most of the Indian Americans are the highly educated Indian migrants. One of the lesser-known *desk* success stories is the proliferation of the management studies. Even a cursory look at the top 5 or 10 Business Schools will reveal that 5 to 15 percent of the faculty and students are Indians.

Overseas Indians have tasted success in the hospitality industry. It was jokingly said that Indians do not play football because if they were awarded corer they would open a teashop. From the *chai human* of the past to the revolving restaurants of today Indian hoteliers have come a long way. They not only serve the *desi* (*Madrasi*?) idli, vada and masala dosa but also the now global burgers, roll, hotdogs, and what not? Many Indians either work or own (inter-) continental hotels. Their success also lies in good educated cooks, chefs, and appealing ambience.

Naturally the brain drain phenomenon (the exodus of educated workers and academics) has got a shot in the arm; it is now viewed as a phenomenon of overseas arm of Indian culture and prosperity. This is because of the new equation: India + 'Outside' India = Greater India.

In the field of entertainment industry, the most likely candidate for a force of bonding would be the Hindi feature film, a phenomenon unique to Indian Diaspora. Perhaps, what Hollywood is to Western Europe, Bollywood is to the Middle East and East Africa. Indian film and TV crew visiting America, Europe, and Africa etc for shooting and stage shows is a trend today. Indian matinee idols have a large fan gathering in these places. Even the themes and stories of several Indian cinemas and commercials have an NRI or PIO framework: *Dilwale Dulhaniya Le Jayenge, Jeans, Pardes, Kal Ho Na Ho, Bend it like Beckham, Monsoon*

Wedding, Swades, Veer Zara... the list seems never ending. Suddenly (Celluloid) India seems to have fallen in love with its Diaspora.[15]

What is positive about these films, however, is that they depict Indians at home in the globalised world, despite the trials and tribulations arising out of two different cultures. Indian films, Indian clothes and several other ethnic products are now very much in demand among the diasporic communities. For India this fetches handsome revenue too. Thus, several social and economic factors have intertwined in a changing Indian Diaspora. This has been leading to growth of wealth and welfare, although not in the same degree for both.

It is an admissible fact that the idea of Welfare State itself has undergone a sea-change in the diasporic evolution. Despite the still strong notion of nation state, the concept of Welfare State is fast losing its country-uniqueness and is acquiring sharing complementarities with divergent production regimes. This was bound to happen, sooner or later, because the role of the state itself is being redefined under globalisation.[16&17]

Emerging Issues

With increasing open-ness and renewed focus on Indian Diaspora certain pertinent issues are emerging. A few of them are considered here.

One of the most important issues is related to the call for *swadeshi* (indigenous) in the light of the so-called *videshi* (foreign) invasion of Indian culture. There is the danger of treating all Overseas and Non Resident Indians as invaders of culture and missionaries of conversion. An identity crisis –at least for the sake of discussions – has cropped up. Their identity is lost, Indians at home fail to recognise them when they return; in their adopted country they are still considered as Indians. For the diasporic Indian, "to be or not to be?, that is the question". For those who carry on with the tradition there is no escaping India. But the diasporic Indian cannot afford to be averse to the culture of his host country. His loyalty must be not suspected, while his individuality must be respected. Where does the East meet West? How to draw the contours of convergence? Is culture stronger than civilisation? Are the methods of maintaining one's cultural identity ever the same? What is the reciprocity of cultural exchanges? These are relevant questions.

Many diasporic Indians find that they cannot hang on to their own culture and are therefore, in a state of panic. They want Mother India to help them hold on to their children and grandchildren. This cultural help is very important to the Overseas Indians. The Indian Diaspora has reached a stage, where, on the one hand it is trying to maintain its continuity as a community while on the other, it fells that its identity is at stake (even though the fact is that the definitions of national identity are never fixed).[18] Solutions to these problems must be worked out within the ambit of globalisation, without forgetting the traits of Indian civilisation. Only then globalisation becomes meaningful – globalisation that is inclusive, not exclusive, globalisation for integration – a comprehensive integration at that. This state has to be reached to have a healthy diasporic relationship. That requires dialogues between diaspora and India n a healthy environment.

The second issue is that of the rights and privileges and expectations of the PIO and NRIs. In some places the Diasporic Indians face a denial of their rights as workers and/or as citizens. Americans of Indian descent have, in the past, been targets of racism by members of all ethnic groups - though it has dissipated substantially. Some of it is overt, perhaps the worst example being the New Jersey dot busters - groups of thugs who sought ethnic Indians and mugged them or attacked their property in the late 80s and early 90s, the 'dot' referring to the *bindi* worn traditionally by Hindu women on their forehead. It is said that these attacks were racially motivated, and alienated the Indian population from the American mainstream. This lack of assimilation has created many problems for both ethnic Indians as well as non-Indians. Another peculiarity: most children of these immigrants - also called as "ABCD" - American Born Confused Desi. This term (usually used as something of an insult) reflects the fact that these first generation Americans find themselves stuck between traditional parents and upbringing at home and the more liberal and open community outside. This 'in-between-ness' can leave them with uncertainty about their own role in society - neither Indian nor American.[19]

In UK, the second and third generation of Indians has started inter-marrying with the rest of the population, to the point where this has in itself become a stereotype. In a few local areas, ethnic tension has resulted in ill-feeling and racist violence against immigrants, and groups such as the British National Party have exploited this. (However, in general, racism towards people of Indian origin has greatly reduced from the early days of mass immigration after Partition). Further there is the "X = X + 1 Syndrome" (Syndrome of postponing returning to India every year), and "NRI Syndrome" (Talking ill of India and Indians, once having exposure to other countries). A feeling of mutual respect is what is required in this regard. An introspection by the diasporic Indians as well as their kith and kin in India will help in neutralising these syndromes.

The third issue is of policy touching upon rights, remittances and return to India by the far-away Indians. The policy changes in recent times have, by and large made way for greater collaborative investments in India by diasporic Indians. While the production/protection aspects are clear, the distributional effects are quite ambiguous. As far as foreign exchange inflow is concerned some feel that though the government gets inflow of money, it is not liable. Should we all not be reliable? Are the policy initiatives 'enabling' the diaspora or (although unintentionally) 'constraining' them?[20] Is there a win–win situation in the diasporic relationship today? Has India done enough for its diaspora? Whatever has been done so far was it what the diaspora needed? Is the Overseas Indian feeling that here is a mere milch cow?

Then there is the China vs. India issue Often the Indian NRI is compared with his Chinese counterpart, stating that the former is not contributing as much as the latter to one's homeland. But let us not ignore the fact the while the Chinese Diaspora is known for its sizeable FDI Indian

Diaspora is known for its professional and entrepreneurial spirit. Moreover, Indian Diaspora has much more than money to give to its Motherland and money is not mother's first priority. What more can the diaspora do? What better can we do for them? At the same time one cannot be blind to the economic realities of Indians in the diaspora.[21] So when we gauge the diasporic potential and contributions to India's economic development both income and non-income indices have to be used. Knowledge of its social and economic status should precede any effort at inviting them or their money to India. We need to be sensitive to their problems such as these faced by the Gulf-Indians today. A diasporic-friendly stance is what is called for. Our first agenda in the dialogues for diasporic development should be proving (that we care for) them rather than wooing them.

Epilogue

The Indian Diaspora is today an incontestable fact of world culture. Under globalisation era it is beginning to occupy a greater place in transnational economic and cultural exchanges (Lal, 2004). To some observers, the Indian Diaspora is mostly visible in its cultural face, but for many – at least – in the LPG era it is the socio-economic dimension that is uppermost. But there has to be compromise here, we cannot ignore culture for anything else. Political and cultural discrimination are clearly issues of considerable importance. At the same time, economic and social abilities do determine the gains and pains of the diasporic communities. The constraints of globalisation have to be confronted with our abilities India has a very long history of migration and diaspora. Today is the time to know what kinds of histories of 'continuity' are assumed by claims of 'origins', both for economic growth and social good. Whether in Sydney or in Singapore, Saudi Arabia or San Francisco, at the core of the diasporic domain is its socio- economic motives. This is the truth for the indentured Indian labourers of the 20th century as well as for the global savvy coolies of today. Like the model religious missionaries of yore, now we need missionaries who can give the economic and social witness of Indian for diasporic life today, who can break the wall, and work for wider fellowship. The purpose is to rediscover Indian witness for the commitment of globally reformed Indians in the economic and social realities of or times.

There are huge energies to be unleashed on both sides of the fence, synergy is what is required. Hence in the spheres of India and its Diaspora there should be no room for 'dominance-dependence syndrome'. Perhaps the 'host-guest' expressions could do (this is another research matter, altogether). Our researchers and policy-makers should, therefore, take into account then social and economic perspectives of the Indian diaspora not only while emphasising its historical context but in its future interests as well. The celebration of Pravasi Bharatiya Divas becomes more meaningful when the Anivasi and Nivasi celebrate it together as profound vishwasis. The common goal at focus should be the global Indian family. Dignity, Identity and Unity should be the watchwords for collaborative development of India and its diaspora. This is in-keeping with the need-based development and warding off the greed-based development. Our favourable factors like the vast and economical labour force a sophisticated and vibrant IT sector a bi market etc., should made our strengths in reaching common goals.

We need to go beyond nostalgia and political niceties. Members of the diasporic communities should be able to live happily 'here' and 'there', with Indians here having a healthy relationship with them. To accomplish this there is an urgent need to re-examine and (re)capture the emerging phenomenon of communities in the transnational space. All these are possible in the global arena. A new world is possible even with a changing diaspora. In the seventies development thinkers spoke of a New International Economic Order. Today they speak of global village. It means globalisation is not only economics. The world needs both economists and sociologists, particularly who teach and practice cooperative globalism and not simply corporate globalism and the role of diaspora in it.

Notes

1. Governments have also changed at the crucial periods. Between 1991 and 2000, the government in India changed five times. Despite strong opposition from nationalists, NGOs, and others, successive governments have affirmed that reversal of outward orientation is ruled out. This may appear to be a compromise among key policy-makers and institutions (Alamgir 2003).
2. Diaspora, nation-state and religion are often assumed to be mutually exclusive categories since all the three demand a high degree of loyalty and identification. Does life in a diasporic situation, characterised by the maintenance of material and symbolic links with cultural and religious traditions outside the country of residence, inevitably lead to a socially disintegrative stance and a threat to national cohesion? The history of religions provides cogent examples of the successful perpetuation of diasporic religious-cultural identities alongside a full identification with the national symbols, society and country of residence. Like political freedom, diasporic development has often not, however, been achieved without considerable struggle, mobilisation and adjustment among both diaspora and 'host' communities. We have examples from South Asian religious diasporas.
3. Citizenship and the Indian Diaspora is another important stream in diasporic discussions. However, a detailed discussion on citizenship and national communities is not within the scope of this paper. For a very explicit discussion on the topic see Mitra et. al., 2005.
4. There is, however, even more gain in going beyond geopolitical and economic contours to the 'historical sociology' approach to understand Indian Diaspora today. This view itself much older than contemporary globality. Halliday, Hobson and Shaw have long insisted on this approach. See Hobson (ed.) *Historical*

Sociology of International Relations, particularly 'Globality and Historical Sociology: State, Revolution and War Revisited'; and 'A New Field of Study: Modern Diasporas in International Politics', by Sheffer Gabriel in Sheffer (ed.:1986) *Modern Diasporas in International Politics*, Kent: Croom Helm Ltd.

5. There are, in fact, several interlinked debates. One other, for instance is over trade barriers. This debate dates back to British Corn laws. Enacted to protect land barons, the Corn Laws were finally repealed in 1846. This made way for what Martin Wolf has called "the first age of globalisation" (Hufbauer and Paul Clyde Grieco: 2005.

6. A non-resident Indian (NRI) is an Indian citizen who has migrated to another country. Other terms with the same meaning are overseas Indian and expatriate Indian. For tax and other official purpose the government of India considers any Indian national away from India for more than 180 days in a year an NRI. In common usage, this often includes Indian born individuals who have taken the citizenship of other countries. A Person of Indian Origin (PIO) is literally, simply a person of Indian origin who is not a citizen of India. For the purposes of issuing a PIO Card, the Indian government considers anyone of Indian origins up to four generations removed, to be a PIO.

7. Diaspora, a Greek Word originally referred to the wide dispersal of the Jewish community beginning from the 70 AD. Over the years the term has acquired a generic meaning and it is now referred to as 'community of people living outside the country of origin, assuming that the community is aware of its origin and identity and maintains linkages with the mother country.

8. The term was first used by Parag Khanna, when he guest edited the UK's ethnic lifestyle magazine Another Generation in Fall 2004 (www.anothergeneration-mag.com). The entire issue

was based on the theme of Bollystan, This was subsequently then used in an article in *The Globalist.* The London-based Foreign Policy Centre think-tank has also recognised Bollystan as a form of diasporic diplomacy'. In the January/February 2005 issue of Foreign Policy magazine, Mitra Kalita of the Washington Post writes, "Finally there is a name for where I live: Bollystan."

9. Dual citizenship will be extended to all overseas Indians who migrated from India after January 26, 2005. An announcement that was first made at the first Pravasi Bharatiya Divas in 2003by the then Prime Minister Atal Bihari Vajapeyee was pronounced by the present Prime Minister Man Mohan Singh while inaugurating the 3rd Pravasi Bharatiya Divas in Mumbai. The procedures have now been made use-friendly.

10. We had no reserves. We had to turn to economic reform in 1991. The reforms of 1991 which were crisis driven are now success driven. That is the big difference which is taking place (Nath, Kamal: 2005)

11. Scholars have used different terms to capture this interconnectedness: network societies', 'global village', 'global ecumen' and so on.

12. GOPIO, founded in New York (1989) is a pan-global organisation trying to unite the PIOs. Its main aims are to address the concern s of the PIOs in their countries of settlement and to utilise the expertise of the Indian expatriates for the benefit of people in India and the countries where the PIOs are settled. (Correia: 1999) GOPIO has been organising conferences and conventions in different parts of the world to mobilize the global NRI/PIO community. In 2004-5 alone, GOPIO organised five international conferences, in January 2004 in New Delhi, in March 2004 on Human Rights in New York, in October 2004 in Brussels, in January 2005 in Mumbai and in November 2005 in Brussels again. Besides providing a globally recognized platform for dialogue and discussion to the worldwide Indian Diaspora, GOPIO

conferences and conventions continue to help bring the Indian Diaspora closer to mother India and strengthen the inherent bonds between mother India and the scattered Diaspora. The conference in Hyderabad on January 5th and 6th, 2005, is another of its continuing efforts to mobilise the global Indian community and facilitate their networking. (GOPIO) has scheduled its Conference 2006 in Hyderabad on January 5th and 6th, in conjunction with Pravasi Bharatiya Divas 2006. The theme of the conference is "Global Indian Diaspora: Today and Tomorrow" (Indolink: 2005).

13. As per the figures available in rupee terms, in 1991 total amount of FDI approvals was Rs. 534.11 crore, while in 2000 it was Rs.37,039.44 crore. This has, however, declined later. The decline has not much to do with number of approvals but with the 'size' of the investment projects. Most of the projects/proposals after 2000 have ranged from about Rs.1 crore to Rs. 50 crore, each (Dasgupta: 2003).

14. In the year 2000, 175 million persons were living outside of their country of birth making one in every 35 persons on earth an international migrant, up from one out of every 40 in 1960. International migrants account for 2.5 per cent of world population since 1960. For details see *World Economic and Social Survey 2004* op.cit.

15. Indian culture has been constantly referenced within wider British culture, at first as an exotic influence in films like My Beautiful Laundrette, but now increasingly as a familiar feature in films like Bend It like Beckham. Indian food is now regarded as part of the British cuisine.

16. As far as economic choices are concerned, for some this has meant "less government and more market", and for others an equal share of both. This is the famous market vs. state debate. The question of 'governance' enters here. While states are ruled, markets need to be managed. There is also school of thought advocating market governance. Governance

is a suitable option for both state and the market. However, power sharing equations, governing policies, terms of negotiations and exchanges etc are but only a few of the host of issues that emerge in the context of managing open-ness in India. This is an area of immense research possibility today.

17. Some like Swank feel that welfare is withering under globalisation. This is the 'political logic' of globalisation, whereas business spokespersons and neo-liberal economic orthodox use the 'economic logic' of globalisation while arguing for restructuring of the welfare state (Swank: 2003).

18. One reason for the identity crisis is the very process of globalisation. For centuries, changes in the diaspora were fed by continuous migration. In every continent migration keeps producing fresh diaspora. But diasporas do not quickly assimilate into the receiving society. Through a combination of preference and social exclusion, they maintain their identity and solidarity over extended periods. In moist countries there are older diasporas and new diasporas. Even within the same ethnic group, mutual support and solidarity may be strained by tensions and conflicts between the earlier and later arrivals. For an elaborate discussion on motivations to maintain solidarity and to exert group influence by the diaspora, see Esnan, Milton, J., 'Diasporas and International Relations' in Sheffer Gabriel (ed), 1986 op.cit. For intra and inter ethnic conflicts and the role of religion and caste and local sentiments thereof read Chandrasekhar Bhat's views in Frontline November 6,1999, and NRIOL .com Special Feature, December 2002.

19. This may have something to do with the 'diverse' nature of the Indian Diaspora too. It is constituted of such diverse elements as South Asian Hong Kong Muslims, Punjabi Mexican Californians, Gujarati East Africans, South African Hindis, and so forth. When in clusters, these Indians look apart and become targets of racial attacks. Recall that the

native dress and symbols like turbans, kirpans etc cam e up for public scrutiny and discussions in some countries recently. Therefore, "who is an Indian" is a relevant question and any discussion on 'Indian-ness' needs open-ness.

20. For instance, the diaspora has little or no control over decision-making, and domestic outcomes – in short their room to man(oeuvre) and capacity to 'govern' – are still restricted over a narrower terrain. Moreover, like everybody else, diasporic Indians are also caught in the dilemma of "price or plan mechanism" of decision-making and development. Can everything be left to the market? Is the state able to keep market stable? Some feel that markets too need adult supervision and that the danger of privatisation is privatisation of everything and the possible rise of 'Gangster Capitalism'. See Sainath: 2004.

21. All is not well for the Indians in foreign countries. For example, while the Indian American is rarely found without a job, the number of American women in the labour force is smaller than comparable White or American women. White are 70 per cent and Indian American are 58 per cent. The question raised here is: is not globalisation perpetuating or even extending gender segregation of work and thus marginalising the female population and preventing them from joining the mainstream? (Shanthi: 2005). About 12 per cent of Indian Americans live below the poverty line. So there is a poverty line in America too!+

References

Alamgir, Jalal. 2003. 'Managing open-ness in India: the social construction of a globalist narrative' in Linda Weiss (ed.). 2003, *States in the Global Economy- Bringing domestic institutions* back *in*, Cambridge: University Press, pp.225-244.

Bhat, Chandrasekhar, and Ajaya Kumar Sahoo (2003), 'Diaspora to Translational Networks: The Case of Indians in Canada', Occasional Paper 7, Retrieved February 14, 2005) from http://www.uohyd.ernet.in

Bolcskei, Gustav (Bp) et.al., (2005 March) 'The Economic and Social Witness of Calvin for Christian Life Today', *Reformed World*, 55 (1):3-8.

Correia, Eugene, 1999 'With roots in India' *Frontline*, November, 16 (23): 1-29.

Dasgupta, Ishani (2003 August25) 'India again big in the Silicon Valley' http.//www.indianchambers.com (Visited 2005 February 14).

Hans, V.B., 'Indian Diaspora in the Globalisation Era: Avenue for New Dialogues in Development', Paper presented to the International Conference "Indian Diaspora: Trends, Issues and Challenges", 24-26 February 2005, Centre for Study of Indian Diaspora, University of Hyderabad, Hyderabad [Session IX, Indian Diaspora and Policy Dialogue]:1-12.

Hufbauer, Gary Clyde and Paul L.E. Grieco (2005, December), *The Payoff from Globalisation.* www.iie.com/publications/papers/haufbauer0505.htm (Visited 2005 January 6).

Indolink (December (29, 2005), 'Global NRI Conference Starts on Jan 6' http://www.indolink.com (Visited 2005 December, 30)

Kalyani, Shankar (2003 January) *WelcomeHome.* http://pib.nic.in/feature/feyr2003/fjan2003/fo80/2003/htm (Visited 2005 December30).

Kiranmayi, B., 'Understanding Transnational Identity through Consumption: Issues and Methodologies' Paper presented to the International Conference "Indian Diaspora: Trends, Issues and Challenges", 24-26 February 2005, Centre for Study of Indian Diaspora, University of Hyderabad, Hyderabad [Session V, Indian Diaspora and Translational Networks]: 1-14.

Lai, Chung-Hsiung, Winter 2002, 'Encountering the Cultural Aporia: Multiculturalism as a Global/Local Nexus' *Journal of Contemporary Thought* 16 (Special Number): 63-81.

Laxmi Narayan, K. (2005), 'Indian Diaspora: A Demographic Perspective' Occasional Paper 3. Retrieved on February 14, 2005 from http://www.uohyd.ernet.in

Mitra, Subrata K., Alexander Fischer and Lavanya Regunathan-Fischer, 'Who is an Indian? Territory, Community and Citizenship in the Indian Constitution', paper for delivery at the International Conference "Indian Diaspora: Trends, Issues and Challenges", 24-26 February 2005, Centre for Study of Indian Diaspora, University of Hyderabad, Hyderabad: 1-12.

Nath, Kamal, (2005 December), 'India: The New Paradigm' (speech) http://www.indiaday.org/speeches/html (Visited 2005 December 30).

Sainath, P (2004) 'The globalisation of Inequality' Seminar 533 (1), pp.79-84.

Shanthi, K (2005), 'Indian Diaspora in the Unite States of America: With Specific Reference to Changing Labour Market Dynamics' Paper presented to the International Conference "Indian Diaspora: Trends, Issues and Challenges", 24-26 February 2005, Centre for Study of Indian Diaspora, University of Hyderabad, Hyderabad [Session: IV: Indian Diaspora: Old and New].

Sheffer Gabriel (ed.) (1986) *Modern Diasporas in International Politics*, Kent: Croom Helm Ltd., pp.1-15.

Swank, Duane, (2003) 'Withering welfare? Globalisation, political economic institutions, and contemporary welfare states', in Linda Weiss (ed.), op.cit. pp.58-82.

Weiss, Linda 'Introduction: bringing domestic institutions back in' Linda Weiss (ed.), *op.cit.* pp.1-33.

Wikipedia (2005, December17) 'Non-resident Indian and Person of Indian Origin' http://www.en.wikipedia.org/wiki/Indian_diaspora.html (Visited2005 December30).

Table-1
Non-Resident Indians - a numerical glimpse

Territory	NRI Population
Asia	6,716,000
Middle East	2,990,000
Africa	4,421,000
Europe	207,500
North America	326,500
Latin America	502,000
Oceania	580,000

Note: Figures are approximation of NRI population in the given territories.

Source: http://en.wikipedia.org/wiki/Non-resident_Indian_and_Person_ of_Indian_Origin

Table-2
Trends in International Migration

Number of Migrants (in millions)	*Period*		
	1960	*1990*	*2000*
World	75.9	154.0	174.9
Developed Countries (excluding USSR)	32.1	89.7	110.3
Developing Countries	43.8	64.3	64.6
Asia	29.3	41.8	43.8
Europe	14.2	26.3	32.8
USSR (former)	2.9	14.0	29.5

Note: Figures are for selective for territories and years
Source: 'Trends in total Migration Stock: The 2003 Revision', in World Economic and Social Survey, 2004 – International Migration, Dept. of Economic and Social Affairs, UN, New York, 2004.

11

The Rise and Growth of the Indian Communities in Trinidad

Mukesh Kumar

Migration is accepted as a global phenomenon. It is defined as the physical transition of an individual or a group from one society to another. The impulse for this transition varies according to the situation, but one thing is clear that, it involves abandoning of one social setting and entering the other, and a different one which more often adopts a hostile and an apathetic attitude towards these new social players. Many factors have been instrumental for such movements. The 17th and 18 th centuries witnessed a new dimension in the European Imperialism and far off places were brought under direct – indirect influences. The Caribbean was one of these areas which were later developed for sugar plantation. African slaves were brought in and the Atlantic Slave Trade flourished. Abolition of slavery and subsequent emancipation of the slaves created a vacuum in the plantation whose existence was threatened due to shortage of labour. The Colonial economic compulsion decided the fate of thousands of Indians who were sent to the Caribbean States for the sake of sugar plantation.

A new system was devised to replace the slave trade and legal contracts were signed in a language alien to the Indians. The terms and conditions of the nature and the place of work were hardly known to them. They had also no idea about the journey and the destination. The "coolie cargo" started in 1845 when Trinidad, British Guyana and Jamaica received their share of cheap and docile labourers from India. The system remained operational till 1917 when due to various factors the Colonial govt. put an end to the practice. In Trinidad Indians were imported on a large scale and even today they are present in a considerable number in the Trinidadian population. There are around 500,000 Indians[1] in Trinidad constituting around 40 per cent of the total population. The European imperialist expansion had thus created conditions for large scale migration from all over the world for the plantation works in the Caribbean. As a result race, colour, culture, ethnicity and class have been intertwined in complex ways in the Caribbean society. The presence of these factors resulted in sharp contrast of culture, status and social organization among the different categories of population has initiated the study of race relations.

The present paper seeks to analyze the existence and growth of a mobile and dynamic nation that took place in a far off space particularly when it had lost touch with their place of origin. It examines the cultural divides in the historical perspective along with the Colonial practices which abetted the suspicion, fear and hatred towards each other. Traditionally different communities exhibited different socio-economic orientations and it was the economic rivalry that lay mainly at the roots of the racial problems and brought into play the colour bar in social and political relations. Locating this micro-study of Caribbean race relations within the context of Indian-Black relations in a plural colonial society, the paper highlights the historical foundation of racial antagonism in the region in order to explore and analyze the various possible ways to effect the construction of mutual trust and social harmony among the different cultural groups for providing tools for making of a multi-cultural society in the Caribbean.

A migrant is a stranger unacquainted with the ways of the receiving group and unknown to its members. Indians were a special kind of strangers who had migrated from one large social group into another with the active support of the government. At the time of their arrival, they found themselves in a bewildering state of strangeness and ignorance with regard to the socio-cultural outlook of the receiving society. The plantations hardly allowed them to mix with the Black people nor was there any attempt from the Indian side to socialize with them as the Indians viewed the Blacks as impure by the Indian standard. The Blacks, on the other hand, right from the beginning cursed them for their (Blacks') economic woes.

In the Caribbean society importation of indentured Indians perpetuated anachronistic economic and social structures and created a class of sub-citizens whose civil liberties, economic security and human rights were tenuous.[2] Though the system was of a legal nature, the migrants were thrown at the mercy of the old Colonial guards who treated them as the bonded labourers. The planters wanted more and more output and cared little for their welfare. They always wanted Indians as the indentured labourers and not as free men.[3] Rather they kept close vigil on their movement which was a punishable crime without a valid pass – *livrate.* An Indian was required to possess a certificate of his working under the indenture system in the plantation or working as a free person after the completion of his indenture period.

Indians were segregated in the Trinidadian society for the immediate benefits of the planters. The managers wished to get the labour force ready for work and therefore kept them tied with a number of rules and regulations.[4] After the end of the indenture period they were offered money or land or both money and land in lieu of the sanction of their repatriation to India. Most of the Indians thought it wise after living there for so many years to acquire land and to start a definite life there. It was beneficial for the planters to keep an acclimatized work force adjacent to the plantations because mostly the nearby less fertile land were allotted to the Indians. However this did not end the legal control because they had to show the discharge document at any time both in public and private places. Naturally they found themselves in a micro minority and were harassed by the Whites and the Blacks alike.

The Blacks thought Indians as inferior creatures who had accepted what nobody had agreed to do and that too for very low wages, and thus they had further downed the dignity of labour. The ambivalence of the receiving countries towards labour migration is built upon a foundation of economic gain and social tension. It has raised fears among indigenous workers of depressed wages, higher unemployment, and deteriorating working conditions. Migrant who belong to racial, ethnic, or linguistic groups that are different from the indigenous population became easy targets of discrimination, hostility, or even violence.[5]

Indians were anxious to make themselves economically independent and this opportunity came with the allotment of swamp land. They cultivated rice on the piece of land that was hitherto considered useless by the planters and was sold to them. But after the abolition of the indenture system in 1917 the planters again feared the labour - crisis and the price of the swamp land was at once doubled that of the good land. As early as in 1914 the McNeill and Chiman Lal Committee Report had made it clear that some impediments were made for the Indians in acquiring the land. To start with the Indians were at first concentrated in the rural areas. Gradually they moved towards the urban settings and worked as petty traders, hawkers, milk-men, vegetable –sellers, shop-keepers etc.[6]

The Blacks had a bitter experience in the plantations and had refused to work there after their emancipation. So they viewed the Indians with much contempt for accepting this work and lowering the wages. In their eyes Indians were the meanest creatures living in the world with the minimum income. The Indians were termed as an inferior human species who would accept conditions of life that other races would reject.[7] The Blacks also did not like the general Indian mentality of thrift and acquiring land after the termination of the indenture period. For an Indian acquiring a piece of land and owning a business was a great thing which provided him/her the feeling of security and pride. They had left their country with the determination and then making something definite from zero was a great feeling for them. The Blacks resented Indians' prosperity in what they thought to be Blacks' socio–economic space and attributed Indian success to "coolie deviousness". They also feared being deprived of the little they had. They charged the Indians of helping in the furtherance of the "White Power Structure" and creating assets out of these. On the other hand for an Indian, "The Negro is too interested in feting: dancing, carnival, and expensive clothes........(to) know how to save money."[8] Indians believe no Black would scruple to steal. 'The Niggers sleep during the day and at night they walk around and steal. Stealing and killing – that's their work.' The clash in their attitudes resulted in many attacks on Indians business establishments during the Black Power Movement in 1970.[9]

> These people have done considerable damage to business property owned by Indians....... These wanton and lawless acts do not show that the Black Power Movement has any sympathy, brotherliness or incorporation with the Indians of this country, as it pretends to profess.[10]

All these activities were centred around the joint family system which remained the pivot of the Indian culture and tradition. However in a distant land they had to compromise in the face of proselytizing efforts of the Canadian Presbyterian missionary. The missionary started its work in Trinidad in 1868 and from there it was extended to Grenada in 1884, St. Lucia and British Guyana in 1885 and to Jamaica in 1894.[11] Indians were considered as recalcitrant and were unyielding to accept the Christianity because they had been successful in maintaining their religion and were proud of a rich and vibrant culture at the place of their origin. The missionary did not find it smooth while working among the Indians in comparison to the Blacks.[12] The Blacks were transported to the Caribbean from Africa during the period of slave trade. They were physically as well as culturally uprooted from their place of origin and were subjected to severe inhumane practices. In the process they had lost any memory whatsoever was of their culture. After their emancipation as there was nothing reminiscent of their origin and they were ashamed of even at the mention of their African connections, they started to imitate their Colonial masters. The process of westernization among the Blacks was so intense that once C.L.R. James remarked that, "West Indian uniqueness consists in this, that of all of these hundreds of millions of formerly colonial coloured peoples, West Indians are the only ones who are completely westernized, they have no native language, no native religion, no native way of life.[13] It was only during the *Black Power Movement* that they vehemently adored and glorified their African origin.[14] The indentured Indians, on the other hand, had moved away from their country with just one thing – their strong conviction in their culture and tradition. However in the outset under the unfavourable circumstances they were not comfortable in observing their socio–religious practices. They used to find whatever little time was there to keep their culture vibrating. The Blacks ridiculed the Indian socio–cultural and religious practices which they found quite strange and un-Catholic. Under the force of westernization the Blacks viewed the Indian customs with much contempt. They considered Indian way of life primitive, their food unhealthy, their family system nasty, and every sugar-cane worker a criminal.[15] The Colonial Government was also not sympathetic towards the Indian culture and the first cremation ceremony on one single personal application for permission was reformed as late as on 24th Sept. 1940.[16] The Govt. did not recognize the Indian marriage – bamboo marriage, until the enactment of an Indian Marriage and Divorce Bill in 1946.[17] These socio–psychological pressures forced the Indians to consider themselves quite exclusive in the society.

Indians were not averse to the process of westernization and the well-to-do families mostly in the urban and semi-urban areas are becoming more and more westernized, but not at the cost of the Indian value system. For them westernization does not mean acceptance of the

'Creole' way of life. Morton Klass observes, "Among rural Hindu East Indians the creolized individual is rare to the point of non-existence, traits and values deriving from India take precedence over those deriving from the non-Indian environment"[18] Indians insisted that they are not adopting the Negro way of life: though they are becoming westernized, they are different from the Negroes.[19] They remained separate because they have little in common with the Negro people.[20] The Africans also know that the Indians are not going to give up their culture as they are satisfied with their culture. Heightened by isolation, ignorance, and fear, these differences have endangered negative, persistent, and inclusive group stereotypes.[21]

The Indians introduced in an alien society, were not allowed to socialize with the general people by the Colonial Masters and were kept under the strict conditions of the slavery period. As a common practice where Indians were, Creole departed. In Trinidad the society is divided on the racial lines which developed as a plural society with the Blacks and the Indians as the two major players. Indians were generally the agriculturalists while the blacks preferred oil-fields and government and other white collar jobs in the cities. Indian have always been under–represented[22] in civil services, police force and other professions during the Colonial rule because they were first of all concerned about their economic stability and their rise as independent workers.[23] They kept themselves away from the western education due to fear of conversion to the Christianity. The government and the planters did not want to lose their plantation labour and deliberately neglected Indians' education.[24] But education is always considered as the major factor in the social, cultural, economic or political empowerment of a society. Everywhere it has served as the principal pathway to power and in Trinidad the Indians wished to secure state's support to establish their own schools in response to a growing rise in ethnic consciousness in the thirties. But these efforts were frustrated by the plantocracy, the Colonial authorities and the Creole Christian establishment which wished to preserve their own dominance.[25] The Indian move for the denominational schools was hailed as divisive for the Trinidadian society.[26] The Indian quest for the spread of education among them was resented because the Blacks feared them of grabbing the economic as well as the political power which would adversely affect the interest of the Blacks.

> ...the linkage of a major political party to a Hindu religious body which had been a prime mover in the education movement caused a multiple alarm reaction across the country. The alarm was racial, religious, political, social and economic. Indians, largely of non-Christian background, were visualized as capable of attaining political power. Some renowned racialists were heard to say, 'these Indians came to Trinidad with job assured and the promise of land, usurping the rights of the Negroes as they emerged from slavery. Now they are educating themselves fast, fast and organizing themselves politically fast, fast. They are much too fast. We must contain them...[27]

However, from 1950 onwards steps were taken to establish these schools in the Indian localities. At one place this helped in the survival and continuation of their religious beliefs and traditions. Assimilation into the national curriculum has created entry for Indians into the professions and positions of leadership in the wider society.[28]

Nehru's advice of 1950 to Indians to get settled in the countries of their adoption and not to consider themselves Indians baffled them, and this spurred the process of their Creolization. Education provided them the much needed social mobility and they aspired to civil-service and white-collar jobs once exclusively held by the Creoles. Through their demand for equality in civil-service employment Indians lay claim not only for jobs but also to status and power hitherto denied to them. The Blacks resisted Indian demand for civil-service entry on a proportional basis. In Trinidad Indians were also discriminated in police force where deliberate favouritism apart from the minimum criteria of height and girth, and bachelor-hood ousted automatically them.[29] The civil services, both at home and abroad, are staffed with the Blacks[30] who placed in the senior positions in civil services deliberately make the admission of Indians difficult.[31] Entry into these fields being restricted, the numerically sound Indians could very well adhere to themselves on the ethnic lines. Ethnicity helped them in organizing themselves in a powerful way to make their presence felt at every walk of life. Indians now aspired to be a part of the policy making body and tried to enter the politics in a big way. This was thought as the only way to ensure them a definite footing in the socio-political space of the island.

Many overseas Indians complain against the Nehruvian policy which denied them moral and material support of the motherland in the period of crisis when they were marginalized in the Trinidadian society. But it is true that India was not in a position to intervene in their affairs and it would not have been fruitful for them. Even today Indian intervention is not possible in Fiji or British Guyana where the Indians had to suffer a lot under the racial assaults.

In Trinidad a rich Indian businessman Bhadase Sagan Maraj started organizing Indians on the religious line with the formation of Sanatan Dharma Maha Sabha in 1952 and in 1953 launched the People's Democratic Party (P.D.P.).[32] He was the leader of All Trinidad Sugar Estates and Factories Workers Trade Union whose membership included virtually all the Indian sugar workers. In Trinidad, the colonial Office had conceded a considerable measure of self–government whereby the functions of the government would be transferred to a Chief Minister who must have the confidence of the legislature.[33] At this time Eric Williams had made his entry and in the election of 1956 made a populist appeal to all the have–not Trinidadians to vote for his party, the People's National Movement (P.N.M.) and won a clear majority. The trend of result showed that the P.N.M. got massive support from the predominantly Black population but it could not manage to win support in the rural areas where Indians were in majority. Trinidad suffered under the leadership of Williams as its Chief Minister whose administration was based on the racialism and its development. He brought the civil-service, police, education, press, business etc under strict control.[34] The opposition then united to form the Democratic Labour Party (D.L.P.) to challenge him and in the election of 1958 for the Federal Legislature, the D.L.P. captured six seats while the P.N.M. bagged four.[35] This infuriated Eric and he publicly denounced them as a "hostile and recalcitrant minority."[36] Williams declared the Indians as the greatest danger facing the country and thought them as the impediment to West Indian progress.[37] He aroused racial feeling talking about the danger of Indian takeover and managed the constituencies in order to keep Indians in minority in those areas. He denounced the new DLP leader Dr. R.N. Capildeo's pretensions to be the 'Coolie Prime Minister'.[38]

In the General Election of 1961 the PNM captured thirty seats and the rest ten seats were won by the DLP. The PNM put forward the demand for independence before the Colonial Office. While the DLP maintained a multi-racial stance at the conference, the Indian Association demanded for election on proportional representation system and parity in civil-service and police recruitment. Trinidad achieved independence in August 1962, but the Indians' demands were not entertained. The predominantly Black-led PNM party remained in power for over three decades since the attainment of the independence. In this phase Indians focused mainly on trade and commerce and worked hard to achieve full incorporation in Trinidadian society in order to overcome the much abused notion of '*never trust a coolie*'. They resented the Blacks' 'habit of looking at Trinidadians of Indian origin as Indians and not as Trinidadians............. When a Negro does or says something, he is a Trinidadian, or a West Indian. When an Indian does or says something, he is an Indian. .... 'Bread is no more West Indian than Roti is. Cricket is no more West Indian than hockey is. And James [C.L.R.] is no more West Indian than Bhadase Maraj is.'[39] For the Indians integration should be a two way path and it should not be forced upon them. They want integration but do not conform to the idea of assimilation to the point where their identity is at stake.

Though the access to state resources and state patronage at the disposal of a Black-dominated party such as the PNM for such a long period have conferred an enormous electoral advantage on the latter, there has been a definite change in the consciousness of the Indo-Trinidadians as well as in the general attitude towards Indians. Over the years the Indians held many significant state office e.g. that of President, Chief Justice, the Speaker (three times), the President of the Senate, senior cabinet posts, Deputy Political Leader. Their workings and commitment were rewarded and the United National Congress, a party formed in Oct. 1988 by an Indo-Trinidadian Basdeo Panday came to power on the Nov. 7th 1995. However, until 1995 even in Trinidad and Tobago a government headed by an Indian was a taboo topic to be discussed in the conferences because 'it could have led to rivers of blood flowing throughout Trinidad'.[40] Indian dominance in the middle levels of bureaucracy and in the professions was already evident.[41] They proved to be one of the most prosperous and organized ethnic groups and emerged as a secular acceptable identity at the international level. As the globalization has reduced the territorial rigidity, multiple loyalties are now accepted and thus, the Indians tasted the success. From the shadow of a sub-ordinate group and a powerless faction, Indians have come up to enjoy equal rights.

Under the able administration of Basdeo Panday not only the under-representation of Indians in the white collar jobs has been corrected but the relationship between the Indians and the Blacks has also undergone a remarkable change. Interaction between them was always decided on the ethnic lines. In Trinidad Indianness requires the reiteration of Indian ancestral glories and Blacks bolster their African roots. This ethnicity scarcely replaces the general yearning for the things European, but the cloak of ethnic equality validates acerbities of colour in the 1970s.[42] But the triumph of the Indians in the election of 1995 necessarily highlights the change in attitude and emphasizes the need to treat all these cultural pockets as the integral parts of the Trinidadian society whose prosperity lies in the total participation of its peoples. The participation of a minority group certainly enriches public discourse while simultaneously bringing groups that are otherwise marginalized into the mainstream. It will be a powerful tool for defining public norms and creating deliberative consensus to achieve proper assimilation of an immigrant group in the host society. This social system offers freedom of choice to those who want to be carefully different in one or several aspects, such as religious or political beliefs, occupation and ethnic identity. Under this system of multiculturalism, various communities have opportunity to participate in the political process, set agendas and voice their specific point of view. Different groups and subgroups coexist side by side with mutual respect, allowing the necessary acculturation and integration to occur at a natural and spontaneous rate. However, at the same time, all groups are consciously members of the same single, large comprehensive socio-cultural group, the society, which also constitute the political nation. This provides us with the much-needed socio-political prescription in the present era of globalization. A multicultural structure would foster better social tolerance towards minorities, make them more visible and thereby ease ethnic and religious tensions and conflicts.

Notes

1. *Report of the High Level Committee on the Indian Diaspora*, Govt. of India, New Delhi, 2002, p. 1.
2. Tinker, Hugh, *A New System of Slavery*, Oxford University Press, Oxford, 1974.; Saha, P., *Emigration of Indian Labour (1834-1900)*, People's Publishing House, New Delhi, 1970.; Gangulee, N., *Indians in the Empire Overseas*, The New India Publishing House Limited, London, 1947.
3. Kondapi, C, *Indian Overseas (1838-1949)*, ICWA, New Delhi, 1951, p.7.
4.. Tinker, Hugh, *A New System of Slavery*, op. cit.

5. Newland, Kathleen, *International Migration: The Search For Work*, Worldwatch Paper 33, Nov. 1979, pp.18-19.
6. Singh, Kelvin, "East Indians and the Larger Society", in La Guerre, J.G. ed. *Calcutta to Caroni: The East Indians of Trinidad*, Longman Caribbean, Trinidad, 1974, p. 43.
7. *Ibid.*
8. Klass, Morton, *East Indians in Trinidad: A Study of Cultural Persistence*, Columbia University Press, New York, 1961, p. 244.
9. Maharaj, Grace, 'To The Black People in T'dad', *Embryo*. Vol.2, No.19, 24 March 1970, p.9. See also Nicholls, David G., East Indians and Black Power in Trinidad, *Race*, XII, 4(1971), pp.443-460.
10. *Trinidad Guardian*. 08 March.1970.
11. Grant, K. J., *My Missionary Memories*, The Imperial Publishing Co., Halifax, 1923;Samroo, B., "Missionary Methods and Local responses : The Canadian Presbyterians and the East Indians in the Caribbean", in Bridget Brereton and Winston Dookeran edrs., "*East Indians in the Caribbean : Colonialism and the Struggle for Identity*", Kraus International Publications, New York, 1982, pp.93-116; Steele, Beverley A., "East Indian Indenture and the work of the Presbyterian Church among Indians in Grenada", *Caribbean Quarterly*, Vol. 22, No. 1, March 1976, p.31.
12. The real difference between Indian immigration and the others was a cultural one. The practices and aloof obstinacy of the Hindus were thought to be a sad example to the Creoles. Wood, Donald, *Trinidad in Transition*, Oxford University Press, Oxford, 1968, p.110.
13. James, C.L.R., *Federarion: 'We Failed Miserably' How and Why*, Tunapuna, Trinidad, 1960, p.2.
14. Nicholls, David G., "East Indians and Black Power in Trinidad", *Race*, XII, 4(1971), pp.477-494.
15. Klass, Sheila Soloman, *Everyone in this House Makes Babies*, Doubleday, Garden City, New York, 1964, pp. 128-29.

16. Kondapi, C., *Indian Overseas (1838-1949)*, op. cit. p.383.

17. Ibid, p.372.

18. Klass, Mortan, "East and West Indians: Cultural Complexity in Trinidad", *Annals of the New York Academy of Science*, Vol. 83, Jan.1960, p. 858.

19. Malik, Yogendra K., *East Indians in Trinidad: A Study in Minority Politics*, Oxford University Press, Oxford, 1971, p.10.

20. Jagessar, Ramdath, 'Indian Iceberg', *Tapia*, No. 3, 16 Nov. 1969, p.7.

21. Lowenthal, David, *West Indian Societies*, University Press, Oxford, 1972, p.156.

22. There are only nine Indian Justices of Peace out of about 230 for the whole island and I understand that there is no Indian Justice of Peace in such areas as San Fernando, Chaguanas, Penal, Siparia, Cedros, and La Baria. It is difficult to believe that there is no suitable Indian gentleman in those areas." Tyson, J.D., *Memorandum of Evidence for the Royal Commission to the West Indies*, Port of Spain, 1939, p.41.

23. Grant, K.J., *My Missionary Memories*, op. cit., p.82; Morton Sarah E., *John Morton of Trinidad*, Westminster Co., Toronto, 1916, pp. 41-2.

24. Kirpalani, Murali J., *Indian Centenary Review*, Guardian Commercial Printery, 1945, p.54.

25. Ryan, Selwyn, *Race and Nationalism in Trinidad and Tobago*, University of Toronto Press, Toronto. 1972.;Mohammed, Carl, "Indian Education in Trinidad", in *Celebration of 150 Years of the Indian Contribution to Trinidad and Tobago*, ed. Brinsley Samaroo et al, Cariflex Ltd., Trinidad and Tobago, 1995.p.43.

26. Ryan, Selwyn, *Race and Nationalism in Trinidad and Tobago*, University of Toronto Press, Toronto. 1972, p.123.

27. Mahabir, Winston, "Our Diasporas: Sowers and Seed", in I.J. Bahadur Singh, ed., *Indians in The Caribbean*", Sterling Publishers Ltd., New Delhi, p.75.

28. Mohammed, Carl, "Indian Education in Trinidad", in *Celebration of 150 Years of the Indian Contribution to Trinidad and Tobago*, ed. Brinsley Samaroo et al, Cariflex Ltd., Trinidad and Tobago, 1995.p.95.
29. Collins, B.A.N.,"Racial Imbalance in Public Service and Security Forces", *Race*, Vol.VII, 1965-66, pp.235-53.
30. Gomes,Albert, "Race and Independence in Trinidad", *New Society*, 27 Aug. 1964, p.16.
31. Niehoff, Arthur and Juanita, *East Indians in the West Indies*, Milwaukee Public Museum Publications in Anthropology, 1960, p.52.
32. Tinker, Hugh, *The Banyan Tree*, Oxford University Press, Oxford, p.63.
33. Ibid.
34. Ibid.; Malik, Yogendra K., *East Indians in Trinidad : A Study in Minority Politics*. op. cit.
35. Ibid.
36. Mahabir, Winston, *In And Out of Politics*, Inprint Caribbean Limited, Trinidad, 1978.
37. Ibid.
38. Tinker, Hugh, *The Banyan Tree*, op. cit. p. 65.
39. Singh, H.P., *The Indian Enigma*, Port of Spain, Trinidad, 1964, pp.11-14.
40. Papers presented at the conference, *Celebration of 150 Years of the Indian Contribution to Trinidad and Tobago*, op. cit.; Dubey, Ajay, "Indian Diaspora in the Caribbean and Africa : Identity Issues and Responses of India", in Dubey, Ajay, ed. *Indian Diaspora: Global Identity*, Kalinga Publications, Delhi, 2003, p.123.
41. Ryan, Selwyn, *Pathway To Power :Indians and the Politics of National Unity in Trinidad and Tobago,* Caribbean Paper and Printed Products 1993 Limited, San Juan, Trinidad, 1996, p. XXXIII.
42. Lowenthal, David, *West Indian Societies*, op. cit. p.177.

12

The Strategic Framework for Engaging India with Indian Diaspora

Jeetendra D. Soni
and
Surendra D. Soni

Introduction

Migration is an old age process of human civilization. People move from one part of the globe to another due to various reasons. These migratory movements can be the result of changing climatic scenario, differential economic opportunities, political turmoil and civil war, for better standard of living and other push and pull factors working at the places of origin and destination. Indians also moved in the different parts of globe in almost all directions. In the last two centuries this movement was much bigger and its speed and spread was wider than the previous experience. If the people retain the sense of affection and belongingness to their homeland along with such types of international movement than it gives birth to the diasporic community. In the similar manner evolution of Indian Diaspora has taken place.

The Indian diaspora is one of the *oldest diaspora* in the world. It is the *third largest* diasporic community (20 million), spread in more than110 countries of the world. In many parts of the world, Indian community has become an *influential minority*, one that is known for their professional accomplishments as IT professionals and entrepreneurial skills as big businessmen and seen as well-educated and well-earning group.

In India, Indian diaspora are *important development agents*. This community is acting as catalyst in the process of strengthening India's bilateral relations with many countries where they are residing.

In the long run this segment of the Indian family would play a vital role not merely on *economic front* but in activities related to *cultural dimension*, on *diplomatic side* in strengthening Indian ties with foreign nations and in enhancing the prestige of India at the global scale. Their role in above stated manner depends on the *nature of contact* between diasporic community and state.

India has its current interest in the overseas Indians in *two ways*. Firstly for *older diaspora* India's interest is primarily cultural, patchy and patronizing. Secondly for *recent migrants* to the West, its interest is largely economic and political with the intention of attracting their capital and skills.

Indian Diaspora

The term *diaspora* is of Greek origin. It referred originally, to the Jews. It is now commonly used in a generic sense for communities of migrants living or settled permanently in other countries, aware of its origin and identity and maintaining varying degrees of linkages with the mother country (*L.M. Singhvi Report, 2001*). It is in this sense that the term "Diaspora" is used to refer to Indians who migrated to different parts of the world and have generally maintained their Indian identity.

The term "Indian diaspora" includes in its ambit both non-resident Indians (NRIs) and persons of Indian origin (PIOs). Where as

Non-resident Indian refers to

A citizen of India, who has, at any time after the 25th March, 1947 being staying in India but who has gone out of, or stays outside India in either case:

(a) For or on taking up employment outside India, or

(b) For carrying on outside India a circumstances as would indicate his intention to stay outside India for an uncertain period business or a vocation outside India, or

(c) For any other purpose in such circumstances as would indicate his intention to stay outside India for a uncertain period.

Person of Indian Origin refers to

A 'person of Indian origin' means a foreign citizen not being a citizen of Pakistan, Bangladesh and other countries as may be specified by the Central Government time to time if.

(i) He/she at any time held Indian passport, or

(ii) He/she or either of his/her parents or any of his grand parents or great grant parents was born in and permanently resident in India as defined in the Government of India Act, 1935 and other territories that became part of India thereafter provided neither was at any time a citizen of any of aforesaid countries, or

(iii) He/she is a spouse of a citizen of India or a person of Indian Origin covered under (i) or (ii) above.

EVOLUTION OF INDIAN DIASPORA

The *Buddhist monks* migrated to Sri Lanka, South East Asia and East Asian parts of the globe for the cause *of preaching and propagation of their religion since the 5th Century.*

During the classical age (from 320 to 740 A.D.) of the Gupta period trading community flourished and trade relations were established with many foreign countries in Central Asia and East and South East Asia as well as with the Roman Empire.

During the *colonial era* large scale migration took place in the form of *indenture labourers, under kangani and maistry system and through free and passage emigration.*

Indenture labourers migration: "Indenture was a contract by which the emigrants were bound to work for a given employer for a 3-5 year term, performing the task assigned to him for a specified wage. At the end of the contract, the labourer was free to reindenture. After ten years, he was entitled to a subsidized return passage (Prakash C. Jain, 1993).

Indenture labourers (after the abolition of slavery in the colonies in 1833-34) - to colonies such as Mauritius, South Africa, Fiji, Malaysia, Guyana, Trinidad and Tobago, Surinam and Sri Lanka. From Chotanagpur region, West Bengal - Hindi speaking zones of Bihar and Eastern U.P. - Tamil and Telugu speaking people. This however officially ended in 1920.

The Kangani and the Maistry System: Under this system, a Kangani, (himself an Indian emigrant) used to recruit the coolies in India paying them in advance for expenses. The Maistry system was also similar to the Kangani system except that the Maistry system was characterized by a gradation of middle man- employers and the innumerable illegal deductions" (Prakash C. Jain, 1993).

The South Indian labourers (Tamil speaking Hindus) were supplied through Kangani system to Malaysia and Sri Lanka and under Maistry system to Burma. The Kangani system was abolished in 1938 after more than a century.

Free or Passage Emigration: It includes emigration of trading castes and classes within the British Empire. It was predominant in South Africa and East African countries like Kenya, Tanzania and Uganda. Most of the emigrants to East African countries were Gujaratis and Punjabis.

The workers who emigrated from India during colonial period were largely uneducated and were from depressed and backward classes both socially and economically. Most of them were Hindus. They all preserved their social, cultural, religious and ethnic identities. They were divided on the lines of caste and class and because of this did not have much political strength to bargain on issues related to them.

Brain Drain: From the late 1960s a strong wave of well-educated and professionally competent immigrants from India, started towards the industrially advanced countries of Western Europe and North America and recently in the countries like Australia and New Zealand. It was totally voluntary in nature. This stream was pioneered by Sikhs. The individuals who are migrating to these advanced countries representing to educational and professional expertise.

Labour immigration to West Asia: The oil boom of 1970s had created acute labour shortage in this region. A perceptible growth in the construction sector and other social and economic infrastructure developments had created a huge demand for professional, skilled, semi skilled and unskilled workers. About 3 million Indians are present in this region with more than half from Kerala (Prakash C. Jain, 1993).

Governmental Efforts

In the recent years the Indian attitude towards oversees Indians have undergone important changes because of two primary reasons. *Firstly,* the overseas Indian community is neglected for long. They struggled to improve their miserable conditions with their hard work and entrepreneurial skills and still retain their cultural identity. So for the recognition of their struggles and achievements Indian authorities realize a desire to reciprocate. *Secondly,* in the recent past they have made sizeable contribution in various Special Borrowing Schemes and sent good amount of remittances to their homeland.

In March 1999, Government of India launched *Persons of Indian Origin (PIO) card scheme* for all PIOs up to the fourth generation. This scheme was further rationalised recently with lowering of fee charges, simplifying the process and they are thinking about the extension of this beyond forth generation.

Realising the constructive economic, diplomatic and philanthropic role played by the Indian Diaspora, the Government of India set up a *High Level Commission* headed by, notable jurist and Indian former High Commission to U. K., Dr. L. M. Singhivi in 2000 in this regard. For the recognition and appreciation of the work of Indian Diaspora the committee recommended.

- *Pravasi Bhartiya Divas* should be held on 9th January every year. On this line Pravasi Bhartiya Divas is being organized from 2002 every year.

- *Dual Citizenship* for Indian Diaspora towards forging a broader relationship with PIO's, both emotionally and economically. In this regard the Government of India issued Overseas Indian Citizenship to two PIOs on 9th Jan. 2006 during 4th Pravasi Bhartiya Divas in Hyderabad. This step will help transnational Indians in forming better linkages with their home land.

On May 27th 2004, government of India has established a separate Ministry, *Ministry of Overseas Indian Affairs.* This Ministry is looking after the issues related to admission of Non-Resident Indians and Persons of Indian Origin to educational and cultural institutions, scholarships to NRIs and PIOs under different schemes, organization of Pravasi Bhartiya Divas, coordination with the State Governments on matters related to Overseas Indians and many other areas related to diasporic community.

Today government is giving thought to extend voting rights to them. The government is also working on modalities to establishing a separate university for diasporic youth and large scale exchange programs for strengthening links with young Indian diaspora. In this process of engaging diasporic community in the developmental scheme following multilevel strategy can be helpful.

Strategic Framework

According to R.R Ramchandani (2001), with the changing map of international power equation and international production relations after the end of the era of cold war, it is the time to evaluate the whole set of NRI and PIO issue in the new world environment. Their role in raising India's empowerment successfully in the era of globalisation has to be discerned and steps should be taken for providing institutional framework to the reform agenda. He again stated that, the guidelines should be flexible enough to incorporate changes along with the changing world scenario. P. V. Rao (2001) also talked about the promotion of foreign policy constituents, role of civil societies and a strategy for extension of educational services, which may contribute in enhancing the cooperation between India and the Indian diaspora. He also emphasized that with the vast size and geographic diversity of Indian diaspora a common policy regime cannot address the diasporic issue rationally and suggested that the government should take a regional approach for this.

The Indian diaspora is an invaluable asset for India and India should formulate strategies for the responsive and productive engagements of this Indian community in multifaceted fields. This diasporic community has a great influence to mould the international opinion at different platforms on many issues in favour of Indian interest. At the top level both PIOs and NRIs can contribute through their direct support and knowledge transfer in the areas of national importance. They can provide their services in the fields of space research, atomic energy research, biotechnology, genetic engineering, nano technology, mega infrastructural projects, IT, trade, diplomatic sphere in strengthening bilateral relations, social sector etc.

Fig. 1: Multilevel Modular Scheme for productive engagement of Indian diaspora

National Level

Both PIOs and NRIs can contribute in sectors like space research, mega infrastructural projects, IT, trade, diplomatic sphere in strengthening bilateral relations, social sector etc.

↑↓

Regional Level

Both PIOs and NRIs can contribute in sectors like major infrastructural projects, IT, trade, social sector etc.

↑↓

State Level

Both PIOs and NRIs can contribute in sectors like major infrastructural projects, IT, trade, tourism, promoting local handicrafts, social sector etc.

↑↓

District and Local Level

Mainly NRIs can contribute in sectors like micro infrastructural projects, strengthening rural infrastructure, social sector etc.

At the regional level their contribution can help in the sectors such as major infrastructural projects as multipurpose projects, opening of engineering and medical colleges, other professional courses, IT, trade, tourism, social sector etc. At the state level also this community can provide its services in the areas like major infrastructural projects as ports and airports, IT, trade, tourism, promoting local handicrafts, social sector etc.

At the district and local level the NRIs are having better linkages and they can work as catalyst in the process of rural transformation. NRIs can contribute in sectors like micro infrastructural projects as small irrigational projects, hospitals, opening of educational institutes and training centers, strengthening rural infrastructure, social sector etc. They can adopt small villages of their districts and can help in the rural development process. They can help in the promotion of local handicrafts and can provide it international recognition.

In this multilevel strategic framework for engaging Indian diaspora for Indian cause there should be equal representation of members from civil societies, people from diasporic community and government officials at each level. The government officials should work for advising them regarding functional aspects for execution of different plans. Civil Society people can assist them in implementation of projects at grass root level. This framework is carrying checks and balance system itself. There should be functional autonomy and transparency in the working of these bodies at each level. These bodies should be organically linked with each other and should follow the principle of single window system. There should be speedy process for developmental plan formulation, ground survey and execution of these plans.

Future Strategies

"India's emergence as modern society, destined to play a role in the knowledge based industries, particularly in the field of information technology. It has helped to change the image of the Indain diaspora globally. It is no longer considered as an economically disadvantaged, salient minority in western world. It has even started playing a role in molding public opinion in them. It is no coincidence that the last two decades have seen the emergence of members of the Indian diaspora in their adoptive homelands. This period has coincided with India's resurgence as a global player and a country of stature in the comity of nations" (L. M. Singhvi Report, 2001). To strengthen the ties between India and Indian diaspora we can follow the sectoral approach as it is given in the following schematic diagram. Here, in this approach sector specific units have to be eastablished to deal with specific issues. According to this approach there should be different units at each level both centre and state according to the requirement to deal with the specific issues. Administrative reforms are required at all levels and this is the most urgent need to achieve these objectives. This approach can help in making more pragmatic understanding in the problem areas faced by the diasporic community and can be helpful in making adequate strategy to deal with these problems.

The Indian efforts are still not appreciable in collection and dissemination of the information related to the Indian diaspora. There is a great scope of research in this area to trace the potentials, capabilities, aptitudes and attitudes of the Indian diaspora and in getting deeper insight in the problems of the Indian community living abroad.

Relevance of This Strategy

There are two facets of the relationship between India and Indian diaspora for the search of responsive and productive engagement.

Relevance for Indian state – This is in diverse areas such as social, economic, science and technology cultural and diplomatic spheres. In these fields the contribution of diasporic community is needed in terms of their knowledge and skill transfer, resource canalisation, philanthropic support etc. This exercise is very similar to the trickle down and spread effect suggested by Myrdal and Hirschman in the theories of regional development.

The Indian diasporic community is important in the areas of bilateral dialogue process and to enhance the economic development of India with their direct contribution

Figure-2: Strategy for Strengthening the ties between India and Indian diaspora

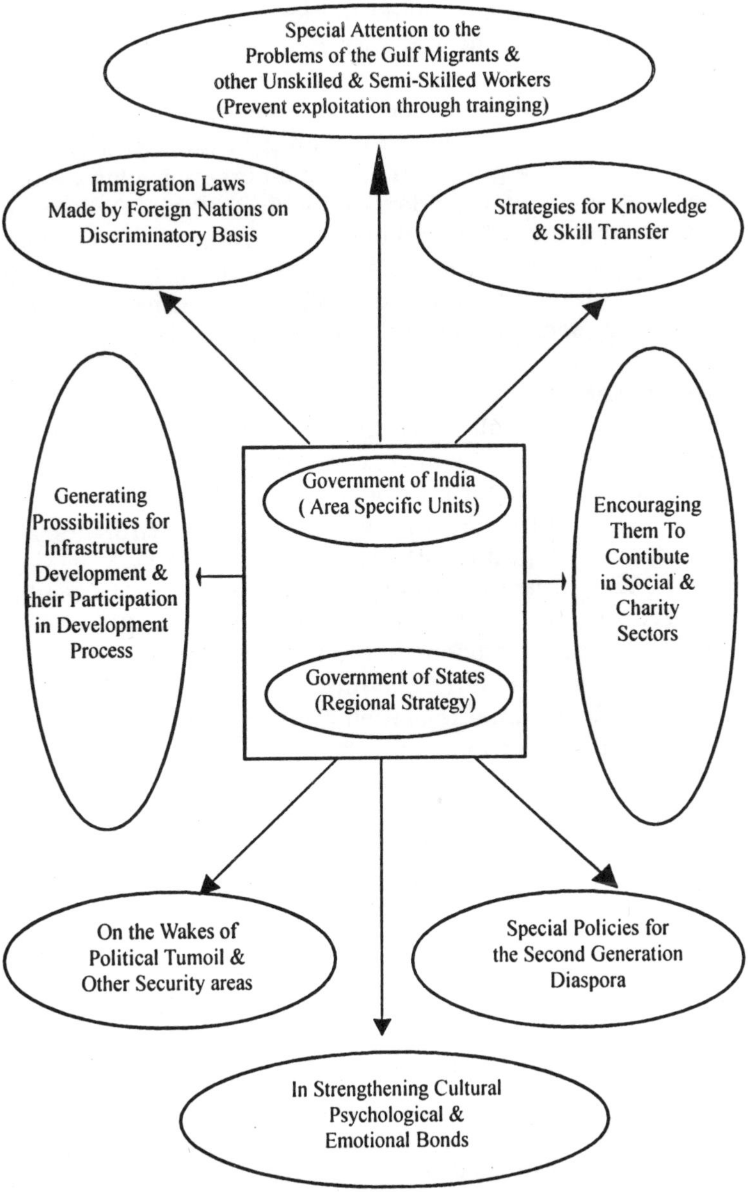

and through transfer of knowledge. For the better interaction and integration between the diasporic community and their motherland, especially with young Indian diaspora, strategies should be framed to increase their participation for Indian cause and to revive their diminishing links with India.

Relevance for diasporic community – The Indian state can help them to protect an identity and seeking role of Indian state as a guardian during emergencies {as we have seen incidents of Uganda (1972), Fiji (2000), France and Iraq recently etc.}. The Indian state can also play an effective role in other areas where diasporic community is facing lot of problems such as racial violence, discriminatory behaviour, social concerns, immigration laws etc.

Conclusion

Inspite of all these above stated problems, a high social and economic status, comfortable standard of living and opportunities for advancements in diversified areas in developed countries are attracting the Indians and employment in gulf countries.

The present strategy is an endeavour to explore historical, cultural, social, economic, political and psychological dimensions of the Indians. It is an attempt to explore potentials of this community for social, cultural and economic developments of their motherland and reciprocate to their problems constructively. In such type of work, their opinions should be taken to formulate a more pragmatic strategy for their more productive engagement with their homeland and responsible role of Indian state.

India should conduct a detailed survey of the areas of occupational expertise of PIOs and NRIs after formulating a detailed occupational structure of the Indian diasporic community. Government should frame a pragmatic policy framework to utilize this potential in different sectors which may help in accelerating the pace of India's development. Along with this the Indian Government should also identify the problems of the Indian diaspora and take initiatives for the resolution of such problems to make the life of Indians abroad smooth in their adaptive lands. Most of the work in this field has been done at macro level only. No doubt it is appreciable but there is an urgent need to look into this issue with micro perspective.

Bibliography

Agarwal, Priya. (1991), "passage from India: Post –1965 Indian immigrants and their Children- Conflicts, Concerns and Solutions", Yuvati publications, California.

Bhat, Chandrashekhar. (2001), "India and Indian Diaspora; Linkages and Expectations, with special reference to the field of education", Paper presented in Seminar on 'India and Indian Diaspora: Linkages and Expectations, University of Hyderabad, Hyderabad.

Binod, Khadria. (2001), "Harvesting the New Indian Diaspora and the Old; in Praise of A Single Generic policy objective vis a vis Multiple Policy interventions", Paper presented in Seminar on 'India and Indian Diaspora: Linkages and Expectations', University of Hyderabad, Hyderabad.

Jain, Prakash, C. (1993), "Five Pattern of Indian Emigration" in 'Global Indian Diaspora: Yesterday, Today and Tomorrow', ed. by Dr. Jagat K. Motwani et. al., GOPIO, New York.

Jain, Prakash, C. (2003), "Indian Diaspora in Canada", in 'Indian Diaspora Global Identity', ed. by Ajay Dubey, kalinga pub, New Delhi.

Jain, Ravindra, K. (2003), "A Civilisation Theory of Indian Diaspora and its Global Implications", in 'Indian Diaspora Global Identity', ed. by Ajay Dubey, kalinga pub, New Delhi.

Krishan, Gopal. (2003), "Indian Diaspora" in 'Population Geography', Vol. 25, No. 1 & 2, June-December.

Lessinger, Johanna. (2003), "Indian Immigrants in United States: The Emergence of a Transnational Population", in Culture and Economy in the Indian Diaspora' ed. by Bhiku Parekh et.al., Routhledge, London.

Pant, Girijesh. (2001), "Gulf NRI's: From Expatriates to Entrepreneurs", World Focus, Vol. 22(3), March, New Delhi.

R.R. Ramchandani. (2001), "People of Indian Origin and India's Post Cold War Policy Perspective", Paper presented in Seminar on 'India and Indian Diaspora: Linkages and Expectations, University of Hyderabad, Hyderabad.

Rao, P. V. (2001), "India and the Indian Diaspora: Strategies of Cooperation", Paper presented in Seminar on 'India and Indian Diaspora: Linkages and Expectations', University of Hyderabad, Hyderabad.

Singhvi, L. M. (2001), "High Commission Report On Indian Diaspora", Government of India, New Delhi.

Singla, Surinder, Kumar (2001), "Recognising Indian Diaspora's Contribution", World Focus, Vol. 22(3), March, New Delhi.

Reports

Proceedings of first, second and third Pravasi Bhartiya Divas published by FICCI and Ministry of External Affairs, Government of India.

GOPIO Resolution Passed during the 2006 Conference, January 6, 2006, Hyderabad, India.

Reports, PIOs Dialogue with India, Third and Forth Annual Conference, 10 January 2005 and 2006, India.

Sites Internet

http://www.indiandiaspora.nic.in
http://www.meadev.gov.in
http://www.nrilinks.com
http://www.indiaday.org

13

Studying Diaspora Online: Migration, Community Formation and Transnational Networks

Ajaya Kumar Sahoo

The early usage of 'diaspora' whose meanings are conceptualized in terms of dispersion from one place to another, permanent settlement in host society by adopting new languages, culture and life styles even though it's painful, sometimes objectionable, no longer prevails today. Today its meaning has changed, as the immigrants developed a different and multiple networks simultaneously with the societies of origin and host society by communicating with their kith and kin. They have experienced a different life that goes beyond the boundaries of one nation-state and brings both the host and mother culture into one single place for interaction (Sahoo and Bhat 2003: 97). This new type of migrants refers to as '*transmigrants*' and the process in which they are involved is called as '*transnationalism*'. The basis behind this sudden transformation is due to the globalization, deterritorialisation, and intensification of international migration flows, development of communication technology, and the internationalization of nation states in the modern world.

Diaspora: The Concept

The etymological meaning of 'diaspora' is derived from two Greek words, '*dia*', means through, and '*speiro*', means scatter. The word was specifically used to indicate the experience of the Jews exile to Babylon after Nebuchadnezzer's conquest over Jerusalem in 587 BCE.[1] Though the concept has assumed different meanings and interpretations since its early usage, it is currently employed to imply a wide variety of contexts, from *dispersion diaspora* to *trade diaspora* and *worker/ migrant diaspora* (see Cohen 1999: 178). These terminologies are increasingly used in the present day transnational studies.

For Tololyan (1991: 6), diaspora communities now serve as "...exemplary communities of the transnational moment", where the diaspora culture goes beyond and challenge several national borders. However, from a pragmatic point of view, the High Level Committee on Indian Diaspora (2002), under the Chairmanship of Dr. L. M. Singhvi, M.P., employs this concept in a generic sense for "...communities of migrants living or settled permanently in other countries, aware of its origins and identity and maintaining varying degrees of linkages with mother country".

Studies on diaspora communities often dealt on the issues of emigration, processes of settlement, persistence of culture, the extent of assimilation or adaptation, socio-economic and political participation in the host society, etc. Also implicit in this approach is the assumption that the displaced or deterritorialized groups negotiate their life and culture with that of their hosts and other immigrants, with limited interaction with the motherland/ homeland especially in the case of 'old diaspora'.[2] Interactions with the motherland were essentially imaginary since the immigrants lacked access to resources and modern technology (Bhat and Sahoo 2003: 144).

The past few decades has witnessed a phenomenal dynamism among the diaspora communities, made possible by the recent advancement in technologies of travel, transport and communications. Not only did these developments could bring the diaspora communities and their motherland closer but also has facilitated in bringing the members of their community dispersed around the world together. The emerging social formation, following the fusion of real and virtual community transcends the boundaries of all nation states. It is essentially *transnational* in nature.

Transnational Networks

'Transnational' generally implies migration of people across the borders of one or more nations. It also refers to the deterritorialisation of population along with their material and non-material cultural commodities. The term came into prominent use for the first time in the study of international relations in the context of international organizations, relations between non-governmental bodies' *in particular* (Vertovec and Cohen 1999: xx). In fact, the term 'transnational network', 'transnational communities' and 'diaspora' are often used interchangeably in many of the contemporary studies. Transnational networks form a precondition to the emergence of transnational communities and the process of this transformation is generally designated by 'transnationalism'. An excellent analysis of this process is promoted by Portes (1997) in his paper on *Globalisation from Below: The Rise of Transnational Communities.* He states, quoting Basch and others (1994: 4) that transnationalism is "...a process by which immigrants forge and sustain multi-stranded social relations that link together their societies of origin and settlement. We call these processes 'transnationalism' (*especially*) to emphasize that many immigrants today build social fields that cross-geographic, cultural and political borders". They actively engage in multiple spheres of life in host countries as well as in the countries of their origin. Such involvement is further extended to include other countries too, where members of their community have dispersed.

Transnational relations have important implication for both the sending and receiving society. According to Tambiah (quoted in Sek Pei LIM 2000), there are two types of transnational relations' i.e., vertical and lateral. The 'vertical' relations refer to the "...participation of immigrants in the host country to improve and impact the host nation". In this form of relationship, the diaspora actively participates in the social, economic and political domains of the country and thus becoming an important social and economic force in the host society. On the other hand the 'lateral' relations are manifested in the form of "...maintaining, reinforcing and extending the relation between the emigrant communities and their places of origin". For instance, sending remittances by the immigrants to their families back home, arranging and participating in marriage and other ceremonies, sponsoring for home festivals and events and so on. The scholars of transnational approach call this relation as 'Transnational Global Networks'. When we use the term 'transnational global networks', it simply refers not only to the relationship between the diaspora and home state, but also between members of the other diasporic community in other countries.

One of the factors leading to the emergence of this transnational network is the ease and speed of communication network and travel what David Harvey call "compression of time and space" (1989: 240). As compared to earlier dispersions, where immigration often led to isolation from homeland and kin, the contemporary immigrants can easily sustain their family and kinship network globally, promote religious, economic and political activities on a transnational space. They also maintain their cultural identity and linkages with the places and countries of their origin.

Developments in the field of transportation and communication technology have made tremendous changes in the transnational linkages. These developments have made it possible for immigrants to network with each other while simultaneously staying at different places. Further, the continuous circulation of people, money, goods and information between various settlements of immigrant population has given rise to the formation of a 'single community' [virtual community]. A person can now feel nostalgic to talk in their mother language wherever and whenever he meets with his community people, and in the process the whole community becomes a 'global village'.

Importance of Studying Diaspora Online

Over the past few decades Information & Communication Technology (ICT) has come to transform the boundaries and brought distant communities into a single platform where immigrants can share their own ethnic identity and able to preserve their regional culture and language *virtually*. ICT is integrated into virtually every aspect of commerce, education, and governance worldwide.[3] The Internet, Email, Chatroom, Webcam, etc. has important implication in this regard to connect people and community virtually all over the world. Studying diaspora community online or what we call *digital diaspora* is one of the major aspects in the contemporary scenario, as information becomes a key ingredient in amalgamating unity between the homeland and diaspora. The Internet with its various offshoots as well as the worldwide satellite TV broadcast technology have been identified as cheaper and popular means of communication in order to establish effective diasporic linkages. Among other Internet segments, Oriya portals (e.g., www.sambit.com, and www.orissa.net) in this regard effectively serve as an individual forum for the exchange of communication between the homeland and diaspora. The following section will deal with the methodology and the subject of Oriya diaspora in a transnational perspective.

Methodology

Diaspora discourse is *far away* geographically from the motherland, but *near* in terms of contact, with the help of self-administered e-mail questionnaire. The respondents for this article are chosen on the basis of snowball sampling. This technique is a way of broadening sample size by asking participants to give details of other respondent or forward the request to others (those who are interested). Initially a 'request questionnaire' was sent to various associations, student communities' within and outside India to get the addresses of Oriyas those settled abroad. In the course of my survey I also become the member of Oriya groups on the net (especially Odiya.org, Orissa.net and Mahanadi.com) to get the details of diasporic Oriyas. These sites are helpful for me in the sense it has *member directories* with regards to Oriyas all over the world. I collected 500 email addresses out of my first inquiry into the field. In the second phase of my query, I sent 400 email solicitations - out of the addresses given by various members, as well as from the member directory - requesting them to respond to my research topic *in general.* Approximately 180 addresses returned 'undelivered' or 'vacation messages', resulting in a contact group of approximately 220.

The 220 remaining respondents were contacted by further email to respond to my specific research questions, of those 63 (28.63%) replied during the data collection period between May 2002 - July 2003, 11 gave incomplete answers with missing data, resulted in the total survey response rate comes down to 52 (23.63%). The target population was Oriya family members, professionals, businesspersons, and students those who stayed more than three to five year abroad and, those who have access to Internet as a medium of communication. The sample distributions are as follows:[4]

Gender - Out of the total sampling 23.07 percent of the respondent are females including working women and doctoral students, and 76.92 percent are male respondents (See Figure-1).

Figure -1: Gender

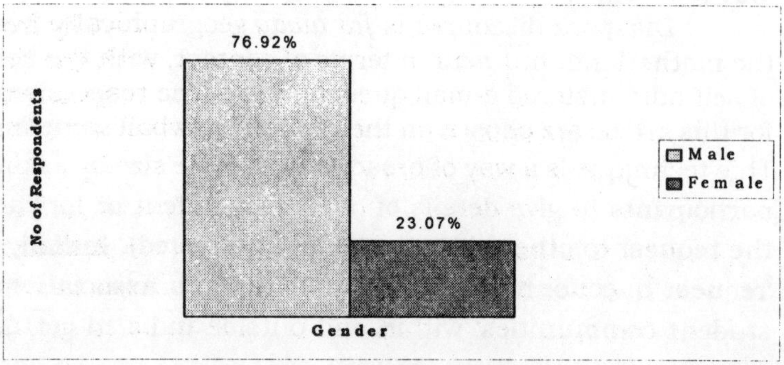

Profession - 34.61 percent of respondents are faculty members in academic institutions, 23.07 percent are students and post-doctorate researchers, 15.38 percent are software professionals, 13.46 percent are business persons (not specified), 7.69 percent are medical doctors, and 5.76 percent of the respondents are engineers and architectures (See Figure-2).

Figure-2 : Occupation

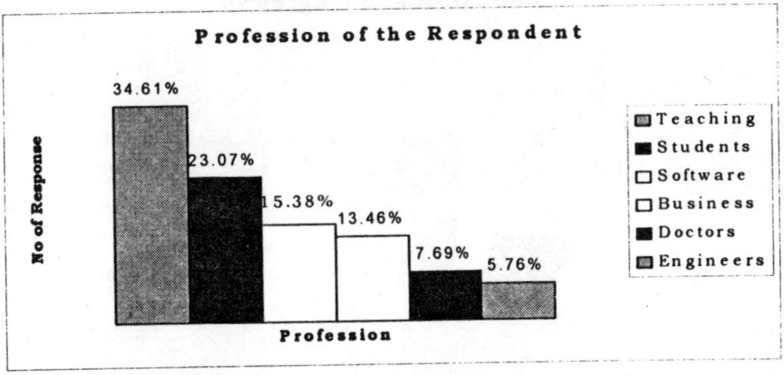

Country of Residence - Majority of the respondents i.e., 51.92 percent belongs to the United States, 13.30 percent from UAE, 15.38 percent from Australia, 7.69 percent from Germany, 3.84 percent from Singapore and 3.84 percent of respondents are from Japan (See Figure-3).

Figure – 3: Country of Residence

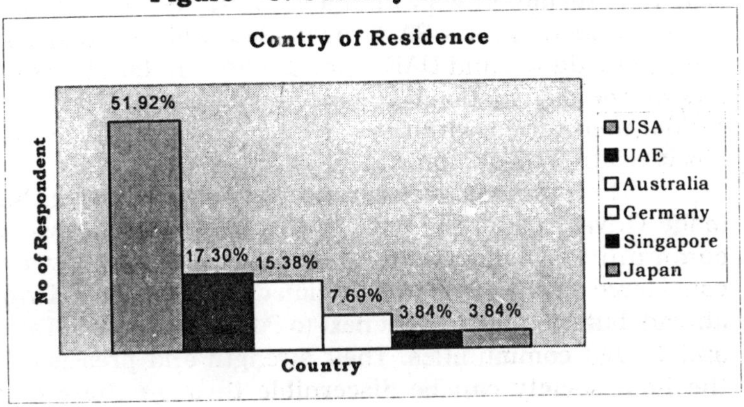

Educational Background - 48.07 percent of the respondents had Master's degrees, 25 percent had Doctorate degrees, 15.38 percent had Post-doctorate degrees, and 11.53 percent of respondents had graduate and post-graduate diplomas (See Figure-4).

Figure – 4: Education

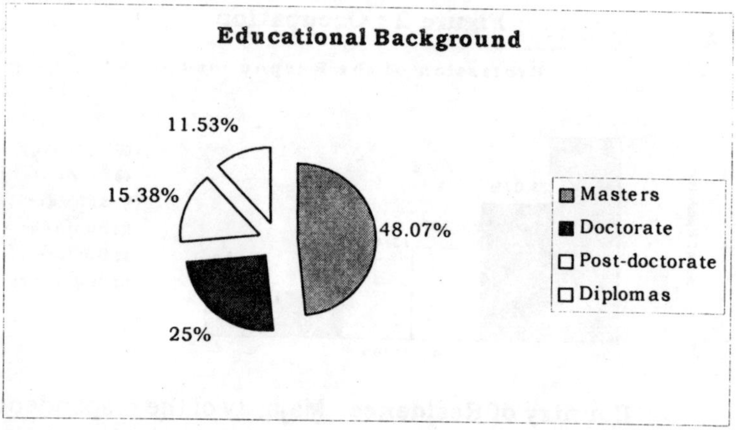

Oriya Diaspora

The diasporic Oriyas constitute sizeable number in several countries around the world. They are significant in number in countries such as Indonesia, Java, Sumatra, and Bali and are 'minorities within a minority' in the European countries such as UK, USA, Canada, New Zealand, Australia, Singapore, Japan and UAE. They are now in the process of forging the transnational community by building linkages amidst themselves, with the kith and kin around the world albeit relatives back home in Orissa.

The ethnic consciousness of being an 'Oriya' has made Oriyas one of the most successful Indian diasporic communities around the globe. Of course, they are considered as one of the least Indian diasporic groups living abroad, but they must count next to Punjabi, Gujarati, Tamil and Telugu communities. Their strength and presence in the host society can be discernible through the ethnic associations, temples or *Mandirs* (place of worship) they formed in the countries of their residence. These associations and temples are one way or the other helps Oriyas to retain their familial and socio-economic networks with the homeland and other Oriyas around the world. The network among the Oriyas further become easier as a result of the revolution in the field of information and communication technology, which has tremendously altered the whole world during last few decades.

The Oriyas, settled abroad, migrated from the state of Orissa, which is bounded by the Bay of Bengal on the east, West Bengal and Bihar on the north, Madhya Pradesh on the west and Andhra Pradesh on the south (Rath 1983: 1-2). The language spoken by Oriyas called 'Oriya' which is an anglicized version of *'Odia'*. The word *Odia* is a modern name for the *Odra* or *Udra* tribes who inhabits in the central part of modern Orissa. In India, over 30 million people speak the language. It is one of the official languages of India and the major language of Orissa. Oriya language has spread to the other parts of the globe such as Myanmar, Malaysia, Fiji, Indonesia, Java, Sumatra, the USA, UK, Canada, Australia, New Zealand, Singapore, Japan and UAE.

Oriya Migration

Migration from Orissa has a long history. The Oriya merchants had trade links with other parts of the country during the ancient and Middle Ages. Being a coastal state [Orissa], maritime trade played an important role in the development of Oriya civilization, where cultural, commercial and political contacts with Southeast Asia, particularly southern Burma, Malaysia and Indonesia were especially extensive.

Archaeological evidence from Sisupalgarh in Orissa suggests that the trade contact between ancient Orissa and Rome dates back to the first and second century AD. The trade contacts between eastern India and Thailand date as far as back from 3rd and 4th century BC. Himanshu Ray's "*The Winds of Change-Buddhism and the Maritime Links of Early South Asia*" mentions that, at least eight oceanic routes linked the eastern coast of India with the Malaya country.

Around the 7th century AD Kongoda Dynasty from central Orissa migrated to Malaysia and Indonesia. Tome Pires says that, Oriya and the Portuguese merchant traders were active at the ports of Southeast Asia during ancient time.

The chronicles of Huen Tsang refers to Orissa's overseas contacts in the 7th century, and by the 10th century Orissa's trade with the east began to proliferate (Rath 1983). During the Sailodbhava dynasty through ports, merchants from Orissa reached distant destinations in Sri Lanka, Burma, Thailand, Java, Bali, Sumatra, Borneo, Malaya and Cambodia. Historians point out that the links between the Sailodbhavas of Orissa and Sailendras of South East Asia dates back to antiquity. The rituals of Balijatra and Khuduru Kuni Osa[5] today are the best example of the great maritime past of Orissa.

During the colonial period, when British ruled Orissa, a significant change took place in the region. The first British factories were established at Hariharpur in Orissa. Subsequently other factories were established in *Balasore* on the river *Burabalanga* and *Pipil* on the river *Subarnarekha.* These two Orissa harbors formed the bases for maritime trade. In fact, at the same time, the British rule has had a severe impact on the social and economic life of the Oriya people. Numerous categories of craft workers, especially weavers and dyers became bankrupt and were reduced to abject poverty.

The shrinking of the cottage industry, which created large number of unemployed workers along with the abject poverty and severe draughts and famines pushed Oriyas to the far away lands in search of a better future. Oriyas during these days migrated to East African countries as indentured labour[6] to work on the plantations. They also migrated to Malaya, Burma and Indonesia and Caribbean countries as unskilled labourers. As Sheila Rampersed (1998) in her article *Jahaji Behen* says "...the migration to the Caribbean took place mainly from northern India, where 90 percent of the people migrate from the Gangetic Plane, the former United Provinces, Central Provinces and Oudh, Orissa and Bhiar".

Migration of the Oriyas to the industrially developed country is a recent phenomenon. During the 1960s and 1970s in the state of Orissa, a number of technical and engineering colleges and institutions came up in major cities such as Rourkela, Bhubaneswar, Talcher, Berhampur, Cuttack, and Baripada. These institutions produced large number of engineers and professionals but unable to get employment in India many Oriyas migrated to the United States, Canada and Australia and so on looking for a brighter future.

This period was often called as the 'Brain Drain', which pushed large number of engineers, doctors, scientists, and teachers from India to the developed countries. The migration did not stop, further as a result of the developments in the field of transport and communication, it has led to unprecedented migration of Oriyas since the late seventies.[7] Presently Oriyas could be found in many parts of the world. They are not only in business but also are highly educated, having gained professional qualifications in such fields as science & technology, medicine, economies, business management etc. On the threshold of the 21st century, the Oriya community seems to be at the crossroads in every sphere of life. On the one hand, it has become transnational, and on the other, it is struggling to retain its culture.

Transnational Perspective

Oriyas are not only successful in maintaining close contacts with the families and relatives back home, but also are very much successful in maintaining the transnational networks with their kith and kin around the globe. For instance, the super cyclone of Orissa 1999 that made millions of people homeless, was the worst in the history of Orissa as well as India. To rebuild Orissa again, the Oriya NRIs and NGOs have played an important role by raising funds from all over the world through institutions, associations, and personal networks. Thanks to the modern means of cheaper transportation and faster means of communication technology, which has made possible closer networks among the family and community members around the world. The Oriyas continue to keep in touch with their relatives and old friend in Orissa and in other countries. Their personal linkages are maintained through telephone calls, writing letters, Internet, Email and through personal home visits where as the socio-economic linkages are manifested through the form of marriage arrangements, kinship networks, remittances and religious ceremonies. In this way the Oriyas have succeeded in reviving some of the old ideas and values. Further due to the development of Internet, it has now become possible to create an Oriya 'Virtual Community' where the people of Oriya community all over the world can participate in the global community. The Worldwide Satellite technology now has allowed Oriyas, wherever they located globally, to have access to Oriya TV programs.

Oriyas in diaspora would like to keep their traditional values including religious practices and family customs through marriage obligations, attaining religious functions as well as cultural festivals within the community, side by side want to adopt the western culture. The institution of Oriyas will be examined in this context.

Culture

Culture is an abstract symbolic system, which is composed of values, meanings and beliefs. In the diasporic context, the Oriyas have remained attached to their invaluable culture, which finds expression in the form of traditional festivals and ceremonies. Oriyas perform various festivals in diaspora such as *Rath Yatra, Holi, Diwali* and *New Year* in which large number of Oriyas participate. Another aspect of outward manifestation of a cultural tradition, is the dance form. For example, *Oddissi*[8] the traditional dance form of Orissa is seen as a powerful method of promoting common interest. Besides *Oddissi*, other important dance and theatre forms of Orissa such as *Chhau* dance,[9] drama, stage shows of the story of Ramayana and Mahabharata etc., are also performed in the diaspora. Today specialized dance troupes are invited from Orissa to perform in several special occasions. These cultural activities of

Oriyas abroad give a sense of nostalgia of being a member of the great civilization and also frequently reinforced the contacts with motherland. Wearing of ethnic dress is one part of immigrants' maintenance of cultural identity in the new alien culture. Given the preference of wearing ethnic dress, western dress or both, the study shows that 83 percent of the respondent manipulate both Western and Indian dress side by side (see Table-1, following endnotes). Only 4 percent respondent adheres to the Indian traditional dresses as part of ethnic marker. And 14 percent does not give importance when it comes to preference of wearing ethnic dresses.

Table-1: Preference of Clothing

When it comes to preference for wearing ethnic clothes, which one do you prefer?	*Percentage of Respondent*
Indian	3.84
Western	*
Both	82.69
Does not matter	13.46
Total	100

Family and Marriage

The traditional family system of Orissa - in general and India in particular - is joint family or extended family. It consists of a group, usually two to three generations with a complex set of mutual obligations. It includes affinal relations through marriage, as well as by one's descent. The same is noticed in the diaspora despite the pressure for change in the host society. Oriyas continue to maintain their familial and affinal linkages back home with the help of new communication and information technology (See Figure-5&6).

Table-2. Concerning the issue of Marriage

Do you think it is better to marry within own group?	*Percentage of Respondent*
Agree	62.23
Disagree	3.84
Does not matter	26.92
Total	100

One important aspect of families in Orissa is the nature of marriage that binds community together and helps to maintain Oriya tradition well intact. When a marriage takes place it made through the consent of parents between two families rather than between two individuals, which is the offshoot of western society. In the present survey it was asked to the respondents about the preference of marriage - marriage within the own group (See Table-2). Majority of the respondent i.e., 63 per cent answered that, 'it is better to marry within own group', while 27 per cent of the respondent gave fractured views, in the sense, the question of marriage does not bother much to them. It is worth noting here that among the 27 per cent, most of the respondents are young research scholars and doctorate students. Only 4 per cent of respondents disagree with the statement of marriage. It may be conclude that the parents of Oriya community had attitude towards endogamy than the younger generation who wants to marry according to their individual choices regardless or caste or religion because of the modern education and more important due to effective communication technology *especially* Internet. For example, at present, marriages are performed transnationally. The matrimonial advertisements, which are now available on the Internet, facilitate further in searching for brides/ grooms, often based on caste preferences. One can now find the matrimonial ads of Oriya speaking community belonging to all castes from all over the world. There are certain web sites exclusively made for Oriyas, which include Oriya magazines, newspapers, and matrimonial ads. Among such web sites one reads as follows:

> *The Sambit.com: - The first transnational Oriya magazine on the web. It locates the Oriya speaking peoples, friends and relatives worldwide. This site also provides an opportunity to the Oriya speaking community of the world in finding suitable marriage alliances. It displays matrimonial ads for Oriyas who are looking for the marriage alliances either for themselves or for their kith and kin. On the web site, one can find matrimonial ads of Oriya speaking community belonging to all castes from all over the world. Apart from the matrimonial site, it also helps Oriyas to search for Oriya people around the world to create the 'Virtual Community'.*

During the marriage ceremony - which is taking place in the Oriya diaspora unlike the marriages in Orissa - relatives from far away place come together and meet each other. Of course, there are some variations in the nature and extent of marriage ceremonies according to caste and religious affiliation, and region of origin in Orissa among the diasporic Oriyas (qualitative answers).

Religion

Religion offers one of the most significant aspects of cohesiveness among the immigrants and for Oriyas it is very much important in one's everyday life (See Table-3). It is not only the basis of creating ethnic consciousness, but also it helps to establish communication network in a larger scale, which is now cut across national boundaries. For example, the devotees of religious preachers/Gurus like Sathya Sai Baba, Sankaracharya, Swami Premananda, Vivekananda and so on meet every now and then during birthday anniversaries, religious conferences and preaching activities across the world.

Table-3. Issue of Religion

How do you rate the importance of religion in the everyday life?	*Percentage of Respondent*
Very important	53.84
Fairly important	42.30
Not important	3.84
Total	100

Concerning the issue of consistency in attaining the places of worship - *Mandirs* - Oriyas are more akin towards attaining places of worship for various purposes. As the study shows one third of the respondent i.e., 62 per cent attain regularly the religious rituals and festivals in the temple or in the home shrines (See Table-4). Only 23 per cent of the respondent never attain religious festivals as they assume religion does not have any value in today's context, while 16 per cent of the respondent attain religious festivals and functions very rarely.

Table-4. Intensity of Attaining Religious Rituals and Festivals

Do you attain religious rituals and cultural festivals of Oriya community?	*Percentage of Respondents*
Never	23.07
Rarely	15.38
Regularly	61.53
Total	100

Regarding the question of 'occasion to meet each other', most of the respondent mentioned about the important Oriya cultural festivals such as *Rath Yatra of Lord Jagannath, Ganesh Puja, Durga Puja* and family celebrations and college students get together. Among these occasions

Oriyas give more importance to religious festivities in the sense it celebrate with more fan fare in diaspora unlike in home. Apart from this Oriyas also meet together during Christmas/New year days, holidays and *Kumar Purnami* occasions. Most of the respondent also raised their.concern about the 'mother tongue' which according to them as the 'integral part of religious and cultural consciousness', as during the occasions of get together most of them speak Oriya language, besides English as a mode of communication in the alien land. It is also apparent from the study that Oriyas settled abroad have 'Oriya' as their major language of communication in their homes (qualitative answers).

Role of ICT

Information and communication technology plays an important role connecting Oriyas in Orissa and their counterparts in the Oriya diasporas. The transnational Oriya newspapers, which are now readable online such as *Samaj* (www.thesamaj.com), *Dharitri* (www.dharitri.com), *Sambad* (www.orissasambad.com), *Samaya (*www.thesamaya.com), and Internet portals like 'Orissa 4 You', 'Orissainfo', 'Orissa' etc., have become more accessible to those who are kin to know more about Orissa and its culture. Besides that the Internet sites and newspapers provides opportunity to Oriya speaking community of the world in finding suitable marriage alliances. It also helps Oriyas for finding Oriya people around the world in order to create the 'virtual community'.

Table-5: Number of Relatives out side the Country of Residence

Do you have relatives outside the place of residence, including motherland?	*Percentage of Respondent*
Yes	80.76
No	*
Does not know	19.23
Total	100

Oriyas unlike any other Indian communities abroad have their relatives out side their current place of residence, because communication network become more crucial when there is distance of geographical boundaries.[10] The study found that 80 per cent of the respondent have relatives outside the current place of settlement besides having kith and kin in the homeland (See Table-5). They frequently network with their relatives in the homeland as well as other relatives outside the geographical boundaries where they settled. Table-6 shows that, 45 percent of Oriyas network with their relatives on a regular basis and 33 percent network within a time span of one month, while 24 percent weekly once maintain network with their relatives.

Table-6. Frequency of Networks With the Relatives

How many days in a month do you contact with your relatives?	*Percentage of Respondent*
Never	*
Once in a Week	23.07
Once in a Month	32.69
Regularly	44.23
Total	100

The major mode of communication network among Oriyas to exchange information on both sides is through Email, sending letters, and through telephonic calls besides personal visits (See Chart-5&6). The easy and cheaper transportation, airfare in this regard contributes a great deal in connecting Oriyas with their homeland. As the study shows (See Table-7) 60 percent of Oriyas paid a visit to the homeland in between six month to one year. This shows the economic conditions of Oriyas abroad, which is more comfortable according to their own life styles. The major purpose of the visit to homeland is during leisure times and holidays. The other purposes of visit are to attain marriage festivals, conducting religious rituals, and to attain birth/death ceremonies beside business activities (See Table-8).

Table-7. Number of Visit to India During Last Five Years

Duration of visit to the homeland 'Orissa'	*Percentage of Respondent*
Before one month	3.84
Last 6 months	11.53
6 to 12 months	59.61
More than one year	15.38
Does not know	9.61
Total	100

Table-8. Purpose of Visit to Homeland 'Orissa

Purpose of visit to the homeland 'Orissa'	*Percentage of Respondent*
Business purpose	3.84
Religious purpose	19.23
Marriage purpose	30.76
Birth/death ceremony	11.53
Leisure purpose	64.61
Total	100

Figure - 5: The Modes of Communication Used to Network with the Relatives

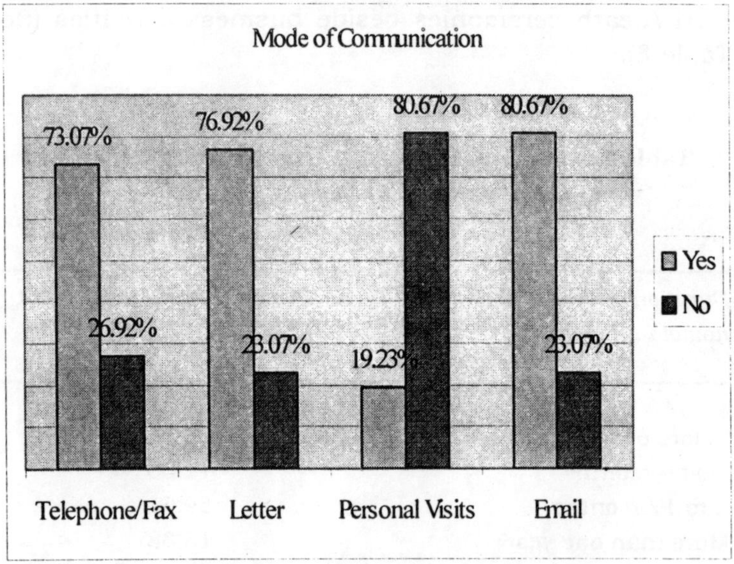

Figure - 6: How Frequently do you use this Mode of Communication to Network with the Relatives?

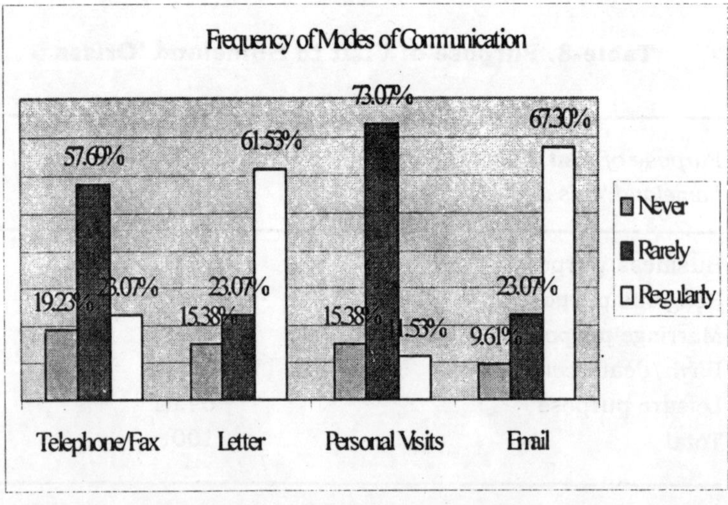

Association

The first thing Oriyas did when they migrated overseas was to form the ethnic associations with the co-operation of other Oriyas. Through the associations they retain the invaluable culture of Orissa. Presently there are many Oriya associations found around the world wherever a sizable number of Oriyas settled, and they extended their boundaries to all Oriyas settled abroad. One out of three Oriyas outside Orissa is a member of the Oriya association in their place of residence.

Table-9. Membership in Oriya Association

Do you have membership in any Oriya Cultural Association / Organization in the current place of residence?	*Percentage of Respondent*
Yes	69.23
No	30.76
Total	100

Table-10. Oriya Associations Abroad

Do you think that, Oriya associations do not meet the problems of Oriyas abroad?	*Percentage of Respondent*
Agree	44.23
Disagree	51.92
Does not know	5.76
Total	100

Table-9 shows the membership in Oriya associations, where 70 per cent of the Oriyas have membership in one or other Oriya associations' abroad. As the question asked (see Table-10) how far Oriya associations abroad meet the needs of Oriyas, some contrasting - positive and negative - qualitative answers drawn, which are given below for some general observation:

> ...it is one of the important aspect to preserve the Oriya culture and tradition.
>
> ...it is not at all important as these associations are just for time pass. They are too political and badly exploit the Oriyas living abroad.
>
> ...while talking about Oriya Society of Americas[11] (OSA), its aim is pretty limited and they have not done any great work for Orissa other than sending some money during super cyclone. Whereas 'Odiya Samaj' another institution has been created by a group of enthusiastic Oriyas whose aim is broader and they did some good relief work collaborated with various NGOs in Orissa.

However, as most of the respondent i.e., 52 percent viewed that Oriya association in the diaspora meets the basic problems of Oriyas, other 45 percent agreed that it does not meet the requirements of Oriyas abroad.

In summary, this article does not provide a comprehensive analysis of Oriya identity question in the larger diasporic context, but gives a clear picture on how these immigrants maintain networks through various means of new communication technology in a 'transnational space' (Portes 1995). However, there is much work to be done, when it comes to *Oriya Diaspora* and other communities like *Bengali Diaspora* in which not a single work executed till today, focusing on the diasporic perspective, whereas a whole gamut of literature available in case of Gujaratis, Punjabis, Telugus, Tamils and Bhojpuris. As the title shows, in this article I have brought only a brief sketch of transnational networks of Oriyas based on selection of samples through *online*. The article is brief in conclusion and warrants more for empirical study on these communities in a transnational perspective, which I think, should initiate by researchers and academicians in various social science disciplines.

Notes

* The paper was first appeared in the journal *Man and Life*, Vol. 29, No.3&4, July-December, 2003, pp. 159-180. I sincerely thank the editor of the journal for kindly giving me the permission to reproduce the article.

1. See the history of Jewish exile from 'Israel Science and Technology Homepage': http://www.science.co.il
2. A distinction can be made between the 'old diaspora' - formed as a consequence of indentured labor during the colonial period - and the 'new diaspora' formed following the emigration of skilled labor and professionals to the developed countries (See Bhat, 1998: 2).
3. See African Diaspora web page: http://www.ddn-latinamericacaribbean.org/about.htm
4. While analyzing the data inside the text (excepting methodology part), percentages are taken as rounded to the nearest whole number for easy understanding and a star symbol (*) used in case of zero (0) percentage in the tables.
5. *Bali Jatra* is a festival of Orissa which is observed among unmarried girls and the *Khuduru Kuni Osa* is observed to keep the memories of the past transnational trading especially in reference to Bali.
6. Indentured labor was invented by the British to recruit cheap labor from Asia, India in particular. It was a form of "...contract by which the immigrant was bound to work for a given employer for a three to five year term, performing the task assigned to him for a specified wage" (Jain 1993: 30).
7. It is worthwhile to mention here that, the respondents, which covered in this study, are mostly recent migrants (called new migrants) who have migrated after independence.
8. *Oddissi*, is an ancient dance form of Orissa, which has received worldwide recognition with its beautiful footwork and theatrics. Among the well-known performers who have transnationally acclaimed today are such as Bagmi Das, Natasha Rao,

Siddhartha Mohaptra, Satish Mishra, Mrunali Das, Rajashri Mishra, Prerana Pradhan, Shashwati Das, Suman Ojha and so on.

9. It is a folk dance from of western Orissa now become popular dance form in Orissa as well as in Oriya diasporas.

10. For the sake of reliability on respondents' network, the following question asked, as Oriyas may have their relatives within the geographical periphery and might have frequent communication with them, which the study finds no importance in transnational networks.

11. OSA was founded in 1969 at Boston. It is a non-political, non-profit and voluntary association, in the United States. The association has fourteen regional centers, which operate as a social umbrella for different regions in the United States and Canada. These centres arrange religious festivals, social get together, cultural events and participate in the cultural life of the local community as representatives of Oriya culture. See more details about OSA: www.orissasociety.org

References

Basch, Linda et al., 1994. *Nation Unbound: Transnational Projects, Postcolonial Predicaments and Deterritorialized Nation-States.* Amsterdam: Gordon and Breach.

Bhat, Chandrashekhar. 1998. *Context of Intra and Inter Ethnic Conflict among the Indian Diaspora Communities.* Occasional Paper-5: Centre for Study of Indian Diaspora, University of Hyderabad.

Bhat, Chandrashekhar and Ajaya Kumar Sahoo. 2003. Diaspora to Transnational Networks: The Case of Indians in Canada. In Sushma J. Varma and Radhika Seshan, Eds., *Fractured Identity: The Indian Diaspora in Canada,* Jaipur, Rawat Publication, pp. 141-167.

Cohen, Robin. 1999. *Global Diaspora: An Introduction.* London, UCL Publication.

Harvey, David 1989 *The Condition of Postmodernity: An Enquiry into the Origins of Cultural Change.* London, Basil Blackwell.

High Level Committee on Indian Diaspora. 2002. The Report of the High Level Committee on Indian Diaspora (*Executive Summary*). New Delhi: Ministry of External Affairs.

Jain, P. C. 1993. Five Patterns of Indian Emigration. In Jagat K. Motwani, Mahin Gosine and Jyoti Motwani, Eds., *Global Indian Diaspora: Yesterday, Today and Tomorrow*, New York, GOPIO Publication, pp. 29-32.

LIM, Sek Pei. 2000. *The Question of Diaspora in International Relations: A case study of Chinese diaspora in Malaysia and South-East Asia.* University of Sussex: Dissertation, MA in International Relations.

Portes, Alejandro. 1995. Segmented Assimilation among New Immigrant Youth: A Conceptual Framework. In R. G. Rumbaut and W. A. Cornelius, Eds., *California's Immigrant Children: Theory, Research, and Implications for Educational Policy,* San Diego, Center for U.S.-Mexican Studies, University of California, pp. 71-76.

———— 1997 *Globalization from Below: The Rise of Transrational Communities.* Paper at the ESRC Transnational Communities Programme, University of Oxford. See web page: www.transcomm.ox.ac.uk

Rampersad, Sheila. 1998. *Jahaaji Behen? Feminist Literary Theory and the Indian Presence in the Caribbean.* Occasional Paper-2, Centre for Study of Indian Diaspora, University of Hyderabad.

Rath, B.K. 1983. *Cultural History of Orissa.* Delhi, Sundeep Prakashan.

Sahoo, Ajaya Kumar and Chandrashekhar Bhat. 2003. Transnational Networks among Punjabi and Gujarati Diasporas in the USA. In R. Gopa Kumar, Ed., *Indian Diaspora and Giving Patterns of Indian Americans in USA.* New Delhi, CAF India, pp. 95-128.

Tololyan, Khachig. 1991. 'The Nation-State and Its Others: In Lieu of a Preface'. *Diaspora*, Vol. 1, No.1: 3-7.

Vertovec, Steven and Robin Cohen (Eds.). 1999 Migration, Diaspora and Transnationalism. Cheltenham, Edward Elgar Publishing Ltd.

Index

C

G

H

S

T

U

V

W

Y

Z